R.

WITHDRAWN

MUSIC AND MARX

CRITICAL AND CULTURAL MUSICOLOGY
MARTHA FELDMAN, *Series Editor*
Associate Professor of Music
University of Chicago

ADVISORY BOARD
Kofi Agawu, Ruth Stone, Gary Tomlinson, Leo Treitler

MUSIC AND THE CULTURES OF PRINT
edited by Kate van Orden

THE ARTS ENTWINED
Music and Painting in the Nineteenth Century
edited by Marsha L. Morton and Peter L. Schmunk

THE AFRICAN DIASPORA
A Musical Perspective
edited by Ingrid Monson

BETWEEN OPERA AND CINEMA
edited by Jeongwon Joe and Rose Theresa

MUSIC, SENSATION, AND SEXUALITY
edited by Linda Phyllis Austern

MUSIC AND MARX
Ideas, Practice, Politics
edited by Regula Burckhardt Qureshi

MUSIC AND MARX
IDEAS, PRACTICE, POLITICS

EDITED BY REGULA BURCKHARDT QURESHI

ROUTLEDGE
NEW YORK AND LONDON

Published in 2002 by
Routledge
29 West 35th Street
New York, NY 10001

Published in Great Britain by
Routledge
11 New Fetter Lane
London EC4P 4EE

Routledge is an imprint of the Taylor & Francis Group.

Printed in the United States of America on acid-free paper.

10 9 8 7 6 5 4 3 2 1

Cataloging-in-Publication Data is available from the Library of Congress.

ISBN 0-8153-3716-7

Contents

Series Editor's Foreword

General Introduction to *Critical and Cultural Musicology*

MARTHA FELDMAN

Musicology has undergone a sea change in recent years. Where once the discipline knew its limits, today its boundaries seem all but limitless. Its subjects have expanded from the great composers, patronage, manuscripts, and genre formations to include race, sexuality, jazz, and rock; its methods from textual criticism, formal analysis, paleography, narrative history, and archival studies to deconstruction, narrativity, postcolonial analysis, phenomenology, and performance studies. These categories point to deeper shifts in the discipline that have led musicologists to explore phenomena which previously had little or no place in musicology. Such shifts have changed our principles of evidence while urging new understandings of existing ones. They have transformed prevailing notions of musical texts, created new analytic strategies, recast our sense of subjectivity, and produced new archives of data. In the process they have also destabilized canons of scholarly value.

The implications of these changes remain challenging in a field whose intellectual ground has shifted so quickly. In response to them, this series offers essay collections that give thematic focus to new critical and cultural perspectives in musicology. Most of the essays contained herein pursue their projects through sustained research on specific musical practices and contexts. They aim to put strategies of scholarship that have developed recently in the discipline into meaningful exchanges with one another while also helping to construct fresh approaches. At the same time they try to reconcile these new approaches with older methods, building on the traditional achievements of musicology in helping to forge new disciplinary idioms. In both ventures, volumes in this series also attempt to press new associations among fields outside of musicology, making aspects of what has often seemed an inaccessible field intelligible to scholars in other disciplines.

In keeping with this agenda, topics treated in forthcoming volumes of the series include music and the cultures of print; music, art, and synesthesia in nineteenth-century Europe; music in the African diaspora; relations between opera and cinema; and music in the cultural sensorium. Through enterprises like these, the series hopes to facilitate new disciplinary directions and dialogues, challenging the boundaries of musicology and helping to refine its critical and cultural methods.

Foreword

JACQUES ATTALI
TRANSLATED BY ELIZABETH MARSHMAN

Music is an invention at least as ancient as language.[1] Until the time of the great empires, like all other human activity, it was a part of religious practice. Then it became isolated as an ambiguous and fragile art, apparently of minor, secondary importance. It was first restricted to venues designed for it, then broke out to pervade the world in mass-produced form. Music is now an enigmatic comforter, a source of profit, a stake in power struggles; it is background noise admired by many who do not really listen, and is bought, never to be really heard. Today, more money is spent on music than on books, films, or any other source of entertainment, and music is at the forefront of globalization.

Many philosophers have contemplated music. Jean-Jacques Rousseau, for example, wrote in "A Discourse on the Origin of Inequality": "Whether we inquire into the origin of the arts or observe the first criers, we find that everything in its principle is related to the means of subsistence (1962)." For Karl Marx, music is "the mirror of reality"; for Friedrich Nietzsche, the "expression of truth," a "Dionysian mirror of the world (1967)." For Sigmund Freud, it is a "text to be deciphered (1958)." And according to Pierre Schaeffer, music speaks from person to person in a language of matter.

But social theories, trapped in structures created before the end of the nineteenth century, weighed down by pre-established terms, cannot explain the essentials: jubilation and violence, chance and confusion, the free and the reciprocal. Music explores the whole range of possibilities in a given code, faster than material reality can. It conveys through sound that which only later comes to be visible, to be imposed, to dominate. It is not only the echo of an era's aesthetic, but something beyond the everyday which heralds the future.

Mirror and crystal ball, medium for recording human creation, indicator of voids, piece of utopia; private memory in which each listener records his or her own feelings, reminiscence, collective memory of order and of

ix

genealogies (1963), music is neither an autonomous activity nor a consequence of economic infrastructure. It is born of communities and artists, of men and gods, of celebration and prayer.

Thus Bach and Mozart each unknowingly and unintentionally reflected in their own ways the newborn bourgeoisie's dream of harmony, the decline of the courts, and the discontent of the people. Moreover, they did it better than—and before—all the political theorists of the nineteenth century. Bob Marley and Janis Joplin, John Lennon and Jimi Hendrix spoke far more eloquently of the dreams of freedom of the 1960s than any theory could ever hope to do. Variety shows, hit parades and show business, clips and samples are the precursors, both pathetic and prophetic, of the forms the globalization of desires will take. Free jazz and then rap foretold the explosion of urban violence; Napster the imminent battle over intellectual property. At the same time, the broad strokes of a future utopia are being sketched out, an image of happiness found in giving pleasure.

Music is thus simply one way of expressing to humans their labors, of hearing and making heard their condition and the scope of their untapped creativity.

Music as Noise of Power

There is no power without the control of noise and without a code for analyzing, marking, restricting, training, repressing, and channeling sound, be it the sound of language, of the body, of tools, of objects, or of relationships with others and with oneself. All music—all organization of sounds—is a method of creating or consolidating a community; it is the link of power with its subjects, and an attribute of this power, whatever its form.

Moreover, there is no freedom without music. It inspires man to rise above himself and others, to go beyond standards and rules, to build an idea—however fragile—of transcendence.

And precisely because noise is at once an instrument of power and a source of rebellion, political powers have always been fascinated by what their subjects listen to. It is through noise that they are reassured, prepare their orders, foresee revolt. The powerful imagine knowing everything; the police dream of recording everything.

From the confessional to Internet tracking, from torture to phone tapping, extortion techniques and sound recording technologies serve as a canvas for every story of power. Totalitarian theorists all aimed to reserve for the power a monopoly on the broadcasting and reception of noise. The French monarchy's repression of regional music, white music executives' ostracism of black musicians, the Soviets' obsession with peaceful, national music, the systematic distrust of improvisation: all of these show the same fear of the foreign, the uncontrollable, the different.

In the market as well there is a monopoly on broadcasting messages and a control of noise, although the means by which this is achieved are less violent and subtler. When the market lays siege to and invests in music, it reduces the musician to a consumer good, an inoffensive show of submission and subversion, the first product of mass production and mass sale, with rebellion as its raw material. One example of this is Muzak, the corporation that since 1920 has been producing and distributing standardized music programs worldwide to thousands of radio stations and millions of elevators, restaurants, airports, and other places in which people are together in their own individual solitudes.

This is a pretext for reasonable people to make money through a senseless enterprise; like Lent disguised as Carnival, the music industry is an instrument of social pacification that gives each person the illusion of tasting forbidden passions. The legion of interchangeable songs and stars—although they may appear violent or rebellious, libertarian or subversive—enforces the limits of a daily life in which no one really has the power of expression, in which music is simply a method of playing at fear, a trivial topic of conversation, a means of preventing serious speech and action.

Understanding through Music

In order to develop a theory of the relationships between music, power, and money, one must first consider theories of music. This can only lead to disappointment, as these theories are a succession of confused typologies that are never without ulterior motivations. Today, the insatiable development and competition of theories, surveys, encyclopedias and typologies of music crystallizes the angst of the era, of music assimilated by entertainment, aesthetics dissolved in futility, senses drowned in the sea of commerce. Classifications with no real bearing on reality, these are only the final attempts to maintain order in a gaudy, demented, contradictory world where time in music is maze-like, cannot be reduced to measurements or categories. The simultaneity of styles, the dynamic interpenetration of forms and the freedom of creators prohibit all linear genealogy, hierarchical archeology, or ideological localization of a musician or a work. Each musical code is rooted in the ideologies and technologies of the era that produces it.

So what road should be followed through the immense forest of sounds that History has to offer? How can we understand what the economy makes of music, and what kind of economy music predicts? How can we trace the history of relationships between music and the worlds of production, trade, and desire?

Writing the history of the political economy of music is essentially an attempt to describe the flow through which sense can appear out of nonsense, music out of noise, trance out of dissonance. This is neither progress nor regression, but simply a sort of meaning, a tension at the forefront of all change in the social order.

Over the course of three distinct periods, music was expressed according to three codes, corresponding to three specific modes of economic organization. In parallel, three ideologies, three orders, dominated one after the other: religious, imperial, market. In between, periods of confusion and disorder prepared for the birth of the next order.

With the twentieth century began a fourth period, of repetitive music forged in the crucible of black American music, supported by the relentless demand of the world's youth and a new economic organization that made possible the recording and distribution of music, first physically, then virtually. In each of these periods, for those able to see it, the practice of music sketched out the times to come.

More than any other human activity, music—born of men and of gods, in the service of preachers and of princes, and then transformed into a commodity—has gone from sacred to profane. Music first showed how all the body's activities could be mastered, how practice could be specialized, how performances could be sold and mass-produced, recordings accumulated, and finally how a method of virtual storage in the form of pure data could be developed. Music was thus the forerunner of a repetitive globalization where nothing succeeds anymore unless it is part of the infinite flow of merchandise that only appears to be real and new.

Music is extremely current in this sense. As a pure sign it reveals one of the principal contradictions of the future: while no society can endure without building differences into its core, no market economy can develop without reducing these differences through the sale of mass-produced items. Music is the first to make audible the essence of these contradictions in tomorrow's societies, conveying an anguished search for lost differences in a logic from which difference has been banished. Today technology permits an infinite accumulation of music and of objects, all the while ensuring their sameness, and commodities communicate in an impoverished language. Some believe that this means the end of music, in much the same way as others have proclaimed the end of History: the musical odyssey has come to an end, the cycle is complete.

And if, on the contrary, it were only the beginning? If new music were once again heralding new societies? If we could, thanks to the music, build a bridge to the future and a renaissance?

In proposing new vistas of music in relation to society this book reaches beyond conventional music scholarship and expands the horizon of explorations considering music as a social force. The focus on Marx and music serves to problematize difference: of music as embedded in its material, social, and technological era, and of music as a human agent of transcending and transforming those contexts.

Note

1. This foreword contains parts of the new first chapter of the forthcoming second edition of *Bruits: essai sur l'économie politique de la musique.*

References

Jean-Jacques Rousseau. 1962. "Discours sur l'inégalité, in *(Oeuvres Complètes,* Bibliothèque de la Pléiade, vol. 2, part 2. Paris: Gallimard.
Friedrich Nietzsche. 1967. *Birth of Tragedy,* trans. Walter Kaufman, 61, 119. New York: Vintage.
Sigmund Freud. 1958. *The Moses of Michelangelo,* trans. James Strachey, standard edition, vol. 13:211. London: Hogarth.
Dominique Zahan. *La Dialectique du verbe chez les Bambaras.* Paris: Mouton.
Michel Serres. 1975. *Esthetique sur Carpaccio.* Paris: Hermann.

Introduction
Thinking Music, Thinking Marx

REGULA BURCKHARDT QURESHI

Some years ago world systems theorist Immanuel Wallerstein noted the striking move of the humanities toward the social sciences, asserting that "social processes matter, that what the humanities have to talk about are these social processes" (1996:6). Marxist theory has since its inception given culture-oriented scholars a means to engage with the social. The results are widely divergent, but they have in common a concern for social critique and what Grossberg and Nelson (1988:1,12) identify as two abiding Marxist priorities: "transgressing the line that has traditionally separated culture from social, economic, and political relations," and "[making] a commitment to revolutionary identification with the cause of the oppressed." The concern for theorizing both the intellectual and political consequences of a socially engaged music scholarship opens a debate that needs to extend across the divide between cultural humanism and social science. To engage Marx is to introduce into this debate a set of materially grounded perspectives unparalleled in scope and interpretive power.

Despite the theoretical and methodological ferment of recent musical scholarship, perspectives explicitly informed by the work of Karl Marx have been conspicuous largely by their absence. Marx's analyses of the commodity and of modes of production form a crucial basis of much recent critical theory, yet music scholars who have increasingly taken an interest in that theory as a means of exploring the cultural role of music have worked with Marx's ideas primarily in derivative forms. Studies of art music in particular have retained a humanist suspicion of materialist treatment. But if Marxist perspectives have rarely found their way into music studies, music, too, has figured only marginally in Marxist social analyses, even though the first work explicitly linking music and political economy comes from an economist (Attali 1987). If music scholarship is to deal seriously with music's place in society, a renewed engagement with the ideas of one of the most influential analysts of society is critical.

Music and Marx: Ideas, Practice, Politics is a response to this imperative. By bringing together scholars whose interest in Marx spans a variety of methodological and topical areas, the book explores the potential to theorize the social in music, or music in the social. This is a relatively new agenda for Western music scholarship, one that has been introduced largely from the margins of the academic establishment by scholars whose musical orientation entails accountability to social and cultural difference. Ethnomusicologists stand out among them in universalizing such accountability beyond particular constituencies, cutting across categorical boundaries set by privilege, technology, and the knowledge of power. Specialists in popular music and a growing number of Western musicologists have been expanding critiques of established cultural and scholarly practices in relation to gender, race, and class. Their collective engagement raises issues of power and hegemony that are increasingly concerned with global capitalism and its impact on people as much as on music.

This is the first time that a distinctly diverse set of music-directed approaches to Marx have found their way into a single collection. Specifically, the book approaches music and Marx from four critical directions:

1. Problematizing musical thinking/theorizing in relation to commodification and fetishism (Gramit, Klumpenhouwer).
2. Problematizing the poetics of musical form and genre as socially mediated by capitalism (Krims, Manuel).
3. Problematizing music-making processes in relation to economic processes via feudal and capitalist relations of production (Olmsted, Qureshi, Stokes).
4. Problematizing Marxist state policies in relation to musicological and musical practice (Judson, Levin, Zemtsovsky).

The essays are remarkable for their individuality and originality, each representing a uniquely situated approach to the general theme but ranging across the theory, practice, and politics of Marxism. Musically, they address scholarly concepts and practices (Gramit, Klumpenhouwer, Zemtsovsky), genres, forms, and repertoires (Krims, Manuel, Judson, Levin), musicians and performances (Olmsted, Stokes, Qureshi) in Western art music (Manuel, Olmsted), African American and Latin American popular music (Krims, Judson), Turkish and Mediterranean musics (Stokes), Uzbek music (Levin), and Indian music (Qureshi). Theoretically, the essays interrogate music through Marx by applying Marxist theory to musical "case studies" (Olmsted, Qureshi, Manuel, Levin), but they also address Marxist theory through music by expanding particular theoretical concepts in reference to musical issues (Stokes, Klumpenhouwer, Krims).

Diversity and difference are clearly a starting point for this book. It is an attempt to expand the terrain of a Marx-oriented engagement with music

beyond the confines of a single disciplinary horizon, and to include even contradictory positions. In so doing, it breaks with the established divisions that
have characterized Marx-related writings on music and on culture generally,
including not only the division between humanist and social science
approaches to Marx, but also between considerations of scholarly and political Marxism.

Another dimension of difference has to do with authorial location and its
interpretive dynamic. The music scholars who are located within the orbit of
the humanities and cultural studies tend to look to social processes in order to
enhance the interpretation of music. This can be seen in the chapters focused
on musical concepts (Gramit, Klumpenhouwer, Zemtsovsky), as well as in
those focused on musical products (Krims and Manuel) and musical production (Qureshi, Olmsted, and Stokes). In contrast, the social scientists look to
music to enhance the interpretation of social processes (Judson, Attali).

Marxist interpretation is far from being a single coherent discursive and
political practice, and boundaries between Marxist and non-Marxist theoretical positions are not easy or even meaningful to draw. The diversity found
in the papers of *Music and Marx* is itself symptomatically linked to the historically divergent strands of Marxist thought that have addressed music
and, more broadly, culture. Identifying three of these strands or intellectual
lineages suggests a broader context for the range of contributions in this
book.

The first and multiple strand of Marxist-inspired scholarship is best
known and most unproblematically associated with music. Variously identified as (Continental) humanist or culturalist Marxism, it comprises "a rich
legacy" of theoretical work in literary and cultural criticism and a commitment to the cultural centrality of music, and references on art more than
music (Norris 2000; Solomon 1974). This scholarship was developed in the
interwar period principally by the Frankfurt School, which uses Marxist concepts mainly on the terrain of ideation, individual consciousness, and the aesthetic (Arato and Gebhardt 1978). Drawing also on Hegelian philosophy and
Freud, the movement's dialectical critique of capitalism addresses mass culture and music from a standpoint of individual interiority, thereby theorizing
what Perry Anderson calls "the stratified consensual structure of bourgeois
hegemony in capitalist society" (Adorno 1978; Cook 1996; Horkheimer
1974; Anderson 1976). Since the 1960s cultural Marxism has resurfaced in
America, mainly through the mediation of Adorno by Fredric Jameson
(1971, 1990), enriched by critical vocabulary through engagement with
semiotics and poststructuralism, and focusing on multiple meanings of culture as experience and consciousness within the reification of late capitalism.
Cultural theorists incorporate Marxist perspectives into considerations of
advanced capitalism and the commodification of culture and music. New
readings of Adorno focus not only on art music but on music of popular cul-

ture (Paddison 1993; Klumpenhouwer forthcoming). In contrast to this Continental-American culturalist lineage, British cultural studies in the 1970s introduced a Marxist focus on class conflict to the theorizing of popular culture and popular music (Shepherd et al. 1977; Garofalo 1987). Within the textually oriented domain of cultural studies, Marxist concepts address largely formal concerns. But they also provide the theorizing of popular culture, including music, with a "political edge" in relation to mass culture in late capitalism and within it the counter-hegemonic expression of marginalized constituencies (Norris 1989).

A second strand of academic Marxism, consolidated in the 1970s in the social sciences, was centered in studies of political economy that addressed structures of capitalist domination and differential economic-political power across societies. Marx's concept of mode of production is theorized and applied empirically by anthropologists, sociologists, and historians, both Western and non-Western (Anderson 1974; Wallerstein 1976; Prakash 1990). Marxist anthropology is marked by structural Marxism, which developed from French structuralism and its tenet of theorizing social structures as centrally linked to structures of ideation (Levi-Strauss, Althusser). This broadly applied and influential approach locates determinative forces in structures of social and political relations, identifying labor and value within economically and culturally diverse societies (Godelier 1977; Bloch 1975), thereby theorizing the articulation of material, social, and cultural domains. Hence material production implicates culture and aesthetics as practices within "fields of cultural production" (Ortner 1984; Bourdieu 1995). Most prominently, culture and ideation are viewed as social processes critically and dialectically linked to class relations and structures of domination (Bloch 1975). Most recently, anthropologists and sociologists have been developing a neo-Marxist approach using the concept of flexible accumulation to deal with increasingly differentiated global capitalist practices, including the music industry and its global decentering, which is most immediately relevant for popular music studies (Blim 2000; Krims forthcoming). Another decentering initiative is the non-Western critique and deconstruction of Marxism's Eurocentric master narrative (Chakrabarty 2000; Chaudhury 1995).

Contrasting with these critical-interpretive approaches is a third strand of what I call "activist," "political," or "state" Marxism. After an initial Marxist phase of theoretically and practically integrated internationalism, the political reality of ideologically divided political systems generated two distinct kinds of Marxist orientations, both of which are further differentiated within national or regional political as well as historical contexts. State Marxism is predominantly associated with Soviet ideation, but it also has its exponents in independent Marxist states, especially China, and in revolutionary movements elsewhere. Contested by academic Marxists, opposed by non-Marxists, and used as negative evidence by anti-Marxists, state and revolutionary Marxism have nevertheless offered alternative applications of Marxist theory to art and music, even if these are intellectually constrained by their activist purpose and legitimized by arbitrarily totalizing implementation (Zhdanov 1950). Since music, along with literature and art, was seen as a tool for shaping communist society and abolishing class hegemony, ideation on music became a political imperative. Articulated by state functionaries and even by Lenin and Stalin, this was literally the knowledge of power, to be elaborated aesthetically and historically by music scholars and realized musically by composers. From the early tenet of music reflecting the life of the people (Lenin 1967; Lunacharsky 1965) to the constructionist imperative of creating people's music with socialist content, musicologists and folk music specialists played a special role theorizing and validating these policies, especially their musical implementation by composers (Schwartz 1983; Solomon 1974; Taruskin 1997).

Considering these Marxist lineages from a contemporary perspective prompts some striking historical associations: cultural Marxism with the "Western" need to be anticommunist; political Marxism with loyalty to Soviet and other communist regimes; and Marxist anthropology with the need to explain colonized non-Western societies. Today's global economy and "global ecumene" (Hannerz 1992) call for acknowledging rather than ignoring the historical dialectic that ultimately links these differently construed modes of thinking Marx and music. *Music and Marx* opens a shared conversation that challenges assumptions and identifies contradictions within all three discourses—as exemplified particularly in the self-historicizing critique of state Marxism by Zemtsovsky, the mode of production critique by Stokes, and, most profoundly, in the negatively dialectical critique by Klumpenhouwer.

Historicizing, finally, leads me to the antecedents of this book, and to contemplating some of its consequences. If Marx and subsequent Marxisms are historically situated, so are the applications of his work in relation to each contributor's particular way of approaching music. This is of relevance especially because the intent here is not only to apply Marxist theory to music, but also to open up space for interrogating the use of this theory as an intersubjective practice within the milieu of music studies.

The idea of this book arises from a pioneering collective engagement with Marx by a group of colleagues and students at the University of Alberta. In 1996 Marx was easily the most contested topic in the co-taught core seminar of our interdisciplinary graduate program in music. Four critically honed colleagues were debating the idea of Marx and music from perspectives of musicology (David Gramit), music theory (Henry Klumpenhouwer, Adam Krims), and ethnomusicology (Regula Qureshi). The outcome was the first-ever panel on music and Marx, presented initially to the Annual Meeting of the Society for Ethnomusicology in Toronto and then, in full form, to the Annual Meeting of the American Musicological Society in Baltimore. The papers caused a stir as well as puzzlement—and Martha Feldman's invitation to do a book. Since then, the University of Alberta has become a center for Marxist studies of music, with Klumpenhouwer, an acknowledged expert on Marxist theory and music (Klumpenhouwer 1998, forthcoming), and Krims, who theorizes popular music through Marx (Krims forthcoming). In a more applied vein, David Gramit (1998) draws on Marx in a socially grounded approach to interpreting music historically. My own engagement with Marx goes back to the late 1970s, the heyday of Marxist anthropology (at the University of Alberta) and its focus on connecting economies and culture (Qureshi 1994, 2000; see also Asch 1979; Olmsted forthcoming).[1]

Explicit orientations toward Marx are a rarity in the current world of music scholarship. The task of identifying other contributors who would enter the demanding thematic orbit of this book was a challenge that revealed both the continued disciplinary ensconcement, and a remarkable commitment to individual theorizing among colleagues willing to expand such boundaries in the direction of socializing music scholarship. The resulting essays are divergent, even contradictory, in approach no less than in topic and emphasis. But by assuming a focus on the unequaled ideational and social scope of Marxist theory, their authors open a conversation about music across disciplinary fences and map out a common space to expand the already ongoing discourse on the "sociality" of music. The authors' interpretive use of Marx is also a conduit for inserting music into the reference frame and discourse of the social sciences, an agenda that challenges humanist notions of music among social scientists, including Marx himself (Qureshi 2000). While *Music and Marx* profiles ways of using Marx for this agenda, it must leave historicizing Marx's own treatment of music to others. The book also deliberately leaves out consideration to the well-known Marxism-inspired discourse within the area of cultural studies (Lipsitz 1994; Nelson and Grossberg 1988).

Finally, I wish to acknowledge and thank my colleagues at the University of Alberta—David Gramit, Henry Klumpenhouwer, and Adam Krims—for providing the nucleus of "difference" on which this book is built, and for broadening my horizon in matters of Marx and otherwise. To all the contributors of the book I extend my sincere gratitude for entrusting their innovative work to this volume, and for their patience. Equally sincere thanks go to series editor Martha Feldman for supporting this project with her expertise throughout. I especially want to thank warmly Stephen Blum for his resourcefulness and Brenda Dalen for her incisive advice. Special thanks go to Kaley Mason for his superb editorial and research assistance, and to Richard Carlin and Lisa Vecchione of Routledge for their highly professional support. Finally, funding from the University of Alberta for travel to Baltimore and for translating the Attali and Zemtsovsky chapters is gratefully acknowledged.

Note

1. A different perspective on this history appears in chapter 4.

References

Adorno, Theodor W. 1978. "On the Fetish Character in Music and the Regression of Listening." In *The Essential Frankfurt School Reader,* edited by Andrew Arato and Eike Gebhardt, 270–99. New York: Urizen Books.

Anderson, Perry. 1974. *Lineages of the Absolute State.* London: N.L.B.

———. 1976. *Considerations on Western Marxism.* London: N. L. B.

Arato, Andre, and Eike Gebhardt, eds. 1978. *The Essential Frankfurt School Reader.* New York: Urizen Books.

Asch, Michael. 1979. "Ecological-evolutionary Model and the Concept of Mode of Production." In *Challenging Anthropology,* edited by Terence Turner and Gavin Smith, 81–98. Toronto: McGraw-Hill Ryerson.

Attali, Jacques. 1987. *Noise: The Political Economy of Music.* Translated by Brian Massumi. Minneapolis: University of Minnesota Press.

Blim, Michael. 2000. "Capitalism in late Modernity." *Annual Review of Anthropology* 29: 25–38.

Bloch, Maurice, ed. 1975. *Marxist Analyses and Social Anthropology.* London: Malaby Press.

Bourdieu, Pierre. 1995. *The Field of Cultural Production: Essays on Art and Literature,* edited by Randal Johnson. New York: Columbia University Press.

Chakrabarty, Dipesh. 2000. *Provincializing Europe: Postcolonial Thought and Historical Difference.* Princeton, N.J.: Princeton University Press.

Chaudhury, Ajit. 1995. "Rethinking Marxism in India: The Heritage We Renounce." *Rethinking Marxism* 8/3: 133–43.

Cook, Deborah. 1996. *The Culture Industry Revisited: Theodor W. Adorno on Mass Culture.* Lanham, Md.: Rowman & Littlefield.

Garofalo, Reebee. 1987. "How Autonomous Is Relative: Popular Music, the Social Formation and Cultural Struggle." *Popular Music* 6/1: 77–92.

Godelier, Maurice. 1977. *Perspectives in Marxist Anthropology.* Translated by Robert Brain. Cambridge: Cambridge University Press.

Gramit, David. 1998. "Musicology, Commodity Structure, and Musical Practice." In *Crosscurrents and Counterpoints: Offerings in Honor of Bengt Hambraeus at 70,* edited by Per F. Broman, Nora A. Engebretsen, and Bo Alphonce, 22–34. Publications of the University of Gothenburg Department of Musicology 5. Gothenburg: University of Gothenburg.

Grossberg, Lawrence, and Cary Nelson. 1988. "Introduction: The Territory of Marxism." In *Marxism and the Interpretation of Culture,* edited by C. Nelson and L. Grossberg, 1–13. Urbana: University of Illinois Press.

Hannerz, Ulf. 1992. "The Global Ecumene as a Network of Networks." In *Conceptualizing Society,* edited by Adam Kuper, 34–58. London: Routledge.

Horkheimer, Max. 1974. *Critical Theory.* New York: Seabury.

Jameson, Fredric. 1971. *Marxism and Form: Twentieth-Century Dialectical Theories of Literature.* Princeton, N.J.: Princeton University Press.

———. 1990. *Late Marxism: Adorno or The Persistence of the Dialectic.* London and New York: Verso.

Klumpenhouwer, Henry. 1998. Afterword. In *Music/Ideology: Resisting the Aesthetic,* edited by Adam Krims, 289–310. Amsterdam: G + B Arts International.

———. Forthcoming. "Late Capitalism, Late Marxism, and the Study of Music." *Music Analysis.*

Krims, Adam. Forthcoming. "Popular Music Studies, Flexible Accumulation, and the Future of Marxism." In *Popular Music and Social Analysis,* edited by Allan Moore. Cambridge: Cambridge University Press.

———, ed. 1998. *Music/Ideology: Resisting the Aesthetic.* Amsterdam: G + B Arts International.

Lenin, Vladimir Ilyich. 1967. *On Literature and Art.* Moscow: Foreign Languages Publishing House.

Lipsitz, George. 1994. *Dangerous Crossroads: Popular Music, Postmodernism and the Poetics of Place.* London and New York: Verso.

Lunacharsky, Anatoly. 1965. *On Literature and Art.* Moscow: Foreign Language Publishing House.

McLellan, David. 1984. *Marxism after Marx.* Boston: Houghton Mifflin.

Nelson, C. and L. Grossberg, eds. 1988. *Marxism and the Interpretation of Culture.* Urbana: University of Illinois Press.

Norris, Christopher, ed. 1989. *Music and the Politics of Culture.* New York: St. Martin's Press.

———. 2001 "Marxism." *The New Grove Dictionary of Music and Musicians,* 2nd ed., London: MacMillan.

Olmsted, Anthony. Forthcoming. *We Shall Overcome: Folkways Records 1948–69.* New York: Routledge.

Ortner, Sherry B. 1984. "Theory in Anthropology since the Sixties." *Comparative Studies of Society and History* 26: 126–60.

Paddison, Max. 1993. *Adorno's Aesthetics of Music.* Cambridge: Cambridge University Press.

Prakash, Gyan. 1990. *Bonded Histories: Genealogies of Labor Servitude in Colonial India.* Cambridge and New York: Cambridge University Press.

Qureshi, Regula Burckhardt. 1994. "Focus on Ethnic Music." In *Canadian Music: Issues of Hegemony and Identity,* edited by Beverley Diamond and Robert Witmer, 343–49. Toronto: Scholar's Press.

———. 2000. "Confronting the Social: Mode of Production and the Sublime in Hindustani Music." *Ethnomusicology* 44/1: 15–38, reprinted in *Border Crossings in Music Scholarship,* edited by John Shepherd, special issue Repercussions (2001).

Schwartz, Boris. 1983. *Music and Musical Life in Soviet Russia.* Bloomington: Indiana University Press.

Shepherd, John, Phil Verder, Graham Vulliamy, and Trevor Wishart. 1977. *Whose Music? A Sociology of Musical Languages.* London: Latimer New Dimensions.

Solomon, Maynard. 1974. *Marxism and Art: Essays Classic and Contemporary.* New York: Alfred A. Knopf.

Taruskin, Richard, 1997. *Defining Russia Musically: Historical and Hermeneutical Essays.* Princeton: Princeton University Press.

Wallerstein, Immanuel. 1976. *The Modern World System.* New York: Academic Press.

———. 1996. "Open the Social Sciences." *Items, Social Science Research Council.* 50/1: 1–7.

Zhdanov, A. A. 1950. *Essays on Literature, Philosophy and Music.* New York: International Publishers.

PART I

Commodification and Music Scholarship

1

Music Scholarship, Musical Practice, and the Act of Listening

DAVID GRAMIT

Produced by the experience of the game, and therefore of the objective structures within which it is played out, the "feel for the game" is what gives the game a subjective sense—a meaning and a *raison d'être*, but also a direction, an orientation, an impending outcome, for those who take part and therefore acknowledge what is at stake. . . . Indeed, one has only to suspend the commitment to the game implied in the feel for the game in order to reduce the world, and the actions performed in it, to absurdity, and to bring up questions about the meaning of the world and existence which people never ask when they are caught up in the game–the questions of an aesthete trapped in the instant, or an idle spectator.
—PIERRE BOURDIEU, *THE LOGIC OF PRACTICE*

I try to put together the two parts of my life, as many first-generation intellectuals do. . . . My main problem is to try and understand what happened to me. My trajectory may be described as miraculous, I suppose—an ascension to a place where I don't belong. And so to be able to live in a world that is not mine I must try to understand both things: what it means to have an academic mind—how such is created—and at the same time what was lost in acquiring it.
—BOURDIEU, *DOXA AND THE COMMON LIFE:* AN INTERVIEW

What does it mean "to have an academic mind" with respect to music? Does it make sense to speak, with Bourdieu, of "what was lost in acquiring it" if we examine the way music is constructed in musicology? To explore these questions, I will begin by drawing attention to an act that is crucial to musicology but nonetheless often taken for granted within it: the act of listening to music—of listening, that is, with rapt attention to the particular shape and details of particular, unique musical works. As one of the central "objective structures within which the game of musical scholarship is played out, that act is crucial to the subjective sense" of the game and has often come to symbolize proper musical scholarship. But this disciplinary loyalty becomes problematic simply because the game of musicology is not the game of music (a pursuit that has its own sense and structures), even if the two have significant points of overlap. Rather than recognizing the differences between these two practices and reflecting on the significance of those differences for musicological practice, musicology has, I will argue, come to privilege the (scholar's) act of listening to the extent that other significant elements of musical practice have been rendered all but invisible. To explain this situation of disappearing practices, I will have recourse to Karl Marx's analysis of the manner in which commodities veil the social relations through which they are produced. From this perspective, what the academic mind "loses" both serves to secure its own institutional position and to naturalize the larger system in which it operates, by so constructing the musical object, the focus of scholarly inquiry, as to locate its significance within the work rather than in the behaviors and relationships that constitute musical activity.

This may seem a meager role for Marx in a collection dedicated to Marx and music, and indeed I make no claim to have forged a theoretical advance that will alter the practice of music scholarship in a way inconceivable without Marx. Rather, I offer the reflections of a music historian whose work centers on musical culture in the society of which Marx himself was a member; considering some of Marx's ideas in relation to musicological practices can explain something about those practices and their origins, clarify Marx's own perspective on the place of music within capitalism, and, finally, offer insight into the social position of musicology and the high musical culture it has helped to construct. Before arriving at Marx, however, I will consider the situation of musicology, and of phenomena that may seem far removed from the world of commodities, production, and class relations. As Bourdieu insists, however, ignoring these symbolic practices in search of an objective account of society is ultimately as deceptive as considering only those practices in isolation (see, for instance, Bourdieu 1990: 17 and 136–41).[1]

I begin, then, with a consideration of a central feature of what might, following Bourdieu, be termed the "academic mind" within music, the structures of thought that produce scholarship whose musicological legitimacy is unimpeachable, even given recent challenges to methodologies and canons.[2] I have elsewhere discussed what I believe to be one crucial component of the field's self-definition (see Gramit 1998a), so I will summarize only briefly here: Acknowledgment of the centrality of the aesthetic experience derived from focused attention to individual musical works is a sine qua non of at least the North American musicological enterprise. This foundational experience has defined the field of musicological study in a way that permits the disciplinary developments and controversies that have been so prominent within the last decade to proceed largely without fundamentally challenging at least this one basic rule of the game. Thoroughly internalized, it is most frequently made explicit when drawn out by a polemical challenge—either in order to defend one's membership in the field or to challenge that of another.

One such discipline-bounding statement provides an admirably succinct characterization of the mode of attention to music that the musicological enterprise privileges. In the context of a discussion of scholarship that he criticized as failing to take account of "what many of us would recognize as the musical experience itself," Ralph Locke (1993: 169) defined that experience as "the active and often critical/creative *internal* participation in the musical artwork." Although unusually direct, Locke's statement is by no means unique. Ellen Rosand, also cautioning against trends in recent scholarship, asserts similarly (1995: 11) that scholarship demands "passionate engagement" and "personal involvement" with music, and writes of "returning once again to the musical work, to discover the affective structures of its operation"; Pieter C. van den Toorn (1995: 1) opens his attack on the practices of "new musicology" by invoking "a consuming interest in music" that results in "an effort to draw ourselves closer to a musical context and enhance our appreciation"; Lawrence Kramer (one of the targets of van den Toorn's attacks), in a polemical exchange with Gary Tomlinson, writes (1993: 27) of "listening with the kind of deep engagement, the heightened perception and sense of identification, that both grounds and impels criticism"; and even Tomlinson, who argues for a methodology that will not necessarily place the criticism of individual works at its center, still acknowledges (defensively) "our love for the music we study," and "our usual impassioned musical involvements"—which, he maintains, we should "dredge up . . . from the hidden realm of untouchable premise they tend to inhabit" (1993: 24).

Nor are such statements limited to polemics of recent years. In the 1980s, Margaret Bent defended traditional musicological practices, especially the editing of music, against Joseph Kerman's advocacy of the primacy of music criticism in part by asserting that editing did indeed involve the crucial element: "learning is a dynamic and shifting consensus of knowledge *that includes aesthetic and musical experience* as well as data in the traditional sense" (1986: 6; my emphasis). A product of the German academic controversies of the 1960s and 1970s, Carl Dahlhaus's *Foundations of Music History* (1983) revolves around the problem of writing a plausible history of music while still acknowledging the necessity of "aesthetic immersion in musical works as self-sustaining entities" (27).[3] And, returning to North America, both of the main participants in the most prominent disciplinary debate of the 1960s, Joseph Kerman and Edward Lowinsky, claimed the musical experience as their unassailable starting point: Kerman wrote of a "passion" for the great composers, of "the essential musical experience," and of "an original commitment to music as aesthetic experience" (1965: 66–67) while Lowinsky countered that "[my] credo has always been: 'the beginning and the end of musicological studies lie in sympathetic and critical evaluation of the individual work of art' " (1965: 226, citing Lowinsky 1961: 72).

Four decades of statements, ranging from almost offhand to fervent and written by scholars of widely differing perspectives, should suffice to make the point: So basic is the aesthetic experience of music—an intense, focused involvement with an individual work of music—to the conception of the object of musicological study that it demands acknowledgment from all sides. In order to establish credibility—even for enterprises (like Bent's or Tomlinson's) that focus elsewhere—it is essential at least to *suggest* that one knows that passionate involvement. To do otherwise is to risk dismissal of the sort given by Charles Rosen (1996: 63) to Tia DeNora: "It would be grand to have a social history of music, but before it can be realized, the sociologists will have to take music more seriously." This formulation lays out the stakes particularly clearly: focused attention to the music itself is what separates legitimate musical scholarship from work in other disciplines that presumes to touch on music (e.g., "the sociologists").

So pervasive a structuring value, I would argue, is part of the *habitus* of the discipline—the structure of thought into which the field disciplines its practitioners and which in turn shapes their perceptions and practices.[4] If this is so, then even attempts to develop new musicological practices would continue to be shaped by it. And in fact, the unmarked presumption that listening—and in particular, concentrated listening to unique works—is the essential musical act is apparent not only in conventional musical scholarship but also in some of the most prominent recent attempts to depart from those conventions. Given this orientation, it is no coincidence that the most prominent and widely discussed examples of "the New Musicology" have been those that have devoted extensive attention to critical rehearings of canonic musical works.[5]

At this point, I should hasten to assure readers who may be wearying of a long parade of examples—one that could easily give rise to the expectation that the old dispensation is about to be dismissed in favor of a new, music-free music scholarship—that I am by no means arguing that musicologists should stop listening to music or writing about "the notes" (a fear given explicit voice by a professional colleague who heard an earlier expression of this position). Rather, I have simply sought to demonstrate that one particular tenet of music scholarship is both pervasive and naturalized: even if individual examples of scholarship may focus on other matters, musicology is ultimately "about" pieces of music to which we listen intently. It may seem disingenuous to proceed to insert my own statement of loyalty—that I too value both the experience of listening to music and the challenge of exploring how individual pieces "work" in various contexts—but it is nevertheless true. I recognize the pervasiveness of the value not only in the words of others but in my own hesitation in making the value itself the object of some of *my* scholarship. For surely, I find part of me objecting, listening to music *is* fundamental, and what we mean by "music" when we name it as the object of our study is self-evident.[6]

And yet, a more reflective part of me insists that it is not in fact so self-evident, and this prompts me to raise the possibility not of a noteless musicology but rather of one that recognizes that the act of listening—especially of listening like a scholar—is only one of the ways through which music becomes significant, and further, that the mode of listening itself can be seen to be as significant as the thing listened to. Before expanding on this position, I will try to convey my sense of its necessity, which arises in part from reflecting on my own experience of music. Simply put, I cannot, with Kerman, claim "an original commitment to music as aesthetic experience," perhaps because I first encountered music that I learned to value for its own sake not through the act of focused listening but rather through the act of playing—specifically, learning an instrument in an elementary school band program. To be sure, I also learned to listen (albeit not immediately, as anyone who has attended an elementary school band concert will understand), but several other modes of listening seem to me to have been at least as important as that of solitary aesthetic participation in a work: listening in lessons to the voice and sounds of the teacher; listening to myself, practicing, in an attempt to internalize that voice and create those sounds; and listening to others in an ensemble situation, whether the direct interaction of chamber music or the larger and overtly hierarchical band or orchestra. Eventually, I also learned to listen to, delight in, and revere "great works" (just as, eventually, playing came to occupy a less significant role in my conception of music) and even to write about those works and their composers. But anyone who can remember listening as a child to an AM easy listening station believing that this was the "classical music" he was beginning to experience in band will perhaps always remain skeptical that aesthetic listening is the necessary center of music.

By introducing this alternative perspective autobiographically, I by no means wish to argue that we replace the aesthetic experience of music with experiential narrative as the mark of legitimate scholarship. Indeed, even my skeletal summary raises issues that reach well beyond the personal. For instance, simply to compare my account with what for Adorno (1994: 328) counted as a "prototypical" (read "autobiographical"?) initiatory musical experience—"a child who lies awake in his bed while a string quartet plays in an adjoining room, and who is suddenly so overwhelmed by the excitement of the music that he forgets to sleep and listens breathlessly"—is to be made aware of the distinction between what Bourdieu calls (1984: 74–75) "domestic learning" ("acquired pre-verbally, by early immersion in a world of cultivated people, practices and objects") and a later, scholastically mediated learning open to those of less privileged origin. What I do hope to have suggested is that even if we limit ourselves to activities that fall clearly within the commonsense definition of musical, a perspective that centers on reflective, critical listening, no matter how socially oriented, will inevitably neglect or marginalize much that is essential to music. The physical activity of playing, of training a body to enact music; the institution of the music lesson, with its highly personalized means of reproducing cultural authority; and the relational and hierarchical dynamics of performance: all of these are inextricably linked to the music that has traditionally been the focus of musicology, yet they fade from view when "music" is implicitly defined as the work of a composer for aesthetic contemplation by a listener. And if we consider as well the relations that bring musical artifacts and events (instruments, printed scores, concerts, etc.) into being, the areas occluded from view still further dwarf that which musicology has defined as its object. As an alternative and supplement, then, I am proposing that we consider music as an activity, and musical works as one product of a set of relationships involving a wide variety of participants. From this perspective, rather than imagining listening, reflective or otherwise, as the center that defines musical meaning, we can suggest that the meaning of that activity too is crucially dependent on one's position amid those relationships. Such a perspective would permit musicology to reflect on its own social relationship to music rather than assuming it within its definition of its object.

There is by now of course nothing novel about the claim that music is an inherently social undertaking, nor that scholarship has often overlooked that sociality; and further, the assertion that music is fundamentally about relations among people has recently been given an eloquent and provocative exposition by Christopher Small (1998). Why, then, reiterate such claims and insist on adding Marx to the mix? Marx himself was certainly never centrally concerned to explore the workings of music within the economic system he theorized; in fact, one of his few explicit discussions of music ([1857–58] 1973: 305–306n.) famously dismissed its performance as productive labor within capitalism with a highly unflattering analogy:

> The piano *maker* reproduces *capital*; the pianist only exchanges his labour for revenue. But doesn't the pianist produce music and satisfy our musical ear, does he not even to a certain extent produce the latter? He does indeed: his labour produces something; but that does not make it productive labour in the *economic sense*; no more than the labour of the madman who produces delusions is productive . . . . Productive labourer [is] he that directly augments capital.

Given Marx's concern to detail the precise role of labor in the emerging capitalist economy he sought to analyze, this distinction is a crucial one, even if

Marx here takes "music" in precisely the sense I have been criticizing. (I will return to the historical context of this view below.) My concern, however, is more limited: Marx's analysis of the nature of commodities and their exchange offers striking parallels to the disappearance of musical activity behind the aesthetic experience, and that disappearance is arguably closely linked to the integration of music into the system whose workings Marx analyzed. To see this demands a review of the starting point of Marx's critical analysis of capitalism, a review that will be so basic as to seem pedantic to readers versed in the social sciences; however, within musicology, it is unfamiliar enough that even my elementary explication may provide material for new reflection.[7]

Marx's massive critique of political economy, *Capital*, begins with what Marx took to be capitalism's most pervasive and fundamental element, the commodity, which he defines in an initially straightforward way:

> The commodity is, first of all, an external object, a thing which through its qualities satisfies human needs of whatever kind. The nature of these needs, whether they arise, for example, from the stomach, or the imagination, makes no difference. Nor does it matter here how the thing satisfies man's need, whether directly as a means of subsistence, i.e., an object of consumption, or indirectly as a means of production. ([1867] 1976: 125)

But this ability to satisfy needs—the commodity's use value—is only part of the story. The second crucial property of the commodity is its abstract value, revealed as a quantity in exchange with other commodities. In this exchange, qualitative (use-related) values disappear, and the value revealed in exchange represents only that which all commodities hold in common: the property "of being products of labour." Moreover, value expressed in exchange cannot represent labor of any particular sort, since different commodities require different forms of labor for their production. What must determine value, then, is "human labour in the abstract": from the perspective of the exchange of commodities, "they are merely congealed quantities of homogeneous human labour, i.e., of human labour power expended without regard to the form of its expenditure" ([1867] 1976: 128).

Such formulations, taken, it is important to note, from the first few pages of a massive work, have done much to give rise to the impression that Marx's viewpoint represents economic reductionism in the extreme, and that the claim of labor as the determinant of value is arbitrary and insufficient. But as Dominick La Capra has noted (1989: 174–79), the opening of *Capital* is anything but straightforward in its stance toward what it appears to introduce as absolute categories: value-neutral language is interrupted abruptly by ironic comments that undercut it, and it only gradually becomes clear that Marx is presenting not transcendent categories illustrated by the concrete example of capitalism, but rather historical but naturalized categories through which capitalism produces—and distorts—its reality. If, then, Marx's appeal to labor as the determinant of value seems a troubling sleight of hand, and if his tone at times appears disconcertingly abstract, we may suspect a strong motivation: this definition of value is not only a part of Marx's analysis of the commodity, but also the heart of the system Marx is critiquing, a system in which abstraction from social relations to objects is essential.[8]

The notions of naturalization and deceptive appearances turn out to be crucial to the functioning of the commodity, because the two distinct forms of value inherent in it lead to a thorough mystification of the system in which commodities function. The exchange of commodities on the basis of quantities of abstract labor value means that what appears as the inherent value of things obscures their critical function within the relations that constitute society: "the commodity seems not to *be* a value, a social mediation, but rather a use value that *has* exchange value" (Postone 1993: 169). In Marx's own terms,

> Since the producers do not come into social contact until they exchange the products of their labour, the specific social characteristics of their private labours appear only within this exchange . . . . To the producers, therefore, the social relations between their private labours appear as what they are, i.e., they do not appear as direct social relations between persons in their work, but rather as material [*dinglich*] relations between persons and social relations between things. ([1867] 1976: 165–66)

Later, Marx succinctly refers to this process as "the conversion of things into persons and persons into things" ([1867] 1976: 209). La Capra comments (1989: 178) that "one might extend Marx's train of thought and argue that meaning divorced from an intimate relation to the work process is projected and fixated in a detached symbolic form into the mystified commodity as fetish."

The location of meaning returns us to the scholarly practices with which I began. Those practices exist within a society in which the straightforward consumption of musical commodities is the norm, notwithstanding Marx's unwillingness to view musical performance as productive labor. This is self-evident in the circulation of recorded music, but even "live" performers also frequently operate under various circumstances as wage laborers.[9] So, too, do salaried academics, despite the social esteem in which their labor has traditionally been held. And one could easily argue that (despite Adorno's claim (1978: 281) that "a Beethoven symphony as a whole, spontaneously experienced, can never be appropriated") musicological publication takes as a raw material—a means of production of its scholarly product—the musical object, the work that is the object of its study. If this parallel seems to conflate capitalists and workers (professors receive wages, but earn the "profit" from their publications as well) it is once again worth adducing Bourdieu and noting that the usual profit realized is cultural capital in the form of professional recognition rather than immediate financial gain.[10]

It would be foolish to argue that a different scholarly focus will materially alter these productive relationships; I mention them rather in order to suggest that they have exercised a strong and often unrecognized influence, which becomes more comprehensible if we consider Marx's discussion of the commodity. In conjunction with institutionalized demands for scholarly productivity, the commodified circulation of musical objects predisposes us to take as the "natural" object of our study those musical objects and the relations among them, rather than the activities and the historically specific systems of social relationships that give rise to them.[11] We thus mis/recognize music's power to mediate social relationships as a power inherent in the (mystified) object. Even analytical approaches that seek to demonstrate how musical processes reflect larger social forces, valuable though they are, also perpetuate this situation to the extent that they posit a separate musical object that represents or models social relations. Again, I am not advocating the abandonment of such scholarship—after all, following Marx, in materializing relations between persons, it in a sense makes works "appear as what they are," that is, as reifications of the social. Rather, I am suggesting that we supplement the intellectual contemplation of musical objects with analysis of the social significance of music as a practice. This must inevitably also involve not only examination of the specific social relations and activities that have allowed musical objects to appear as autonomous, meaningful entities, but also reflection on musicology as a practice in relation to the historical or contemporary objects it seeks to characterize.

From this perspective, the functions of the aesthetic experience of music merit further consideration. That mode of experience—described by Locke (1993: 169) as "*internal* participation in the musical artwork" or by Dahlhaus (1989: 95) as "the mental retracing of musical logic"—is, as I have suggested above, a listener's rather than a participant's mode, reflective rather than active, and directed toward contemplation of the musical object as a whole. Precisely this concern for the whole of the object that focused listening constitutes minimizes awareness of the personal relationships of music-making. To be sure, technology has rendered this disappearance even more literal through the ubiquity of recordings, in which music-making people are not physically present at all. But to the extent that we listen solely to the unfolding "musical logic" (whether as audience member or performer) those relationships are equally effectively obscured from our awareness. (The central role of the piano in the century before recording might also be related to its allowing the performer to substitute musical relationships between parts within a work for the personal relationships of ensemble performance, and the persistence of score-reading requirements in many graduate musicology programs, even granting its undoubted practical utility, also naturalizes the same substitution.) Whether or not one considers music a commodity per se, then, the *act* of listening to the autonomous musical object can be understood as part of the ideological work of music in that it models and naturalizes the veiling of social relationships through its constitution of an ostensibly independent object. The structure of the individual work so attended to plays no role in this process (although this by no means precludes the possibility that the structure of individual works or genres may in particular contexts function ideologically in other significant ways). Indeed, the rich variety of structures and styles that such listening can apprehend and that we are often at pains to point out to our students may serve to focus our attention all the more firmly on the objects themselves and their relationships to one another, turning attention away from both the social relations that bring them into existence and the role of the act of listening itself.

For historians of musical culture, this process of refocusing is of interest not only because it has obscured much of the larger phenomenon of musical practice, but also because the gradual elevation of the reflective listener and the disappearance of musical practice proves to be a significant part of the development of an ideology of serious music in the late eighteenth and early nineteenth centuries—and can lead us back to the dismissal of music with which I began my discussion of Marx. This is not the context in which this process can be traced at length, but the following sketch suggests that the disappearance of music as a field of social practice and the socioeconomic developments Marx traced were more than coincidentally related.

An observation by Charles Burney provides a useful starting point. Visiting Augsburg in 1772, the English scholar-cum-tourist excused the brevity of his account with a revealing generalization:

> I was somewhat tired of going to imperial cities [i.e., free cities not under the rule of a local prince] after music; as I seldom found any thing but the organ and organist worth attending to, and not always them . . . . These cities are not rich, and therefore have not the folly to support their theatres at a great expence. The fine arts are children of affluence and luxury; in despotic governments they render power less insupportable, and diversion from thought is perhaps as necessary as from action. Whoever therefore seeks music in Germany, should do it at the several courts, not in the free imperial cities, which are generally inhabited by poor industrious people, whose genius is chilled and repressed by penury; who can bestow nothing on vain pomp or luxury; but think themselves happy, in the possession of necessaries. The residence of a sovereign prince, on the contrary; besides the musicians in ordinary of the court, church and stage, swarms with pensioners and expectants, who have however few opportunities of being heard. ([1775]) 1959: 42–43)

The expectation that courts were the centers around which music flourished was as unexceptional as the frankness of Burney's pragmatic account of its utility was unusual. But hindsight lends a further casual observation about the city a significance Burney likely never anticipated: "At going out, on the Munich side, there is a very fine building, just constructed, for the use of a cotton manufactory, which is of an immense size, and in a pleasing style of architecture" ([1775] 1959: 43); the old free cities would not be the center of industrial development, but Burney's "poor industrious people" would in the next century begin to accumulate "affluence and luxury" through precisely such means. While it would be misleading to claim—especially for Germany—that industrialization was the cause of the transformation of musical life that followed (and was indeed already under way as Burney wrote), the unchallenged centrality of the courts in musical life was coming to an end.[12]

Musicians, however, were by no means certain what, if anything, could replace the patronage of those courts. Already in 1787 a Viennese commentator noted that, because of declining support for music at courts, "one can scarcely expect the likes of Handel, Gluck, Gasmann, Paisello, Sarti, Naumann, Salieri, Haydn, Dittersdorf, or Mozart in the future" (Schmith 1787: 96–97).[13] Johann Friedrich Reichardt put it much more succinctly in a comment ascribed to him by Ludwig Achim von Arnim: "I am not dumb enough to become a great musician in such a time" (cited in Hartung 1992: 11).[14] For those who sought to support themselves in the face of this uncertainty, the musical press not only offered potential income (as it did for Reichardt, E. T. A. Hoffmann, Berlioz, Carl Maria von Weber, and many others), but also, amid reviews and aesthetic discussion, a wealth of specific discussion concerning the practice of musical life, ranging from discussions of pedagogy to advice to young musicians, and from discussions of new instruments and inventions to counsel on dealing with patrons. Musical discourse, in short, despite the prevalence of idealist interpretations of musical works (see Bonds 1997), made little effort to obscure the practices on which that music depended. Indeed, the musical press routinely carried proposals for developing or preserving adequate support for music and musicians—ranging from modest proposals to provide income for teachers to sweeping reforms proposed in the aftermath of the revolutions of 1848—and music's social significance was frequently discussed as a reason such support should be provided.

Claims for that significance were crucial to the accommodation of music within the new social order that developed throughout the first half of the century, but they also prepared the way for the disappearance of musical practice from musical discourse. For example, the loss of stable court support for musicians was still of concern to a Viennese author in 1818, but a higher motivation for musical patronage has replaced Burney's simple love of affluence and luxury:

> But when the first class of the state [i.e., the nobility], upon which the fine
> arts always formerly depended to support their progress, for the sake of

cultivation of the spirit and of taste, no longer know how to appreciate
their essential value, then the entire burden of supporting the disciples of
the arts falls upon the middle class, and if in the end they prove too weak,
then music, poetry, painting, and sculpture are degraded, and give way to
the rustic. (Ascribed to . . . . r. 1818: 137)[15]

Such gloomy forecasts may seem quaint from our perspective, but conservative commentators did not hesitate to proclaim their fulfillment; according to
Heinrich Paris in 1839, the cause was clear: "because we have destroyed the
worship of all ideas; everywhere we have made only *material* interests the
single mover [*Mobil*] of all social relationships; because in everything *money*
has become our only god" (201–202).[16] In both cases (and many more could
be cited as well), music's value has been translated from luxury to betterment
of the spirit, but at the cost of dematerializing it. Nor was this strategy by any
means limited to musical and political conservatives. Writing in the self-
consciously progressive *Neue Zeitschrift für Musik* in 1845, Theodor Hagen
claimed that a socialist reorganization of factory work could succeed only if
workers also underwent a spiritual regeneration through music, which would
help overcome the debilitating effects of contemporary urban life (194).
When Marx observed that the musician produced only music, not a contribution to the material economy of capitalism, then, he was continuing a tradition already firmly established in musical discourse itself.

Redefining music's value as spiritual in this way could help avoid associations with idle luxury on the one hand and common spectacle on the other
(a frequent metaphor of dismissal for virtuosos equated them with tightrope
walkers [e.g., ... r. 1818: 137]) could be avoided; a corollary was an
increasing focus on a canon of exemplary works shared by conservatives and
progressives alike, as Lydia Goehr (1992) has eloquently demonstrated. But
another corollary was a deepened gulf between the devalued practical details
of musical life and the redemptive value ascribed to those works, properly
understood, and between the world of the increasingly professionalized participant in musical life and the cultivated listener.[17] When the *Allgemeine
musikalische Zeitung* ceased publication in 1848, its publisher, Breitkopf and
Härtel, claimed that under the current chaotic situation of music, "there is no
longer any place for a *general* musical newspaper" (Breitkopf and Härtel
1848: 859–60).[18] This observation is easy to dismiss as an excuse for the failure of an increasingly tedious publication, but both the observation and the
lack of variety and vitality in the paper's last years are symptomatic of the
change in musical discourse I have outlined. Academic music, practical
music, and music for the concertgoer had become increasingly distinct practices, and no one publication could hope to appeal to all these factions. Musicians produced and reproduced works, scholars understood them and
chronicled their history, and listeners were bettered by experiencing them as

autonomous artworks, the means of whose production demanded no more consideration than the manufacture of the upholstered chair in which one might sit to hear them.

Musical works, then, have come to function in relation to the social relations of music-making as commodities do in the social relations of production, both representing and masking the reality of those relations. To the extent that this process is a naturalized one, it persists through its near invisibility. To claim an external function for what appears as self-evidently valuable within the field is to mark oneself as an outsider (hence the current concentration of statements of loyalty to the musical experience around the polemics through which the discipline defines its boundaries):

> In the social fields, which are the products of a long, slow process of autonomization, and are therefore, so to speak, games "in themselves" and not "for themselves," one does not embark on the game by a conscious act, one is born into the game, with the game; and the relation of investment, *illusio*, . . . is made more total and unconditional by the fact that it is unaware of what it is. (Bourdieu 1990: 67)

No one is "born" into the field of musicology (although one is certainly born into circumstances that favor the development of particular modes of attending to music). But to the extent that a discipline avoids reflecting on its presuppositions, it may indeed be nearly as unaware of its investment as Bourdieu here suggests. And from that position of involvement, statements that come close to making the music/commodity parallel explicit—even if they do so in an effort to express the vividness of the aesthetic experience— will likely find little following. Consider, for example, how strangely distant from the standard language of analysis and criticism is this passage by Thrasybulos Georgiades (1967: 94):

> [Schubert's] *Am Flusse* works like a magic box that sounds by itself. It has the magic of an object constructed by a sorcerer's hand and now active by itself. The master who produced it at the same time imbued it with breath. The work of the spirit which is a "work" in the strong sense of the word, is like such an artful object, built by a human—a magic box that spontaneously develops its own life as soon as it is constituted and let free, made independent, set on the table as it were, by the artist who built it. It has the characteristic of the real: it is graspable as if by hand, and yet mysterious.[19]

Georgiades's extraordinary blend of the language of magic and industry, of physical object and spiritual creation, comes uncomfortably close to revealing the tensions of an ideology of the work that demands that it be simultaneously revered with quasi-religious reverence and ascribed an autonomy, a separation conceivable only in physical terms. In them we can perhaps also read some of

Georgiades's own status as an outsider of sorts—a foreigner practicing a historically German discipline within the German university system and focusing
on a central component of the German musical canon—and note as well that
the same work elsewhere shows him to have been unusually aware of sociological constraints on musical styles.[20]

If, as I have argued, the specific relations that constitute music deserve
closer attention than we have most often given them, so too do those that constitute musical scholarship. As John Guillory (1993) has shown in the case of
literature, attention to the institutional site of academic discourse is crucial to
understanding its social role. I have already directed attention to several
aspects of this issue, but in conclusion I would like to return to a familiar institutional context in which the obscuring of musical relationships through the
privileging of the aesthetic experience of music occurs: the university music
department, within which an ability to hear and to talk accurately about "the
music itself" is routinely considered a defining feature over against the studies
of music in other disciplines. I have elsewhere suggested (Gramit 1998a) that
a deep loyalty to the aesthetic experience of music unites performers and
scholars in traditional North American music departments; however, I would
also like to suggest that the same ideology can work to ensure that the partnership of scholar and practitioner will not be an equal one. The denigration of
performance is accomplished without the overt elitism of Boethius ("How
much more admirable, then, is the science of music in apprehending by reason
than in accomplishing by work and deed!" [cited in Strunk 1965: 85]) or
Guido of Arezzo's simple insult ("In our times, of all men, singers are the
most foolish" [Strunk 1965: 117]), but the effect is much the same: the discursive privileging of intellection over purportedly unreflective practice.

When the listener-oriented privileging of the aesthetic experience is
internalized, a hierarchy is established, with "the music" as an abstract, unified entity at its apex and the skills necessary to realize it subordinate to it.
This relationship is succinctly conveyed in Henry Kingsbury's report (1991:
203) of a conservatory sight-singing class which was informed that " 'these
chorales [by J. S. Bach] are not music—they are drills.' " Here the low status
of the practical exercise provides a context that effectively removes the drill's
material from its ordinary category of aesthetic object. In less blatant but
more pervasive ways, the same message—that development and practice of a
skill is distinct from and lower than art—is conveyed by such unremarkable
institutions as music history curricula that teach composers and their works,
or more recently and "progressively," those works in a social context (in both
cases rarely treating performers or pedagogues as historical actors), and by
music theory curricula designed to culminate in the analysis of musical
works.[21] By such means, practicing musicians are trained with the unstated
goal that they will acquiesce to the disappearance of their practice behind the
musical object. This is not to argue that such curricula should be abolished,

but simply to point out that among their functions is to reproduce a hierarchy that figures literate and cultivated knowledge of music as superior to practical skills, thereby perpetuating within the institution an opposition between intellectual and manual labor that pervades our society and provides a prime marker of status within it.

The loyalties and interests that inform the scholarship I have discussed are multiply determined and deeply rooted; I make no claim to be able to loose myself or my own scholarship from them. By drawing attention to those loyalties and interests in this essay, however, I hope to have suggested that, far from being a straightforward response to the nature of music, the act of reflective listening is an important part of the way we make music what it is for us, and that that particular constitution of music is intimately connected to the immediate site of music scholarship, to the dominant mode of contemporary musical consumption, and to the larger systems of relationships that have constituted music and our society. Given this situation, it is difficult to imagine that "the music itself" will at any time soon cease to be the principal focus of musicology. But by maintaining an awareness of the factors that condition our scholarly practice, we may realize the necessity of broadening our interpretations of music to encompass the practices that an unreflective maintenance of our conventional position would obscure from our awareness.

I would also argue that these considerations are relevant to more than the internal squabbles of an academic discipline, absorbing though those may be to its practitioners—and this, finally, is why I continue to find it worthwhile to approach the complex of art music and the musicological scholarship that defines it with explicit reference to Marx. If, as I have suggested, musicology creates its object (music) so that its subject (the cultivated listener) turns out to be none other than the scholar her/himself, in so doing it defines music as a kind of ideal counterpart to the material commodity. And by insisting on its immateriality while reifying it as a thing separate from the relations in which it is enmeshed, musicology has reinforced the place of the culture of art music as an imagined refuge of individual subjectivity in a society whose ruling principle, exchange value, is ultimately inimical to the development of that subjectivity. In short, as unromantic as much musicology may seem, it can provide the ideological justification for art music as a primary locus of what Robert Sayre and Michael Löwy ([1984] 1990), developing an idea found in Lukács, term "romantic anticapitalism": an insistence upon precapitalist values as an alternative to the pervasive impact of exchange, which destroys both traditional community and the freely developing and imagining individual. Over against this threat, properly receptive listeners can be imagined to form a community unified precisely by their "active and often critical/creative *internal* participation in the musical artwork"—an individualized and yet collective act—and as we have seen, this is just the feature of musical experience most privileged by musicological discourse. By presenting an imagined alternative

to exchange-based existence, the high musical culture that musicology has
served to reinforce might indeed play a positive role. But it can do so only if
we recognize the inevitable limits to that alternative by examining as well the
ideologies and practices of music that bind the apparently distinct and purely
musical world of the listening experience to the far more troubled reality of the
society in which it exists as a privileged moment.

Notes

Although no explicit reference to it appears in this essay, Suzanne Cusick's "Gender and the Cultural Work of a Classical Music Performance" (1994) was a considerable influence, especially pp. 80–92; her notion of disappearance has proven
extremely suggestive, although I here develop it differently than she does. My discussion of Marx, in particular, is indebted to the participants in a faculty/student
colloquium at the University of Alberta in 1996; participants included Regula
Qureshi, Henry Klumpenhouwer, Adam Krims, Anthony Olmsted, Vernon Charter,
James Cockell, Tamara Schwartzentruber, and Silvia Yee. Finally, the insistent
questioning of Jean-Jacques Nattiez and Richard Taruskin at a presentation of some
of these ideas at the 1996 annual meeting of the American Musicological Society
led me to rethink and clarify several points. I am grateful for their questions,
although I do not expect that they will agree with the answers at which I have
arrived.

1. Drawing on a scholar as deeply influenced by Max Weber as Bourdieu is may
    itself seem a problematic mix of intellectual traditions, but as Michael Löwy
    (1996) has noted, a diverse strain of Marxist thought going back at least to
    Lukács has integrated Marx and Weber in various ways.
2. I must emphasize that I am here limiting my consideration of music scholar-
    ship to the field of musicology as represented primarily by the practices of its
    North American professional society, the American Musicological Society.
    That is, I am discussing the practices of a discipline whose primary object of
    study has long been the European art music tradition, studied historically—
    leaving alternative approaches and musics to its professional counterparts,
    the Society for Ethnomusicology and the Society for Music Theory. This is
    not only because this is the scholarly discipline with which I am most famil-
    iar, but also because the practices I will describe seem to me crucial to the
    process by which musicology so defined sets its boundaries with other acad-
    emic studies of music.
3. For a discussion of Dahlhaus's position within those controversies, see Hep-
    okoski 1991.
4. For a more detailed discussion of *habitus*, see Bourdieu 1990: 52–65.
5. See, for example, the work of Susan McClary (e.g., 1991 and 1993) and that
    of Lawrence Kramer (e.g., 1995).
6. This presumed security about the object of inquiry could perhaps be posited
    as one of the characteristics that defines musicology as a discipline over
    against ethnomusicology (but see McClary 1991: 19 for a frank questioning
    of this security). For a basic discussion of the ambiguity of the term "music"
    in ethnomusicology in an introductory test, see Nettl 1983: 15–25.

7. The account of Marx that follows is based on my earlier discussion in Gramit 1998b.

8. For further discussion of these issues, see Postone 1993, esp. pp. 63 and 166–71.

9. For examples see Couch 1989 and Peterson and White 1989.

10. To the extent that systems of merit pay for academics rely on quantitative evidence of scholarly productivity for salary adjustments, however, the transformation of such recognition into monetary form can be direct indeed.

11. Clearly, such traditional musicological activities as studies of patronage indicate that some interest in these relationships has long existed, but to the extent that such studies figure as biographical background or social context to "the music itself," they do not challenge the scholarly priorities I have described.

12. This is in some respects an old, familiar story, one told at length as early as 1935 by Eberhard Preußner ([1935] 1950), but also one usefully revisited from the perspective of more recent scholarly concerns. The best recent account of this transformation at the local level is Applegate (1998). A useful overview of the social and economic development of the period (with extensive bibliography) is found in Sheehan (1989). DeNora (1995: 47–48) has rightly warned against the tendency by historians to exaggerate the role of the "emerging" middle classes, but as the sources cited below reveal, the changes to musical life were deep and enduring enough to bring about widespread concern among those whose livelihoods depended on it.

13. ". . . man kaum Haendel, Gluc [sic], Gasmann, Paisello, Sarti, Naumann, Salieri, Hayden [sic], Dittersdorf, Mozart's u.s.f. in der Zukunft zu erwarten hat."

14. "Ich bin nicht dumm genug, um ein großer Musiker in solcher Zeit zu werden."

15. "Wenn aber die erste Classe im Staate, auf welche sonst immer die schönen Künste, um der Ausbildung des Geistes und des Geschmackes willen, ihre Fortschritte stützten, ihren wesentlichen Werth nicht zu schätzen weiss, dann fällt die ganze Last der Pflege ihrer Jünger auf den Mittelstand, und werden diesem die Schultern endlich zu schwach, dann sinken Musik, Dichtkunst, Mahlerey und Bildhauerkunst herab, und machen der Rustik Platz."

16. "Weil wir überall den Cultus aller *Ideen* zerstört; überall nur noch *materiellen* Interessen zum einzigen Mobil aller socialen Verhältnisse gemacht haben; weil überall das *Geld* unser alleiniger Gott geworden."

17. For a useful summary of the transition from participants to listeners, see Schmitt 1990: 71–78.

18. "In diesem Strudel ist kein Platz für eine *allgemeine* musikalische Zeitung mehr. . . ."

19. "*Am Flusse* wirkt wie ein Zauberkästchen, das von selbst klingt. Es hat die Magie des Gegenstandes, der von Zauberhand konstruiert ist, und nun selbsttätig wirkt. Der Meister, der es anfertigte, hat ihm zugleich Odem eingeflößt. Das Werk des Geistes, das im strengen Sinn des Wortes 'Werk' ist, gleicht einem solchen vom Menschen hergestellten, kunstvollen Gegenstand, einem Zauberkästchen, das spontan ein Eigenleben entfaltet, sobald es konstruiert und vom Künstler, der es baute, losgelöst, verselbständigt, gleichsam auf den Tisch gelegt wurde. Es hat das Merkmal des Realen: ist wie mit Händen greifbar, und doch geheimnisvoll."

20. See Georgiades 1967: 125–46: "Schuberts Musik und die Öffentlichkeit: Biographisches und Soziologisches."

21. This practice also has a venerable history in musical discourse: a ubiquitous topos of German music journalism of the early nineteenth century was the contrast of true art and "mere craft" (*Handwerk*).

References

Adorno, Theodor W. 1978. "On the Fetish Character in Music and the Regression in Listening." In *The Essential Frankfurt School Reader*, edited by Andrew Arato and Eike Gebhardt, 270–99. New York: Urizen Books.

———. 1994. "Analytical Study of the *NBC Music Appreciation Hour.*" *Musical Quarterly* 78: 325–77.

Applegate, Celia. 1998. "How Serious Is It? Nationalism and the Idea of Serious Music in the Early Nineteenth Century." *Nineteenth-Century Music* 21: 274–96.

Bent, Margaret. 1986. "Fact and Value in Contemporary Musical Scholarship." In *CMS Proceedings: The National and Regional Meetings*, edited by William E. Melin, 3–9. Boulder, Colo.: College Music Society.

Bonds, Mark Evan. 1997. "Idealism and Aesthetics of Instrumental Music at the Turn of the Nineteenth Century." *Journal of the American Musicological Society* 50: 387–420.

Bourdieu, Pierre. 1984. *Distinction: A Social Critique of the Judgement of Taste*. Translated by Richard Nice. Cambridge, Mass.: Harvard University Press.

———. 1990. *The Logic of Practice*. Translated by Richard Nice. Stanford: Stanford University Press.

Bourdieu, Pierre, and Terry Eagleton. 1994. "Doxa and the Common Life: An Interview." In *Mapping Ideology*, edited by Slavoj Žižek, 265–77. London and New York: Verso. First published in *New Left Review* 191 (January/February 1992).

Breitkopf and Härtel. 1848. "An die Leser." *Allgemeine musikalische Zeitung* 50: 859–60.

Burney, Charles. [1775] 1959. *The Present State of Music in Germany, the Netherlands, and United Provinces. Or, The Journal of a Tour Through Those Countries, Undertaken to Collect Materials for a General History of Music*. Published as *An Eighteenth–Century Musical Tour in Central Europe and the Netherlands*, edited by Percy A. Scholes. London: Oxford University Press.

Couch, Stephen R. 1989. "The Orchestra as Factory: Interrelationships of Occupational Change, Social Structure, and Musical Style." In *Art and Society: Readings in the Sociology of Art*, edited by Arnold W. Foster and Judith R. Blau, 293–306. Albany: State University of New York Press.

Cusick, Suzanne G. 1994. "Gender and the Cultural Work of a Classical Music Performance." *Repercussions* 3: 77–110.

Dahlhaus, Carl. 1983. *Foundations of Music History*, translated by J. Bradford Robinson. Cambridge: Cambridge University Press.

———. 1989. *Nineteenth-Century Music*. Translated by J. Bradford Robinson. Berkeley and Los Angeles: University of California Press.

DeNora, Tia. 1995. *Beethoven and the Construction of Genius: Musical Politics in Vienna, 1792–1803*. Berkeley and Los Angeles: University of California Press.

Georgiades, Thrasybulos. 1967. *Schubert: Musik und Lyrik*. Göttingen: Vandenhoeck & Ruprecht.

Goehr, Lydia. 1992. *The Imaginary Museum of Musical Works: An Essay in the Philosophy of Music*. Oxford: Clarendon Press.

Gramit, David. 1998a."The Roaring Lion: Critical Musicology, the Aesthetic Experience, and the Music Department." *Canadian University Music Review* 19: 19–33.

———. 1998b. "Musicology, Commodity Structure, and Musical Practice." In *Crosscurrents and Counterpoints: Offerings in Honor of Bengt Hambraeus at 70*, edited by Per F. Broman, Nora A. Engebretsen, and Bo Alphonce, 22–34. Publications of the University of Gothenburg Department of Musicology 5. Gothenburg: University of Gothenburg.

Guillory, John. 1993. *Cultural Capital: The Problem of Literary Canon Formation*. Chicago and London: University of Chicago Press.

Hagen, Theodor. 1845. "Die Civilisation in Beziehung zur Kunst mit specieller Berücksichtigung der Musik." *Neue Zeitschrift für Musik* 23: 153–56, 158–59, 165–67, 173–75, 185–86, 189–90, 193–95, 205–206.

Hartung, Günter. 1992. "Johann Friedrich Reichardt, der Musiker und der Publizist." In *Johann Friedrich Reichardt (1752–1814): Komponist und Schriftsteller der Revolutionszeit: Bericht über die Konferenz anläßlich seines 175. Todestages und des 200. Jubiläumsjahres der Französischen Revolution am 23. und 24. September 1989 im Händel-Haus Halle*, edited by Konstanze Musketa with Gert Richter and Götz Traxdorf, 11–21. Schriften des Händel-Hauses in Halle 8. Halle an der Saale: Händel-Haus.

Hepokoski, James. 1991. "The Dahlhaus Project and Its Extra-musicological Sources." *Nineteenth-Century Music* 14: 221–46.

Kerman, Joseph. 1965. "A Profile for American Musicology." *Journal of the American Musicological Society* 17: 61–69.

Kingsbury, Henry. 1991. "Sociological Factors in Musicological Poetics." *Ethnomusicology* 35: 195–219.

Kramer, Lawrence. 1993. "Music Criticism and the Postmodernist Turn: In Contrary Motion with Gary Tomlinson." *Current Musicology* 53: 25–35.

———. 1995. *Classical Music and Postmodern Knowledge*. Berkeley and Los Angeles: University of California Press.

La Capra, Dominick. 1989. "Up against the Ear of the Other: Marx after Derrida." In *Soundings in Critical Theory*, 155–81. Ithaca, N.Y., and London: Cornell University Press.

Locke, Ralph P. 1993. "Music Lovers, Patrons, and the 'Sacralization' of Culture in America." *Nineteenth Century Music* 17: 149–73.

Lowinsky, Edward E. 1961. *Tonality and Atonality in Sixteenth-Century Music*. Berkeley: University of California Press.

———. 1965. "Character and Purposes of American Musicology: A Reply to Joseph Kerman." *Journal of the American Musicological Society* 17: 222–34.

Löwy, Michael. 1996. "Figures of Weberian Marxism." *Theory and Society* 25: 431–46.

Marx, Karl. [1857–58] 1973. *Grundrisse: Foundations of the Critique of Political Economy (Rough Draft)*. Translated by Martin Nicolaus. London: Allen Lane.

———. [1867] 1976. *Capital: A Critique of Political Economy*, vol. 1. Translated by Ben Fowkes. London: Penguin.

McClary, Susan. 1991. *Feminine Endings: Music, Gender, and Sexuality*. Minneapolis and Oxford: University of Minnesota Press.

———. 1993. "Narrative Agendas in 'Absolute' Music: Identity and Difference in Brahms's Third Symphony." In *Musicology and Difference: Gender and Sexuality in Music Scholarship*, edited by Ruth A. Solie, 326–44. Berkeley and Los Angeles: University of California Press.

Nettl, Bruno. 1983. *The Study of Ethnomusicology: Twenty-nine Issues and Concepts*. Urbana and Chicago: University of Illinois Press.

Paris, Heinrich. 1839. "Die Materialität der heutigen Musik und der heutigen Tänze." *Cäcilia* 20/80: 199–244.

Peterson, Richard A., and Howard G. White. 1989. "The Simplex Located in Art Worlds." In *Art and Society: Readings in the Sociology of Art*, edited by Arnold W. Foster and Judith R. Blau, 243–59. Albany: State University of New York Press.

Postone, Moishe. 1993. *Time, Labor, and Social Domination: A Reinterpretation of Marx's Critical Theory*. Cambridge: Cambridge University Press.

Preußner, Eberhard. [1935] 1950. *Die bürgerliche Musikkultur: Ein Beitrag zur deutschen Musikgeschichte des 18. Jahrhunderts*. 2nd edition. Kassel: Bärenreiter.

Rosand, Ellen. 1995. "The Musicology of the Present." *AMS Newsletter* 25/1: 10–11, 15.

Rosen, Charles. 1996. "Did Beethoven Have All the Luck?" Review of Tia DeNora, *Beethoven and the Construction of Genius: Musical Politics in Vienna, 1792–1803*. *New York Review of Books* 43/18 (November 14): 57–63.

Sayre, Robert, and Michael Löwy. [1984] 1990. "Figures of Romantic Anticapitalism." In *Spirits of Fire: English Romantic Writers and Contemporary Historical Methods*, edited by G. A. Rosso and Daniel P. Watkins, 23–68. Rutherford, N.J.: Associated Universities Presses. First published in *New German Critique* 32.

Schmith, Amand Wilhelm. 1787. *Philosophische Fragmente über die praktische Musik*. Vienna: k.k. Taubstummeninstitutsbuchdruck, at the expense of the author.

Schmitt, Ulrich. 1990. *Revolution im Konzertsaal: Zur Beethoven-Rezeption im 19. Jahrhundert*. Mainz and London: Schott.

Sheehan, James J. 1989. *German History 1770–1866*. The Oxford History of Modern Europe. Oxford: Clarendon Press.

Small, Christopher. 1998. *Musicking: The Meanings of Performing and Listening*. Music/Culture Series. Hanover and London: Wesleyan University Press.

Strunk, Oliver, ed. 1965. *Source Readings in Music History: Antiquity and the Middle Ages*. New York: Norton.

Tomlinson, Gary. 1993. "Musical Pasts and Postmodern Musicologists: A Response to Lawrence Kramer." *Current Musicology* 53: 18–24.

"Überden Verfall der Musik." 1818. *Allgemeine musikalische Zeitung mit besonderer Rücksicht auf den österreichischen Kaiserstaat* 2: 135–37. Ascribed to . . . . r.

Van den Toorn, Pieter C. 1995. *Music, Politics, and the Academy*. Berkeley and Los Angeles: University of California Press.

2

Commodity-Form, Disavowal, and Practices of Music Theory

HENRY KLUMPENHOUWER

Commodities are a precondition for capitalism, constituting what Marx calls its "elementary form." The particular character of the current stage of capitalism, a period now generally known, thanks to Adorno and Mandel, as "Late Capitalism," is determined by, among other things, the thorough extension of commodification (in its interlocking consumption, money, and production cycles) into all areas of human society over the globe; the expansion of the real subsumption of labor by capital (which is to say, industrial capital) into all sectors of production; the particular effects on the labor process of the advances brought about by the third technological revolution.

In *Capital* Karl Marx characterizes certain features of the specific form of commodities under capitalism as instances of "fetishism," expressly troping the nineteenth-century anthropological analysis of primitive religious practice, a practice Marx (1975: 189), following Hegel, had earlier in his life suggestively described as the "religion of sensuous desire."[1]

I wish to discuss here the manner in which the phenomenon of fetishism, as an elementary form of ideology, expresses itself in the current practices of music theory, enriching my critique with explicit references to Freud's theoretical writings on sexual fetishism, another equally well-known trope on the anthropological sense of religious fetishism, found within Freud's (1962) catalog of European bourgeois psychosexual pathologies.[2] Conceivably, as a commodity-centered discipline, contemporary music theory is largely determined by the processes that fall under especially Marx's discussion of fetishism.

I draw on Marx (primarily) and Freud not only because both discuss certain aspects of "economic practice," which might be characterized as the transformation by human labor of a natural product into a social one, or the transformation by labor of one social product into another, but because they theorize the styles of thought that characterize modern (unconscious as well as conscious) cognition. In this context, human labor represents the regulated and alienated expenditure of the body's energies along the material pathway circumscribed by drives, wishes, and their vicissitudes. To be clear, the connection here is not drawn on the basis of the common word "economics": Freud's use of the term applies to his third psychological model and is based on what he saw as the quantifiability of increases and decreases in drive energy (Laplanche and Pontalis 1973, s.v. economic).

More important, however, they are both concerned to diagnose in individual consciousnesses formed within capitalist society certain widespread cognitive dysfunctions or processes, whose similarities are suggested by their common figuration with respect to religious fetish. Their shared heritage naturally suggests that shared structures and processes underlie the phenomena of economic and psychoanalytic fetishes, but I will not treat them as a recursive or circular system of metaphors. One needs only to recall that the psychoanalytic trope of religious fetish (like many of Freud's discoveries) is aimed at the development of individuals as they arise within the context of the family, and that Marx's involves more directly the dynamics governing individuals in civil society, which in Hegel's description of the modern state stands opposed to the collection of all families under capitalism by virtue of its function as an outside force of dissolution on individual family relations so as to produce private, purely economic individuals (Kedourie 1995: 144–45).

I must admit that, to my own ears at least, discussions of fetish along these lines come off as annoyingly overdone. In most cases, one frequently has the impression that the term "fetish" is employed in senses outside those provided by anthropology, psychoanalysis, or Marxism, often appearing in the sense of "investing far too much interest," a critical rhetorical figuration that gives the underlying disapproval a certain moral disgust. Typically such uses of "fetish" are directed in the first instance against ideas.[3] In reaction to these uses of fetish, my aim in the initial half of the essay is not only to provide theoretic conditions for the second half, but also to further discuss the phenomenon of fetish itself.

In measuring the effects of fetish—as ideology and as psychological defense—upon the shape of music theory, I wish to focus not on instances of music commodities themselves but rather on modes of ideology that govern practices of contemporary music theory and analysis. In light of the contexts in which music theory arises and its double function as both ideology and technology, an investigation of current styles of technical writing about music provides a reasonable locus for discovering the outlines of the particular styles of cognition that fall under Marx's and Freud's conceptions.

The Commodity

In the opening sentence of *Capital* Marx ([1867] 1976: 125) asserts that the wealth of societies in which the capitalist mode of production prevails is expressed as an "immense collection of commodities" (Marx 1976, 125).

Repeating the categories delimited earlier by classical economists, Marx analyzes the form common to all commodities in capitalist society to be determined by two contradictory sides.

The first, use-value, deals with the properties of commodities that render them socially useful, as suitable objects of consumption. On the face of it, a commodity's use-value appears to arise as its own natural properties, or put another way, it seems to emerge in the first instance as a relationship between a commodity and its buyer, a relationship that may be understood through study of the "natural" characteristics of the commodity in question.

By giving over completely to this impression, many commentators on Marx consequently judge this to be the point at which use-value fails to serve any longer as a worthwhile determinate category in the discussions of commodity form: since use-value engages only the natural, physical properties of commodities, it interacts only superficially with the social and economic nature of commodity form as a whole.

Yet regarding use-value as a purely material instance in commodity form will lead to basic interpretative errors—errors we shall explore in our discussion of the second side of commodity form. For now, it is sufficient to pay attention to the fundamentally social character of use-value. First, use-value is a potential attribute of commodities brought into concrete realization only through purchase and consumption. The production of use-values is always the production of use-values for others. In consumption each commodity obscures important social characteristics by reducing each person who confronts it to the same abstract category irrespective of social and economic distinctions among individuals.

Second, use-values must appear as measured and counted units, as numbers of individual commodities to be exchanged. The particular measuring systems, which are determined anew by each society that makes use of particular commodities and do not arise solely from the nature of the commodity, additionally contribute to the social makeup of use-value. Accordingly, a use-value takes on both a characteristic natural and social form, and rather than constituting the relationship between people and commodities mediated primarily through the abstract category of desire, commodity use-value constitutes a mediated relation between people as buyers and sellers. Although ignored in a great many commentaries on Marx, use-value plays a dominant economic role in the commodity form and, as we shall shortly see, is central to a proper understanding of the nature of commodity fetish, and to the valorization process itself under the styles of commodity production particular to capitalism.

The second side of the commodity form, exchange-value, is the form in which the value of a commodity expresses itself. Value appears to arise out of a commodity itself as an object of natural value, and thus exchange value seems at first best understood purely as quanta-relationships between commodities. In many simplified commentaries on Marx the exchange-value of a commodity corresponds via transformation to its market price.

On Marx's view, exchange-value—the form the value of a commodity takes—is expressible as the ratio between two measured use-values in exchange (four coats = one stereo system). But to exchange any commodity for any other commodity is possible only if there is at least one element that *all* commodities possess, and which accordingly must bestow quantifiable value within the system of commodities. It is important to bear in mind that not only is exchange premised on a single property common to all commodities on a market, but that exchange itself produces the single common property.

Marx identifies the substance of the common element he calls "value" as labor.

> If then we disregard the use-value of commodities, only one property remains, that of being products of labor. But even the product of labor has been transformed in our hands. If we make abstraction from its use-value, we abstract also from the material constituents and forms which make it a use-value. . . . All of its sensuous characteristics are extinguished. Nor is it any longer the product of the labor of the joiner, the mason, the spinner, or of any other particular kind of productive labor. With the disappearance of the useful character of the products of labor, the useful character of the kinds of labor embodied in them also disappears; this in turn entails the disappearance of the different concrete forms of labor. They can no longer be distinguished, but are all together reduced to the same kind of labor, human labor in the abstract. (126)

Exchange-value is just the form in which value is expressed. And abstracted labor, as "congealed labor," serves as the substance of value; labor time, the measure of value. The protocols of measuring by labor time are not features of commodities in isolation from each other, since all commodities (of which labor power is an instance) necessarily must meet each other in the market. All individual labors together constitute a grand system of labor, which in turn regulates them in important ways, including controlling levels of labor intensity and productivity. Accordingly, it is the labor time determined by the characteristics of the total labor system, and not the labor time relevant to the individual commodity, that becomes the measure of value for that commodity.

The ratio in which two commodities exchange is thus determined by the relative productivity of the concrete labors involved (itself determined with respect to collectivized productivity of all labor) and will vary with changes in one or both of those concrete labors, measured in labor time expended. A concrete labor less productive than the social average of all instances of that concrete labor will be able to realize only the value determined by the social average. Introduction of technology may reduce the socially average amount of concrete labor time required to produce a particular use-value. And in general, any change in the value represented by a labor form (due to changes in the value of congealed labor required to produce and maintain it) will determine the measure of value it can create in time.

In all commodity exchange relationships, the value-form itself dissolves into two opposed poles or functions: the relative form and a corresponding equivalent form. In the expression $xA=yB$, where x and y are quantities and A and B are use-values, B expresses (passively) the value of A. The value of any commodity cannot be expressed by itself: it must be expressed by another. The natural form of commodity B becomes the value form of commodity A. Though the relative and equivalent forms are opposed, they are entirely dependent on one another. In particular, each calls the other into being in order to provide its grounding.

The equivalent form of value, the function played by commodity B above, has what Marx calls three "peculiarities." First, the use-value of commodity B becomes the "material bearer," the "appearance form" of its opposite, the value of commodity A. In other words, the natural form (which, while having both social and material aspects, appears primarily as a set of natural characteristics) expresses value, "something purely social" (Marx 1976, 148–49).

Second, in the equivalent form, concrete labor (relevant to commodity B) becomes the appearance form of its opposite, abstract labor, and in particular, the abstracted labor form relevant to commodity A. In other words, the concrete labor appropriate to commodity A creates the value of A only by its reduction to human labor in the abstract rather than by its own distinctive and unique characteristics, while the concrete labor appropriate to commodity B becomes the concrete appearance form of abstract labor, not of commodity B, but of commodity A. Third, private, individual labor "takes on the form of its opposite, social labour" (151).

In simple exchange situations, both commodities have the potential to play the roles of the relative and equivalent forms of value. As the system of commodity exchange expands, one single commodity becomes frozen at the equivalent pole and takes on the form of money. Expanded commodity exchange brings the money form into being because the greater the number of commodities in circulation the more difficult it becomes for the underlying valuation system to express itself, that is to say, in order to stabilize the growing vector of equivalent forms each isolated commodity must adopt. Furthermore, the money form as the general universal equivalent form of value brokers exchanges between all producers and all consumers, generating strings of exchanges between buyers and sellers impossible under pure barter.

As the general equivalent the money-form expresses the value of all other commodities, which in turn become frozen at the relative pole of the value relation. As the money-form becomes paper (instead of gold) its use-value becomes entirely devoted to the expression of the value of all other commodities (gold, of course, had other uses).[4]

Fetishism

Animate and Inanimate Relations

According to Marx, commodities become mystified in a particular way under capitalism, and the outlines of that mystification share something with the anthropological definition of religious fetish worship, in which objects are credited with power they do not in fact have. While commodities appear to possess innate value—either as value determined purely by the psychology of consumers (that is to say, value arising from use-value) or as value emerging from a commodity's natural monopolistic features (which is a potential of any given commodity) appearing falsely as a concrete feature of that commodity (as, say, natural scarcity)—their values are in truth determined by human energies expended in production, and those expenditures are carried out within certain well-defined social relations, so that the expenditures are effectively controlled not by the producers themselves but by capitalists (Cohen 1978: 116–17).

In describing the phenomenon of commodity fetishism, Marx observes that

> [a] commodity is therefore a mysterious thing, simply because in it the
> social character of [human beings'] labor appears to them as an objective
> character stamped upon the product of that labor. There is a definite social
> relation between [human beings] that assumes in their eyes the fantastic
> form of a relation between things. (Marx 1976: 164)

In other words, the characteristics of the social relations governing commodity production appear as properties of the commodity's status as an object. So Marx finds that primitive religious practice, in which "the productions of the human brain appear as independent beings endowed with life, . . . entering into relation with one another and the human race" (162), serves as a suitable analogy to the materialization of social relations he finds in commodity-structure.

What part of the commodity is the source of the fetish effect? Neither use-value or exchange-value on their own as isolated features of commodity form can give rise to fetishism. Instead, Marx tells us that the fetish quality of commodities is produced by the commodity form itself. In other words, the commodity form is not a self-sufficient category: it generates commodity fetish to provide it with a certain essential grounding.

The extension of fetish as a feature of the entire form qua form takes two important directions. First, through the contradictions between the two aspects of the form (use-value and exchange-value)—uncovered in Marx's inquiry into the two categories in isolation and by way of his examination of the forms of value, under which appears the abstraction of labor, the development of social labor, and the money-form—the individual product, once it appears within the commodity-form, projects itself as a self-grounded, self-mediated object of value, whereas under Marx's examination it is just its own value an individual commodity cannot express. Second, the form of the commodity determines the relevant substance, which is to say that the (social) form—its structures, potentials, and tendencies—calls into existence the (material) substance, in order to provide the very foundations of the form itself. Accordingly, the material content of the commodity becomes overwhelmed by the requirements of pure form.

Thus, not only are social relations of production obscured behind object characteristics, but, as Rubin (1968: 6) points out, these relations can be expressed only by way of objects, since under the commodity form, social relations necessarily take on the form of thing relations.

The second half of that formulation has been largely overlooked in many discussions of commodity form and fetish. Taking it seriously (as it ought to be taken) has wide-ranging implications for Marxist-oriented studies. For starters, the formulation undercuts the frequent argument that one may escape the effects of fetishism simply by attending to social relations (often unspecified and thus meaningless) and correspondingly by ignoring altogether the objects that make up the capitalist world. Rather than constituting a properly Marxist perspective, such a strategy is one-sided; it is not just partial or incomplete, but fundamentally misguided, because it ignores basic dialectic movement.

Rubin (1968) takes pains to point out that the way things express social relations is not by way of symbolization, but by way of concrete realization. All products of labor in the commodity economy have a dual essence: material (natural-technical) and functional (social) (12). The "close connection" between the two arises from the close connection between the material-technical aspects of production and the particular social form it takes (13). In the absence of an understanding of the dialectical relation governing form and content assumed in Rubin's formulation, such statements appear to assert connections between fundamentally incommensurate categories closed off to each other (material properties and social relations), which in turn can be connected only by means of rhetorical figuration (metaphor, synecdoche, and so on).[5]

Rubin's two sides relate suggestively to Geras's ([1971] 1990: 209–10) distinction between fetishism-as-mystification, within which relations between producers of commodities are transformed into the natural material properties of commodities themselves, and fetishism-as-(historically specific) domination, within which the production relations of dominance and exploitation are expressed through the materiality of the commodities themselves. Under the mystifactional aspect of fetish, people fail to see the social forms in which products appear and attribute the relevant characteristics to the material content of individual, isolated products. Under the domination aspect of fetish, people fail to see how relations among producers are expressible only through products.

Rubin's own discussion of Marx's concepts of reification and personification is a useful insertion at this point. Reification is "the process through which production relations among people assign a social form . . . to the things by means of which people relate to one another" ([1971] 1990: 22). The personification of things is the process through which people take on the characteristics of the historically and socially determined things they own and through which they express their property relations.

Clearly the two processes are closely connected. The nature of that connection is crucial. While under reification the social form of things emerges from the social relations that produced them, under personification social relations of production are "established" only by means of things with a determined historical and social form (23). The establishment of mutual determination between social production relations and things with determined social forms is both an historical and material process, through which the social forms of things, initially called into being by production relations, become their prerequisite, their grounding. Rubin writes that the

> social form of things conditions *individual* production bonds among particular people only because the social form itself is an expression of *social* production bonds. The social form of things appears as a *condition* for the process of production which is given in advance, ready, made, and permanently fixed, only because it appears as the congealed, crystallized *result* of a dynamic, constantly flowing and changing social process of production. In this way the apparent contradiction between the "reification of people" and the "personifications of things" is resolved in the dialectical, uninterrupted process of reproduction. This apparent contradiction is between the determination of the social form of things by production relations among people and the determination of the individual production relations among people by the social form of things. (25)

It is important at this point to draw Geras's distinction between fetish-as-mystification and fetish-as-domination back into the discussion. The relation between these aspects of fetishism correspond to the dialectical relation between reification and personification, and help foreground what is true and what is false about those two instances.

The relation between reification and personification and the relation between fetish-as-mystification and fetish-as-domination interact dialectically and are thus not coextensive. Under capitalism, a laborer receives the value of his labor (determined, as we have seen, by particular value relations among producers, by the amount of labor congealed in it) in the wage form (a particular form of appearance of value), while the capitalist appropriates the value created by the exercise of the labor power, which is to say, as a result of his purchase of labor's use-value. Reifying the relevant social relations in the thing capital on one hand obscures them, and capital appears to expand on its own, rather than by means of the underlying relationship of exploitation. Yet on the other hand, the thing capital is the only means by which the relevant property relations express themselves. And it is constant capital, "dead labor" in the form of raw materials and machinery, that materially opposes living labor each day. Correspondingly, the personification of capital in the capitalist—which can be brought about only by an initial reification of the relation between producers—both obscures the origins of those characteristics in the capitalist's exploitation of labor power and correctly identifies the dominant instance of the relationship.

The Doubled Ego

Sigmund Freud also finds in fetish-religion an appropriate paradigm for an important conceit within his psychology, and in fact it has become central to recent discussions of "cultural fetishism," both those that make an explicit connection to Marx's analysis of commodity-fetishism, and those that do not.

In Freud's account of sexual practices, sexual fetishism is a product of early male castration anxiety. His first treatment of the subject appears in *Three Essays on Sexuality* (1962), under the rubric of sexual aberration, where Freud classifies sexual fetishism—a practice more common among men than women—as the "unsuitable substitution for the sexual object," under the general heading of "Deviations in Sexual Aim" (17–19). He goes on to describe sexual practices that pay special attention to feet, hair, shoes, and undergarments in place of a person, noting that the procedure is particularly present when "normal sexual aim" is for some reason inhibited.

In a subsequent essay (1963) concentrating exclusively on the practice, Freud focuses on the psychosexual genesis of the use of feet, hair, shoes, and undergarments as substitutes for the sexual object. Here he explains that "the fetish is a substitute for the mother's phallus, which the little boy once believed in and does not wish to forgo—we know why" (215). Specifically, the practice of sexual fetishism "disavows" the loss of the phallic mother, who is replaced by the castrated mother. This loss is deepened for the boy because it generates two further losses: the loss of the non-rivalrous father and the loss of the integrated body, replaced respectively by the castrating father and the castratable self. Thus the fetishized object, whether hair, shoe, foot, or undergarment, serves both metaphorically (via resemblance) and metonymically (via ideational contiguity, or association) as the maternal penis, and in turn by the non-threatening paternal penis, and by one's own non-detachable penis and integrated body. Without the fetish-object, the fetishist is psychologically castrated and incapable of sexual activity. The whole arrangement requires a compromise formation in the subject in which the ego of the fetishist must split into two incompatible parts along the lines of the two doxies: one that must repudiate the loss of the maternal phallus, and one that must acknowledge it.

It needs to be pointed out that the scene depicted by Freud—the little boy's discovery of the non-phallic mother and the castration anxiety that ensues—occurs in every male. Freud (1963: 216) writes, "We cannot explain why it is that some of them become homosexuals in consequence of this experience, others ward it off by creating a fetish, and the great majority overcome it." The observation suggests that fetish practice provides a defense not only against castration anxiety but against homosexuality. One could develop the argument further by suggesting that in the particular defense of homosexuality the partner emerges as the phallic mother, and hence that the partner's penis functions as the fetish object. The fetishist on the other hand is unwilling to give up the paternal identification required to develop into the (neurotically) heterosexual adult.

Expanding on earlier work carried out by Joyce McDougall, Joel White-brook (1995) observes a significant development in Freud's theory of defense in his later writings. Many of the Left Freudians—Marcuse, Reich, even Lacan—committed themselves to the earlier notion that "sexual perversions represent the good Other of the logic of domination and the repressive ego, and can therefore be taken as a cipher for a utopian order beyond the performance principle," Marcuse's term for the current historically specific form of the reality principle based on renunciation, not on account of material lack, but on account of a system of political and economic domination (White-brook 1995: 41). As such, the distinction between perversion and neurotic symptom becomes merely a matter of degree. Later on, however, Freud develops the notion that distinction between sexual perversion and neurotic symptom is one of a kind. Whereas the agency or mechanism of repression generates neurosis, by exiling trauma memories to the unconscious from which they subsequently return displaced or condensed to consciousness, and the mechanism of repudiation generates psychosis, by altering percepts themselves, disavowal generates perversion, by way of ego-splitting (White-brook 1995: 42). Fetishism ends up functioning as the paradigmatic appearance of disavowal, a mechanism of defense under which two contradictory ideations are permitted to exist in consciousness. In tolerating two conflicting ideas side by side, consciousness thus adopts one of the fundamental characteristics of the unconscious system itself.

Economic Psychoanalyisis/Pyschoanalytic Economics

Žižek's (1997b) analysis of the relationship between Marx's and Freud's use of the notion of fetishism is worth inserting at this point. He writes,

> In both cases, fetishism stands for a displacement (relations between men are displaced on to the relations between things; the subject's sexual interest is displaced from the "normal" sexual object to its substitute); this "displacement" is in both cases a "regressive" shift of focus towards a "lower"

and partial element which conceals (and at the same time designates) the true point of reference. The analogy further consists in the fact that for Marx and Freud, the "fetish" is not simply a lower stage of development (of society, of the genital Oedipal sexuality), but a symptom of the inherent contradiction within the "higher stage" itself: commodity fetishism, for example, reveals a crack in spiritual Christianity and in the "mature" free individual of "developed" society itself. (124, fn. 16)

The idea of analogy is certainly a reasonable and useful description of the commodity/sexual fetishism pair. Yet the benefits of the notion of analogy come with a risk in this case, since a relationship thus defined encourages the denial of an absolute priority between the two notions, and hence obscures the totalizing effects of capital, by conceiving psychology and economics as independent spheres of roughly equal determinacy in our current lives. It may be fruitful to think of Freud's particular use of fetish just in the sense he came to in his later writings, namely, as a model for the mechanism of disavowal as one of the characteristic strategies of psychological defense available to individuals under capitalism, alongside repression and repudiation.

As an elementary form of ideology, commodity fetish shares a certain appearance form with all ideological iterations under capitalism. We can describe the form with direct reference to Marx's discussion in *Capital*. He writes, "If I state that coats or boots stand in relation to [money] because the latter is the universal incarnation of abstract human labor, the absurdity of the statement is self-evident. Nevertheless, when the producers of coats and boots bring these commodities into relation with [money] . . . as the universal equivalent, their own private labor and the collective labor of society appears to them in exactly this form" (169).[6] In other words, while all involved will admit it is false, they behave as if it is true: which is why professional wrestling is probably the clearest articulation of ideology form.[7]

Music Theory

There are a number of things to take into account if one is to turn the foregoing discussion into a potentially useful examination of practices that make up contemporary institutional music theory.[8]

First, one should not restrict the phenomenon of commodity fetish to the concealment behind material properties of the isolated commodity of the social relations between producers as the source of value in the strictest sense of those relations. Commodity fetish as a cognitive disruption is not simply a mistake about the origins of commodity value. Although Marx frequently characterized bourgeois economics as he knew it as an instantiation of fetishism, there is no reason the phenomenon does not end at the boundaries of the discipline of economics. All disciplines, especially those that, like music theory, have as their objects of study commodities, must logically be understood as fetish-based modes of thought, however complicated they may become through other mediations.

Second, one must recognize that contemporary music theory is additionally determined by its status as an academic discipline, and thus by social functions played by liberal arts education. Consequently, one must bear in mind both its pedagogical role and its underlying research project. Music theory is not purely an instantiation of ideology but is bound up in the (re)production of its object of study.

Historically, the educational function of modern music theory (in its various forms of appearance as counterpoint, harmony, form, compositional theory, and so on) expanded from its narrow professional base in the newly established state-run (as opposed to the earlier religiously administered) conservatories of the early nineteenth century to appear in faculties of arts by the end of the nineteenth century. And as a human science music theory adopted a role in the education of what Hegel called the universal class, the class of state bureaucrats whose self-interests are to coincide with the interests of the whole, so that that its members could mediate between the demands of civil society and demands of political state.

Both of these roles—the professional and the academic (read: bureaucratic)—continue to lay strong claims on the discipline, regardless of whatever shifts appear in the public articulation of those goals.

Third, there is no broad agreement on the proper object for music theoretical study: the composer's ideation, the work's structure, private aesthetic response of the analyst, the response of a competent (in the linguistic sense) listener, the system underlying composition within a given historical style period. Similar disagreements (with the appropriate changes) characterize other art-interpretative disciplines, but the weak representational nature of music (relative to other arts) allows these distinctions to be obscured within the single category "music study."

Fourth, music—more than other forms of art—is mystified as a transcendent or autonomous practice, in the usual sense of timeless, spiritual. In other words, of all the arts (in the traditional bourgeois sense of that term) music most successfully instantiates the requirements of Kantian aesthetics and hence poses particular problems for music-historical and music-theoretic studies. Accordingly, the status of music as a commodity is generally dismissed. The degree to which Kantian-style categories such as (market) disinterestedness and genius have pervaded bourgeois thinking about music is remarkable.

Finally, a critique of music theory along the lines suggested here is an underdeveloped line of investigation. I can well imagine that a readership genuinely interested in such questions is insignificant even by academic standards: it is difficult to conceive a relevant market, which logically must be made up of either Marxists interested in music analysis or music theorists drawn to undertaking technical analysis from a Marxist perspective. The dormancy of such an interaction (not shared by other aesthetic-critical traditions) is itself suggestive.

With these things in mind, two questions emerge. First, how can we apply the foregoing investigation of fetishism to a properly Marxist critique of the current academic styles of music theory? Second, what would a Marxist alternative to fetishized music theory take?

Proper and Improper Critique

Clearly, providing a thorough answer to the first question is unlikely here, not only because of space, but also because investigations carried out along even loosely related lines are so underdeveloped. In any case, one ought to resist the pressure to simply abstract certain characteristic practices or modes of thought within the discipline (as currently carried out in academic institutions) in order to show them as various instantiations of certain isolated features of commodity fetish. It is hardly as a worthwhile point of departure anyway, since like most phenomena, music theory has multiple determinations.

A reasonable point of departure, however, may be to preempt a discussion of the discipline that claims music theory is fundamentally fetishistic because its central project is to investigate material characteristics of music in place of studying underlying social contexts. I have discussed in previous work the one-sidedness of such a position and will not repeat those arguments here, except to say that in general the error of the assertion is twofold: first, in its belief in the radical discontinuity between the material and social aspects of music (which ironically lies at the heart of Marx's definition of fetishism); and second, in the lack of a coherent definition of the social sphere itself.

Applying the category strictly, one could say that fetishism manifests itself here (as elsewhere) in the belief that the value of the musical commodity (however it appears) arises from its material characteristics rather than the place its producers hold in the totality of social labor—a belief, in other words, that the music commodity's use-value, its ability to satisfy (in this case, aesthetic) needs, the nature of the enjoyment it creates, is the source of its value. The relationship between value in the commodity sense and the aesthetic sense is particularly suggestive and has been discussed by, among others, Barbara Herrnstein Smith in specific connection with canon formation.

By way of the specific mystification of music, aesthetic value emerges as a characteristic displacement of value in the Marxist sense of congealed abstract labor.

One would hope, however, that we could learn more from Marx here than that aesthetic value is contingent and that canons are therefore formed by considerations other than the "material" superiority of certain work over others. While such assertions are not strictly false, they are hampered by the fragmentary nature of their point of departure. To begin with, they fail to recognize the central role music theory plays in both the production and consumption cycles of musical commodities. The fetish nature of institutional music theory lies not only in its examination of material aspects of pieces as the source of value (in the form of aesthetic value or meaning), but also in its concealment of the social nature of consumption or appropriation behind these styles of investigation into the material properties of musical pieces. The putative radical discontinuity between the relevant material forms and social forms generates in turn a radical discontinuity between studies of material relations and those of social relations. Consequently, since it assumes that the material relations it studies are expressing themselves through corresponding material rather than social forms, music theory (in particular) loses sight of the true historical dimension of its various objects of study (the composer's ideation, the work's structure, private aesthetic response of the analyst, and so on) seeking instead to serve as complex multiple order mediation between them. Furthermore, it is easily drawn to positivist epistemological and methodological ethoi that entirely fragment the world into passive objects and correspondingly passive subjects.

The latter development produces in turn a double bind with respect to analytical methodological issues. The ethos of constant technological advance that governs the sciences comes into conflict with the ethos of strict methodological loyalty. The former is determined in part by larger academic institutional demands since the nineteenth century. The latter emerges not only from the especially overwhelming subjugation of music to the commodity form and its disavowal (in the Freudian sense described earlier), but also from the ethos of cultural guardianship dominant in conservatories. As a result, the methodologies most closely associated with these positions, Schenkerian analysis and Set Theory, are subjected to finer and increasingly inconsequential revisions (Klumpenhouwer 1998, 305–306).

Neither the material nor social aspects of music are self-sufficient, self-grounding categories. They appear to be just that, however, and this appearance generates certain "spontaneous, natural modes of thought" fundamental to all disciplines of music study. On one hand, the distinctions between these disciplines (music theory, music history, ethnomusicology) result from tendencies to divide labor stemming from their roles as disciplines devoted in part to professional development. On the other hand, these distinctions result from the fragmentary and metaphysical nature of dominant, fetishized music study. Each discipline represents not only a different isolated fragment of musical life, but is also taken up into a different aspect of fetish thinking.

Beyond Adorno

With respect to the second question posed earlier about the nature of a properly Marxist alternative to mystificational music theoretic practices, one imagines that Adorno's well-known essay "On the Fetish-Character in Music and the Regression of Listening" (1978) might serve as a convenient starting point. The title of the essay itself conveys the outlines of Adorno's methodology. Marxist conceptions (he doesn't invoke Freud's notion of fetishism here at all) are to be applied to an analysis of the production of music—Freudian conceptions (developmental regression) to listening. Given that commodity production itself involves consumption (of which listening is only a part), Adorno ensures the two approaches will become entangled.

Adorno's essay begins by cataloging the extent of capitalism's pernicious effects on music, delivered as a philippic. He is of course correct to complain, though only partially, since there are no good reasons to exempt (as Adorno does) *any* musical context or genre from these judgments. Describing capitalist history as pure cultural decline fails to recognize how feudalism and early capitalism also ruined music, which is to say that they do not constitute states of higher human cultural achievement that capitalism has corrupted over time.

Despite its isolated merits, however, Adorno's critique does not engage fruitfully with the themes engaged in Marx's (or Freud's) conception of fetish. Moreover, one is hard-pressed to find much more in Adorno's essay than the assertion (already made in the essay's title) that music produced in late capitalism is like a sexual perversion and that modern listeners are childish.[9] As such it shares much with the unfortunate Frankfurt method of *Ideologiekritik*, a tradition that rarely rises above caustic lampooning of cultural practices and products, often satisfied with substituting bitter and wounded sententiousness for critical investigation. The many romantic expressions of *Wehmut* over cultural loss (in the narrow sense of the word "culture") that characterize Adorno's work have far too often and too readily (beginning with Adorno himself) been confused with properly Marxist (which is to say, ruthless) critique of "all that exists."[10]

To be fair, we should recall that the essay at hand needs to read synoptically with Adorno's *Aesthetic Theory*, where his ideas about the "illusory character" of art are more developed. According to Zuidervaart, Adorno argues that

> the illusory character of art arises from its demand for unity. To be a determinate negation of society, an artwork must achieve its own unity, but achieving unity makes it illusory in two ways. First, the artwork's unity is feigned rather than fully achieved. Second, such unity covers up societal antagonism, which include the artwork's opposition to society. (Zuidervaart: 178–79)

Unified works are doubly illusory and doubly revelatory. On one hand, the unified nature of artworks (which for Adorno must arise from the parts constituting a totality in such ways that the parts retain their individuality) will, under persistent technical analysis, be revealed as imposed and thus an illusion; and it will further generate the fiction that society is not antagonistic. On the other hand, properly understood, the fiction of an artwork's unity reveals the real antagonistic nature of society; and correspondingly, the artwork gives us a glimpse of what we could be. In this sense, the artwork can represent a utopian breakthrough into the present (Zuidervaart, 179ff).

These are just the aspects of Adorno's work that have attracted the attention of certain strains within New Musicology, although for the most part Adorno's particular conception of social antagonism (which one assumes refers in particular to class antagonism, Adorno's overall inability to integrate class into his analyses notwithstanding) has been redirected to represent in the first instance gender antagonism.

The domination side of fetish—the side that asserts that people fail to see how material relations express social relations—might suggest that the analytical approach of Adorno, and those who base their work on his, represents a reasonable effort to uncover these relations. However, it is quite clear from Adorno's work that technical analysis uncovers relations that are only *symbolized* by structural and formal relations in the piece at hand: the analysis serves therefore merely a structural allegory for more identifiable ideological notions and claims. This is not, however, the nature of fetish as described earlier. The technical features that interest Adorno are not only rhetorically social: according to fetish theory, the technical features, the material aspects of musical pieces, are the very ways social relations materially express themselves. Adorno's bind arises from his (complicated) acceptance of the autonomous, systematically closed nature of musical structure. Accordingly, he has a great deal of difficulty integrating class relations into his discussion of music, except to claim that certain technical features of pieces are marked by certain "class" characteristics. Under Adorno's (1976, 60FF.) analysis, Chopin's music, for instance, is aristocratic; Hindemith's, petty bourgeois; and Stravinsky's, haut bourgeois. Clearly, this is an unsatisfactory approach to both class and music analysis.

Yet what does it mean for the study of music that the material aspects of music express relevant social relations? How do these aspects become a means of expression of domination (in the sense described earlier by Geras)? How do concrete relations call a corresponding material objectivity into being?

The answer to these questions relies on how one understands the nature of "expression" or "called into being" in the formulation, which in turn logically depends on the nature of the concrete relations at hand. However one characterizes these (dialectical) relations, one clearly cannot begin by simply asserting relations in a general sense and then effect a chain of connections to the technical, material aspects of musical pieces.

The very nature of those questions preempts the possibility of a specific music analytical methodology. What one can offer is a sketch of a reasonable approach. Whereas material characteristics appear as self-grounded and self-contained objects, a proper investigation seeks to discover the conditions (both material and social) required to bring about the relevant objects and relationships. Answers to such questions are not generalizable, except to say that investigations along these lines will subsequently be faced with new categories that present themselves as self-contained and suggest particular preemptive resolutions. These appearances, as they come up, are to be met by a rearticulation of the initial questions.

Notes

1. Quoted in Pietz 1993: 133. The immediate context of the remark was Marx's attack on Karl Hermes, who in defense of religion (in general) and in the course of arguing for the censorship of all public religious criticism, described the benefits of even primitive religion, "childish fetishism" as he called it, as the ability to allow humans to transcend their "sensuous desires."

2. The study of social psychology with special reference to both Marx and Freud is a long-standing theoretical strategy, especially among the early Frankfurt School theorists. However, emphasizing commodity-fetishism in *Capital* and placing it suggestively beside Freud's work is, unbelievably, a fairly recent gesture, so that Ellen 1988 has difficulties listing any relevant theoretical attempts along these lines. Emily Apter and William Pietz's 1993 collection, *Fetishism as Cultural Discourse*, contains several full-blown attempts at associating the economic and psychological senses of the word.

3. The following is a particularly good example of what I have in mind, along with a clear indication of its ideological purpose: "The polemical form of my argument contends that the reception of Louis Althusser's work has fetishized his theory of ideology and virtually overlooked, left unread his theory and practice of reading" (Rooney 1995: 183).

4. Marx's discussion of the accidental, expanded, and general forms of exchange is meant to serve as both a logical and an historical sequence leading up to the development of gold as the general equivalent. It is worthwhile observing that the same progression has occurred in the money form, where national currencies have over time developed a general equivalent currency (the U.S. dollar) in which their values are expressed.

5. It should be said here that commodities are not unique to capitalism: the historical development from accidental or isolated exchange to expanded exchange and ultimately to the establishment of the money form completed itself several thousand years ago. What *does* distinguish the commodity and commodity production under capitalism is its compulsory nature, and in turn the transition from the formal subsumption of the labor process by capital to its real subsumption, and correspondingly, the development of relative sur-

plus value production from absolute surplus value production, and the social relations both obscured and expressed by commodities are just these (Wood 1999: 27ff).

6. I have replaced "linen," which serves as the fantasy general equivalent in Marx's discussion, with "money" in order to make the meaning clearer.
7. Teresa Ebert (1999) discusses such matters in connection with Hegels' idea of "unhappy consciousness" and recent work by Žižek.
8. Since institutional music theory has (until very recently) been aimed exclusively to classical musics, I direct my comments to that particular context here, while recognizing the fundamental incompleteness of doing so.
9. It is worthwhile pointing out here how heavily Adorno depends on characterizing practices as perversions and symptoms of serious mental illness. In Adorno's (1978: 278) critique of Stravinsky, for instance, Stravinksy's work is described as sadomasochistic and schizophrenic.
10. Mészáros provides an interesting (i.e., ruthless) critique of Adorno's writings (along with the entire Frankfurt tradition) in Mészáros 1989: 91–167.

References

Adorno, T. 1976. *Introduction to the Sociology of Music*. Translated by E. B. Aston. New York: Seabury Press.
———. 1978. "On the Fetish Character in Music and the Regression in Listening." Translated by Maurice Goldbloom. In *The Essential Frankfurt Reader*, edited by Andrew Arato and Eike Gebhardt. New York: Urizen Books.
Apter, Emily and William Pietz, eds. 1993. *Fetish as Cultural Discourse*. Ithaca, N.Y.: Cornell University Press.
Cohen, G. A. 1978. *Karl Marx's Theory of History: A Defense*. Princeton, N.J.: Princeton University Press.
Ebert, Teresa L. 1999. "Globalization, Internationalism, and the Class Politics of Cynical Reason." *Nature, Society, And Thought* 12/4: 389–410.
Ellen, Roy. 1988. "Fetishism." *Man* (New Series) 23/2: 213–35.
Freud, Sigmund. 1962. *Three Essays on Sexuality*. Translated and revised by James Strachy. n.p.: Basic Books.
———. 1963. "Fetishism." In *Sexuality and the Psychology of Love*, edited by Philip Rieff. New York: Collier.
Geras, Norman. [1971] 1990. "Essence and Appearance: Aspects of Fetishism in Marx's *Capital*." In *Karl Marx's Social and Political Thought: Critical Assessments*, Vol. 4, edited by B. Jessop and C. Malcolm-Brown. London and New York: Routledge.
Kedourie, E. 1995. *Hegel & Marx: Introductory Lectures*. Oxford: Blackwell.
Klumpenhouwer, H. 1998. "Music Theory, Dialectics, and Post-Structuralism." In *Music/Ideology: Resisting the Aesthetic*, edited by Adam Krims. New York: Gordon & Breach International.
Laplanche and Pontalis. 1973. *The Language of Psychoanalysis*. Translated by Donald Nicholson-Smith. London: Hogarth.
Mandel, Ernest. 1975. *Late Capitalism*. Translated by Joris de Bres. London: Verso.

Marx, Karl. 1975. "The Leading Article of the Kölnische Zeitung." *Neue Rheinische Zeitung*.

———. [1867] 1976. *Capital: A Critique of Political Economy,* Vol. 1. Translated by Ben Fowkes. New York: Vintage.

Mészáros, István. 1989. *The Power of Ideology*. Hertfordshire: Harvester Wheatsheaf.

Rooney, Ellen. 1995. "Better Read than Dead: Althusser and the Fetish of Ideology." *Yale French Studies* 88: 183–200.

Rubin, Isaak Illich. 1968. *Essays on Marx's Theory of Value*. Translated by Miloš Samardžija and Fredy Perlman. Montreal: Black Rose Books.

Smith, Barbara Herrnstein. 1988. *Contingencies of Value: Alternative Perspectives in Critical Theory*. Cambridge, Mass: Harvard University Press.

———. 1990. "Value/Evaluation." In *Critical Terms for Literary Study*, edited by F. Lentricchia and T. McLaughlin. Chicago: University of Chicago Press.

Whitebrook, Joel. 1995. *Perversion and Utopia*. Cambridge: MIT Press.

Wood, Ellen Meiksins. 1986. *The Retreat from Class: A New 'True' Socialism*. London: Verso.

———. 1999. *The Origin of Capitalism*. New York: Monthly Review of Books.

Žižek, Slovoj. 1997a. "The supposed subjects of ideology." *Critical Quarterly* 39/2: 4–59.

———. 1997b. *The Plague of Fantasies*. London: Verso.

Zuidervaart, Lambert. 1991. *Adorno's Aesthetic Theory: The Redemption of Illusion*. Cambridge: MIT Press.

PART II

Capitalism and Musical Poetics

3

Modernity and Musical Structure
Neo-Marxist Perspectives on Song
Form and Its Successors

PETER MANUEL

The study of homologies between social structures and formal structures in art has constituted a particularly challenging field of inquiry in the modern humanities. On the whole, scholarly attempts to relate music to broader sociohistorical phenomena have tended to focus on such relatively tangible musical parameters as lyric content, style, or performance contexts rather than formal structure, which, being inherently more abstract in nature, is presumed to have less ideological content. However, a few scholars have persuasively argued that formal structures in Western music reflect a general aesthetic conditioned by social economy. In particular, they have illustrated how sectionally structured, closed, teleological song forms are quintessentially characteristic of bourgeois capitalism (as opposed, for example, to feudal societies). In this essay I review some of the approaches linking bourgeois aesthetics to closed musical structures—especially sonata form and song form—and offer perspectives on the ways that the persistence of these forms, as well as the spread or revival of distinct forms, have been conditioned by the broader socioeconomic contexts of late modernity.

Attempts by music scholars to posit iconicities between form and social context have been at best sporadic and often contested or marginalized in academia. Alan Lomax's well-known cantometrics scheme illuminated a few parallels between form and social structures, noting, for example, the prominence of bardic litanies in "old high cultures," and the Western European preference for "simple, compactly organized melodic forms" (1968: 134–35). However, the cantometrics scheme did not explore the parameter of form in much greater depth, and even these generalizations were problematized by the system's failure to address class stratification within a given region (e.g., South Asia or Western Europe). In the field of popular music studies, Middleton (1990: 141, 150, and elsewhere) has suggested some insightful perspectives, invoking especially the work of A. L. Lloyd and Janos Marothy, to whom we shall return.

For their part, a handful of musicologists in recent decades have shown interest in socially contextualizing aspects of musical form. While Martha Feldman (1995) has explored parallels between ritual and form in opera, other scholars have insightfully related formal structures in common-practice instrumental music to contemporary literary aesthetics. Of particular relevance are the several publications that explore parallels between nonprogrammatic instrumental music—especially sonatas—and narrative prose and/or drama (see Maus 1997; Newcomb 1984, 1987; Treitler 1989; Cone 1989; McClary 1986; and Leppert and McClary 1987). On the whole, these insightful essays, in their distinct fashions, illustrate some of the ways in which the superficially "abstract" sonata form can in fact encode a tightly structured narrative drama. In the most standard interpretation, for example, the protagonistic theme or themes embark on an often tumultuous and exciting metaphorical journey (especially in the development section), eventually to return home safely in the recapitulation, with the reestablishment of order and the domestication of thematic material (second themes) earlier introduced in constrasting keys. The structural parallels with the novel, and with contemporary drama, are self-evident. Nevertheless, with the partial and idiosyncratic exception of McClary, none of these authors attempts to relate the presence of narrative structure in music to the material conditions that generate such an aesthetic of extended dramatic development and closure. Rather, in the tradition of musicological formalism, the use of narrative forms in music is implicitly or explicitly treated as a superstructural phenomenon evolving in a sociohistorical vacuum. It is thus only a small handful of Marxist-informed writers who have explored the socioeconomic factors that have conditioned the emergence of such an aesthetic.

On the whole, musicologists, like most other mainstream scholars, have tended to regard theses about sociomusical homologies with suspicion, if not outright derision. The standard objection, whether implicit or explicit, is that such theories are unverifiable and ideological. Rather, it is sometimes argued, Western art music has evolved in a rarefied, essentially ahistorical milieu in which it is relatively "free from direct social influence" (Temperley 1991: 399). This familiar perspective, treating nonprogrammatic instrumental music as a relatively absolute art form, is occasionally made explicit but is more often implicit, as in writings that treat the evolution of musical styles and structures as purely formal developments. While the question of the autonomy of high art is complex and has been extensively debated, few would hesitate to acknowledge a certain sort and degree of autonomy in an idiom like Western classical music, especially since it is so deeply embedded in a Kantian aesthetic of disinterestedness. Nevertheless, the denial of ideology and of sociohistorical conditioning is of course itself an ideology, and not an innocent one. Implicit in the ideology of absolute music is the notion that Western art music ("Music") is unique among all musics of the world in having evolved as a product of purely abstract, "natural" creation and innovation. All other musics, by contrast, have been somehow stunted or warped in being conditioned—as ethnomusicologists themselves demonstrate—by their sociohistorical contexts. It should be granted, however, that given the inherently hypothetical and speculative nature of homological theories, a degree of skepticism regarding them is not unwarranted. The legitimacy and acceptance of such inquiries in academia has not been aided by the fanciful interpretive conceits indulged in by various post-structuralist writers on music—especially those more grounded in contemporary literary theory than in the rigors of music analysis.

In this essay I limit myself in many respects to what I would consider to be a most obvious and unassailable basic premise: that there is at least an indirect causal relationship between the emergence of capitalist modernity and a coherent bourgeois aesthetic (reaching its classical phase in the eighteenth and nineteenth centuries), one manifestation of which is the predominance of closed, internally structured musical forms, especially sonata form and "song" form. This class of forms uses techniques of symmetry, recapitulation, and internal development to achieve dramatic climax and clear closure. It thus stands in contrast to open-ended, additive, or variative forms that are characteristic, for example, of pre-modern musics (several of which may residually survive in modern societies for various reasons).

If the mere mention of the term "bourgeois" suffices to alienate many contemporary music scholars, it may be useful to point out how unique song form has been to bourgeois societies (or sectors of societies), or more specifically, how uncharacteristic of pre-modern, non-bourgeois societies it is. Thus, in traditional non-Western musics, or in pre-Renaissance Western music, one finds a considerable variety of formal structures, but very little that possesses the features here identified with song per se. These traditional forms would include the following:

- Strophic song (using "song" in the general sense). In this form there is little or no extended musical development. Most typically, the numbers of strophes may vary according to the demands of the particular performance context. Often, as in the case of country blues, the Urdu or Persian ghazal, or traditional flamenco, the strophes need not relate to each other in poetic theme, but are expected to be self-sufficient, independent, epigrammatic entities. Such independence also characterizes genres like *punto cubano* or Puerto Rican *seis* and *aguinaldo*, in which, despite a degree of lyric-thematic unity, each ten-line *décima* strophe is expected to be a conceptually complete and closed entity, with a dramatically concluding final line. For its part, the bardic epic litany sung strophically to a short melody differs in constituting an extended narrative form, rather than a series of discrete verses; however, it shares the absence of *musical* development, or of any formal structure exceeding the length of the strophe itself. Moreover, the bard typically performs fragments rather than the entire work and feels free to omit, rearrange, or elaborate given portions of the internal chapters and passages. The category of strophic song would also include rounds and canons.

- Open-ended "additive" structures. This category includes a variety of forms. One set would comprise entities like the North Indian *khyâl*, in which the exposition of a *râg* could last anywhere from a few minutes to an hour, depending on context and other factors. Here the composition (the *chîz*) is used primarily to punctuate improvised passages, which may vary indefinitely, within certain conventions, in number and length. Also in the "additive" category would fall performances consisting of concatenations of short tunes, as is characteristic of much Irish or Balkan traditional dance music. Conspicuous again is the absence of a fixed formal structure or length, especially in the quintessential traditional dance context.

- Ostinato-based forms. Many of these overlap with the above two groups. As is well known, ostinato forms are particularly characteristic of (but hardly unique to) African and Afro-American traditional musics. They would include the mbira piece consisting of variations on an opening melody, or the drum ensemble music in which a reiterated pattern accompanies the litany of a master drummer, or of vocalists, or is itself subjected to variations.

What is lacking in all these forms, which Marothy (1974) terms "collective-variative" idioms, is a sense of dramatic progression and closure, such as song form achieves through techniques of symmetry, recapitulation, use of arch form, strong and weak cadences ("masculine/feminine," *ouvert/clos*), and/or a conventional, logical sequence and number of internal sections. Pre-modern forms may incorporate such loosely teleological features as a general increase in intensity, as, for example, in South Asian *qawwâli*, or even an alternation of fast, energetic sections with slower, more moderate ones (as in North Indian Bhojpuri-region *chowtâl*). But even these forms are flexible entities whose length and internal structures are open-ended. As in virtually all the forms outlined above, the sense of closure is limited to a general length determined by convention, and achieved at the local level by, at most, a final cadential flourish or figure (e.g., the *tihâî/korvâî* of Indian classical music).

Song form contrasts markedly with these structures. The 32-bar AABA song form and its variants epitomize the closed arch form, and retain this characteristic even if repeated two or three times (but generally not more). As an example of a typical modern Euro-American popular song, one may take the Beatles's "I Want to Hold your Hand," whose form recurs in nine of the eleven songs on the LP *Meet the Beatles*. It may be schematized as follows:

A   verse
A   verse
B   bridge ("and when I touch you . . . ," sung solo)
A   verse
B   bridge (sung duet)
A   verse
(A) repeat of final lines

It should be obvious that rearranging these sections or, for example, adding several more "A" sections at the end would disrupt the logical structure of this song.

For its part, sonata form, with its clear, if flexible exposition-development-recapitulation structure, represents an extended elaboration of this same approach. As in the 32-bar AABA pattern, symmetry and arch form are again evident, and the sense of dramatic motion, climax, and closure is intensified through the tonal wanderings, transformation, and eventual recapitulation of the thematic material.

Naturally, many music genres combine features of the open-ended, collective-variative technique with those of song form. Many of these can be seen from a diachronic perspective as transitional entities. The gradual evolution of song form in Western music, through the lai and virelai on down to the sonata and popular song format, is traced with extraordinary erudition and clarity by Marothy (1974). In my own prior short article on this subject (Manuel 1985), I looked briefly at three traditional collective-variative forms (Urdu *ghazal*-song, Mexican *huapango*, and Cuban rumba) and illustrated how they have acquired certain features of structured song form in the process of being commercialized and informed by bourgeois aesthetics.

Historicizing Song Form

The emergence and spread of song form, and of a general aesthetic in which it is embedded, cannot be attributed to a single historical factor, but to a set of aspects related to modernity in general. One significant, albeit intangible factor presumably involved the advent of a new conception of time that accrued from the invention and spread of mechanical chronometers, especially from the seventeenth century. The advent of timepieces naturally facilitated the ability and inclination to think in terms of temporal blocks and, by extension, of formal sections in music that could be arranged spatially in

various fashions. This ability would be further enhanced by literacy, print-
ing, and, of course, especially by music literacy. Thus, it is difficult to conceive of the creation and spread of sonata form without a well-established
tradition of music notation, facilitating the envisioning, transmission, and
performance of sectional works incorporating repeats, recapitulations, and
the like. John Shepherd's discussion of musical form (1977), which owes
more to McLuhan than to Marx, argues that pre-modern man's pre-literacy,
lack of industrial technology (including clocks), and domination by environ-
mental cycles obliged him to live and think in terms of the sensuous, immediate present and to conceive of time only in cyclical and "Bergsonian"
organic terms rather than in progressive and objective terms. Accordingly, as
Nettl (1956: 80) has observed, musics of technologically primitive societies
tend to be structured in terms of repetition and variation of short motifs, such
that, from Leonard Meyer's perspective, aesthetic gratification takes place
only on immediate, short-term levels (1967: 32). The same could be said of
the collective-variative forms of feudal societies and "old high cultures" as
well. Only with the advent of the related phenomena of literacy (enabling the
storage, retrieval, and rearrangement of blocks of information), technology
(engendering an objective view of time and a greater ability to control
nature), and positivism (with its progressive, rather than cyclical view of history), do Westerners become able (and/or willing) to "stand outside of time
and music" (in Shepherd et al. 1977: 111) and construct formally complex
musical structures involving long-term memory, delayed gratification, and
juxtaposition of lengthy formal sections.

However, the advent of literacy and modern conceptions of time,
although relevant, are not sufficient to explain the spread of the distinctive
features of bourgeois musical aesthetics. For one thing, a McLuhanesque
analytical approach (1962) foregrounding literacy as a determinant of modern conceptions of time could not explain why collective-variative forms
(e.g., strophic forms) have persisted among some predominantly literate peoples (e.g., South Asian bourgeoisies), or, conversely, why structured song format may be popular among semi-literate peoples (e.g., rural Mexicans). In
general, the new epistemologies generated by literacy and mechanical
chronometers must be regarded as preconditions for, rather than primary
determinants of, the new aesthetic.

Most important, the preeminence of song form must be seen as part of a
broader bourgeois aesthetic itself generated by modernity and capitalism—
which, in Western culture, emerged as inseparable entities. This aesthetic can
be seen as part of what has been called a "semiotic revolution" (Witkin 1998)
which accompanied the transition of Western European society from feudalism
to capitalism, commencing in the Renaissance and reaching full fruition in the
nineteenth century. There are several salient aspects to this aesthetic reorienta-
tion, each of which can be seen to condition the emergence of song form.

A particularly important development is the new emphasis on *rationalization* of the formal aspects of the work of art. Arnold Hauser, in his magisterial work *The Social History of Art* (1957: II, 15) grounds this new sensibility in the unprecedented importance of rationalization in socioeconomic life. The key development in this process is the emergence of new urban capitalist modes of production that liberated mankind from the crude dependence on nature experienced by the peasant or hunter-gatherer. The socioeconomic revolution generating the Renaissance, especially as commencing in Italian city-states in the fifteenth century, depended not upon nature but on rational, man-made systems of planning, credit, banking, investment, and the like. Disorder, blind habit, and lack of control were anathema to these institutions and to the ideology that sustained them. As Hauser explains, the capitalist economic developments of the Renaissance confirm

> the rationalism which now dominates the whole intellectual and material life of the time. The principles of unity which now become authoritative in art—the unification of space and the unified standards of proportion, the restriction of the artistic representation to one single theme, and the concentration of the composition into one immediately intelligible form—are also in accordance with this new rationalism. They express the same dislike for the incalculable and the uncontrollable as the economy of the same period with its emphasis on planning, expediency, and calculability . . . . The things that are now felt as "beautiful" are the logical conformity of the individual parts of a whole.

The rational basis of the new aesthetic was explicitly articulated in the fifteenth century by Italian theorist Leone Alberti, who described the work of art as "so constituted that it is impossible to take anything away from it or add anything to it without impairing the beauty of the whole" (quoted in Hauser, 1957: II, 89). As Alberti clarified, the new aesthetic demanded the logical conformity of parts to the whole and highlighted a dynamic dialectic between foreground and background elements.

The aesthetic manifestations of this new sensibility are evident in several art forms. In painting, they are reflected in the new emphasis on creating a unified, complete, balanced, closed formal structure on the painted surface. This approach contrasts, for example, with the busy clutter of so many earlier paintings (see Hauser for illustrations). In literature, the obvious counterpart is the novel, with its tightly knit, rationally structured form. Unlike earlier, non-bourgeois forms of extended narrative, the novel has not merely a beginning and an end, but a coherent internal structure with a clear sense of creative design and logic. It differs in this sense from the short ballad or from an extended narrative epic, which typically is performed only in fragments and which lacks in its internal sections a clear sequential development. Thus, for example, while Homer's *Odysseus* has beginning and concluding chapters, the internal chapters occur in no particular order, and could be rearranged, supplemented, or omitted without impairing the work as a whole.[1] A musical rendition of such a ballad would naturally exhibit the same collective-variative looseness.

It should be obvious that song form, representing the complete expression of a given content, constitutes a musical embodiment of a distinct and new architectural aesthetic. As suggested above, one cannot rearrange or omit sections of a sonata, add a ten-minute coda, or insert several strophes into the middle of a 32-bar AABA song without disrupting the logical form of these entities. Similarly, as noted above, the parallels are obvious between such narrative structures and sonata form, in which the protagonistic themes wander afar and eventually return home, and the disorder and tension introduced along the way are logically resolved.

Another important set of developments underlying the new aesthetic are those involving the replacement of pre-capitalist collective values by a new sense of individualism. As Marx (1964: 96) wrote, "Man is only individualized through a process of history. He originally appears as a generic being, a tribal being, a herd animal." The rise of individualism creates a new dimension of dualism between the self and society that did not exist before capitalism. As with the new emphasis on rationality, the emergence of what Marothy terms the "bourgeois Ego" is not a purely superstructural phenomenon, but is clearly linked to the rise of an economic system based on the output and production of the individual (or nuclear family), rather than the village, clan, or guild. Thus, communal line and circle dances typical of pre-capitalist societies give way (via the minuet, waltz, and *contredanse*) to intimate couple dances. Paintings, with a new sense of realism, increasingly portray ordinary people (especially the bourgeoisie) in everyday street or domestic scenes, instead of focusing on mythological or religious icons and stereotypes. New techniques of chiaroscuro and especially perspective heighten not only realism in general, but also the sense that one is viewing a scene from the vantage point of a specific individual.[2] Literature and drama, from the Elizabethan period on, in a similar trend toward realism, stress sentimental personal situations, often concerning the private lives of ordinary people. (Lukacs highlights the novels of Balzac as epitomes of this trend.) Poetry, especially in the wake of Wordsworth, places a new emphasis on introspection, while Boswell's *Life of Johnson* heralds a new biographical interest in un-heroic bourgeois individuals. The individualism of such bourgeois realism contrasts with the communal heroic values expressed in epics like *Beowolf* or *The Song of Roland*, or in genres like the Persian and Urdu *ghazal* or medieval troubador poetry, all of whose protagonists are generalized stock characters rather than distinct, nuanced, individual personalities. Similarly, poetry and lyric song come to be dominated by portrayals of the relatively new phenomenon of sentimental love between two autonomous, socially free individuals operating in an ahistorical, virtual world of the emotions. Marxists like Marothy would relate this trend to the emergence of the commodity-producing bourgeois. Giddens (1992) supplements this interpretation by grounding modernity's "transformation of intimacy" and the emergence of "confluent" (rather than carnal) love to the liberation of sexuality (especially for women) from procreation (e.g., via contraception), and from danger (e.g., death in childbirth), and a general process in which human agency is heightened and individuals and relationships are increasingly "disembedded" from prior social inhibitions, conventions, and moorings.

As Marothy writes,

> In music, the main formal expression of "ego-centeredness" is the solo song, emerging as the central category of bourgeois music as a whole, and entailing all the other consequences in tonal system, rhythm, polyphony and other formal elements of music. (1972: 16)

Thus, rather than constituting a mere "formal achievement," song form represents a narrative framework typically establishing a tonal, melodic, and thematic "home" (the "little world" of the bourgeois Ego), which is then departed from and ultimately returned to safely. In this sense song form develops an extended dialectic of foreground and background by metaphorically juxtaposing the safe, intimate private world (e.g., of the self, or nuclear family) with the unstable, threatening/exciting dynamics of the external world.

The links between formal structure and sense of social identity are particularly conspicuous when lyric content is considered, as a cross-cultural sampling of traditional vocal genres indicates. Traditional music in North India, for example, falls overwhelmingly in the collective-variative category, whether in the open-ended, elaborated classical *khyâl* or the unpretentious strophic folk song. However different such idioms may seem, in musical terms they share an absence of the distinguishing features of song form, sacrificing long-term development and delayed gratification for such purely foreground features as melodic and rhythmic intricacy and textual interest. Correspondingly, their lyrics, while often amatory, seldom depict the romantic, "confluent" love of two autonomous individuals. Far more characteristic are devotional panegryrics, heroic martial ballads celebrating historical or mythological figures, or, in the case of erotic verse, portrayals of the repressed desire of an essentially one-dimensional stock figure who is explicitly embedded in an inhibiting social environment. Thus, in a typical verse encountered in innumerable folk and classical songs, the young wife expresses the fear that her nocturnal tryst with her lover (or husband!) will be overheard by her mother-in-law. (In traditional Indian rural joint families, married couples typically sleep apart and are expected not to show affection before their parents.)

The protagonists of the Urdu *ghazal* are similarly stereotypical in their condition of unrequited love. Thus, the *ghazal's* archetypical *'ashiq* (lover) rails against social conformity, swoons over a woman he has but glimpsed on a balcony, and weeps over the indifference with which his beloved is obliged to treat him. Ghalib, for example, writes:

> In her case it is a pride in her honour, and in mine a modest concern for self-respect; How could I meet her in the street? How could she invite me to her house?[3]

Accordingly, this lyric and musical representation of a socially grounded stock figure takes place not in the context of an extended song form, but in a strophic rendition in which each couplet is musically and semantically complete and independent, constituting a concise epigram—a jewel in a necklace, or a flower in a garland—relying on a repertoire of stock similes and references. There is neither character development nor long-term musical structure or narrative.

Traditional flamenco is in some respects a more recent product, but tends to illustrate the same lyrical and musical atomism. Flamenco pieces, however sophisticated and elaborate, are essentially collective-variative in character, consisting of strophic renditions of stock tunes; the length of a flamenco piece is loosely governed by convention rather than by any internal structural logic. Accordingly, most lyrics consist of strophes (of three, four, or five short lines) which may be thematically unrelated to each other; even if related, they are expected, as in the case of the *ghazal,* to be epigrammatic statements that are semantically and affectively complete in themselves. As in similarly atomistic genres like blues, or North Indian *thumri*, verse fragments often recur in distinct song lyrics, and may to some extent be freely inserted by singers and poets. In flamenco, in a manner reminiscent of the *ghazal,* the singer/poet rails against social constraints, addresses the world from behind prison bars, shudders with repressed desire as he passes the beloved's house, and portrays himself as grounded in a specific social milieu. For example:

> For you I abandoned my children and hastened my mother's death
> Now you have gone and left me—may God punish you.[4]

What this singer shares with the *'ashiq* of the *ghazal* and the young bride of Indian folksong is that he is portrayed as deeply, indeed pathetically *embedded* in a specific social situation. In this sense all these protagonists differ dramatically from the personae represented in the modern sentimental ballad, whose depiction rigorously eschews any reference to time, place, watchful in-laws, or sociohistorical grounding of any sort.

The transition from open-ended, strophic ballad to closed song form is especially transparent in the replacement of the Mexican *corrido* by the bolero in the early twentieth century. As Mark Pedelty (1999) insightfully notes, the strophic *corrido* was the quintessential folksong genre of pre-Revolutionary Mexico, celebrating the traditional values of a rural, patriarchal, communitarian society via lyrics about great men, great horses, heroic battles, and epic betrayals. Despite its rural collectivist goals, the Revolution (1910–17) had the effect of dramatically urbanizing Mexican society and bringing most Mexicans into the orbit of capitalist socioeconomic relations. Urbanization and capitalist modernity brought not only dislocation and alienation, but new sorts of opportunities, especially in the form of the unprecedented personal freedom from family and community constraints. The archetypical musical vehicle for the new worldview of the Mexican urbanite was not the archaic and quaint *corrido,* but the urbane, sophisticated, and romantic bolero. Unlike the *corrido,* the bolero portrays not historical (and hence socially embedded) protagonists, but abstract, autonomous individuals voicing their intimate sentimental laments in a generally non–gender-specific manner. Accordingly, as Pedelty (1999) observes, whereas the *corrido* was collectively created and transmitted as an oral tradition, boleros were composed by known artists (such as Agustín Lara) and disseminated by a capitalist music industry. A further distinction— not noted by Pedelty, but quite typical of such genres—lies between the strophic, open-ended form of the *corrido* and the closed formal structures of the bolero. These latter, although variable, generally cohere to "song" form in combining a logical, fixed, and finite number of 16- or 32-bar sections to achieve symmetry and closure. Like the sentimental lyrics, the use of such formal structures must be seen not as a slavish imitation of contemporary Yankee trends, but as an abstract musical expression of a new worldview conditioned by new lifestyles and modes of production.

Late Modernity and Postmodernity: The Return of the Repressed

As we enter the new millennium, and indeed for the last several decades, music culture both globally and within the developed West itself have come to represent a set of particularly complex and diverse discursive fields in which no single style or format can be said to dominate, whether in popular or classical musics. Insofar as song form is linked to capitalism and bourgeois aesthetics, one might well assume that such a form would be more pervasive and hegemonic than ever. The communist and socialist blocs, which once comprised a third of the world's population and posed a serious threat to capitalism, have definitively collapsed and no longer serve as

viable socioeconomic models or alternatives. Global capitalism has tri-
umphed and penetrated world economy to an unprecedented degree, and the
mass media fill the world with predominantly bourgeois images of consumerism, individualism, and Western-style fashion and modernity.

There is no doubt that song form, in diverse variants, has accordingly
achieved an unprecedented sort of presence. Whether in locally produced or
imported forms, the pop ballad, invariably combining sentimental love with
standard song structure, has become a substantial component of nearly every
major music culture in the world. While ethnomusicologists (perhaps not
entirely without reason) continue to lavish attention on more distinctively
local aspects of music cultures, the pop ballad—from Chinese *gangtai-yue*
and "pop Java" to the croonings of Julio Iglesias—has become the global
common denominator of contemporary world music culture. In many
regions—particularly East Asia—the pop ballad has come to marginalize all
other forms of traditional and local music. As mentioned earlier, several
collective-variative forms (e.g., rumba, pop *ghazal,* and *huapango*) have
accommodated to song form by adapting some of its features.[5] Similar syn-
theses can be seen in several other genres (such as pop flamenco).

In Western popular music culture, song form continues to be pervasive,
if not quite as unequivocally predominant as during the Tin Pan Alley era.
One might hazard an estimate that around one half of mainstream Euro-
American popular music coheres with song form, particularly some variant
of 32-bar AABA form. This form has pervaded even "rebellious" youth genres like punk and heavy metal, not to mention contemporary rhythm 'n'
blues. As for art music, sonata form has of course been effectively decon-
structed since its apogee of the Classical and Romantic periods, which coincided with the triumphant heyday of the European bourgeoisie in social,
political, economic, and ideological fields. Nevertheless, despite the trajectories of serious composers since 1900, the tastes of the listening public
remain firmly committed to the eighteenth- and nineteenth-century common-
practice styles, themselves pervaded by sonata form, however flexibly interpreted by late Romantic composers.

And yet, even this prominence of song form seems markedly incomplete
in comparison with the all but complete hegemony of global capitalism and
its accompanying ideologies today. Since 1900, sonata form has been perpet-
uated only by the most conservative or neoclassicist of serious composers.
And in the realm of popular music, song form has come to be rivaled, if not
surpassed in quantity, by other forms, particularly those ostinato-based
idioms informed by Afro-American music and its derivatives, including rock.
Meanwhile, of course, many traditional collective-variative forms, from the
mainstream Urdu *ghazal* to Irish traditional jigs and reels, continue to enjoy
considerable resilience and popularity. Given the unprecedented dominance
of capitalism, and, one would think, of the subsequent hegemony of bourgeois ideology, this lack of correspondence would seem to require some

explanation—unless one chooses to discard the entire notion of homology between aesthetics and socioeconomic context.

In many respects, however, the apparent discontinuity between aesthetics and social economy is a superficial one, and belies a deeper correspondence which in its own way affirms the validity of homological theories. The contemporary persistence, and indeed, the dramatic reemergence of collective-variative forms inconsistent with song form can in fact be seen as grounded in several historical developments since the heyday of bourgeois ideology in the nineteenth century. The persistence of traditional idioms (e.g., strophic forms) outside the developed West can be attributed to various factors. Homologies notwithstanding, there is no doubt that artistic forms can enjoy a degree of autonomy and historical momentum, which may ensure their survival even in periods of dramatic social transition. Nostalgia, cultural nationalism, and other attitudes may further contribute to the survival, and even dynamism of genres like Hindustani music, or of the Urdu *ghazal*-song, which have successfully managed the transition from feudal to bourgeois patronage. The markedly uneven nature of capitalism and modernity in such societies—where many aspects of pre-modern socioeconomic life persist—also naturally contributes to such aesthetic conservatism. Further, most music cultures are complex and heterogeneous, allowing modern and pre-modern idioms to coexist side by side. Moreover, a sophisticated homological theory proposes not a vulgar one-to-one determinism, but a relatively loose iconicity in which, for example, song form would constitute the most typical form, but not the sole form, of bourgeois society (or of a society dominated by bourgeois ideology).

By far the most significant cause of the relative decline of song form has been the general undermining of many aspects of bourgeois ideology and aesthetics accompanying the advent of late modernity and capitalism. For although capitalism may be triumphant as never before, the stable, coherent, and comfortably dominant worldview of nineteenth-century bourgeois values has suffered a series of blows. As has often been noted, the advent of world wars, the specter of nuclear annihilation, the ecological despoiling of the planet, and the persistence of poverty and class iniquities have rendered implausible the complacent positivism that animated bourgeois ideology at its peak. Notwithstanding the collapse of socialism, the internal contradictions of capitalism have become in many respects more profound than ever, especially as the mass media promote on a global scale a consumerist desire for unattainable goods. As socioeconomic underclasses become recognized as permanent components of even developed societies, a new form of alienation undermines bourgeois ideology from within.

The ramifications of these developments in the field of elite culture have been well documented, involving self-conscious high-modernist attacks on all the formal achievements of early modern aesthetics—including the proscenium stage, the structure of the novel, and, in painting, perspective and the illusion of three-dimensionality. In art music, they have inspired an abandonment or deconstruction of tonality, song and sonata form, and other essential aspects of common-practice music. In Euro-American popular music—and global popular culture influenced or inspired by that music—the evisceration of classical bourgeois ideology and aesthetics has included the new valorization of music structures based on ostinato and modality (especially the blues scale). The Americas—and particularly Afro-American culture—have played the seminal role here, providing the crucial distinctive ingredients of rock music in all its worldwide variants.

Writers informed by Marxist or neo-Marxist approaches have offered various, often complementary perspectives on these developments. Perhaps least plausible is that proposed in the second half of Marothy's (1974) otherwise brilliant tome. Writing from a sanguine Marxist vantage point during the heyday of world socialism, Marothy heralded reemergent collective-variative forms, like jazz and workers' songs (e.g., "John Henry," or Pete Seeger's repertoire) as anthems of the rising proletariat that was destined to claim sociopolitical power in the foreseeable future. In retrospect, of course, such optimism scarcely seems tenable, given the effective demise of socialism, the irrelevance and marginalization of workers' songs, and the essentially apolitical nature of modern jazz. (It nevertheless finds a quaint echo in the writings of some contemporary cultural studies theorists who purport to find subversive political content in all manner of pop culture phenomena, from rock rhythms to baseball caps worn backward.) What is prescient, however, in Marothy's argument is the dynamic conjuncture of residual and emergent art forms—a consideration to which we shall return.

Similarly controversial, although in some respects more nuanced, is the perspective of Adorno regarding the aesthetic and specifically musical ramifications of late modernity's alienation. Adorno, paralleling the thought of his Frankfurt School colleague Herbert Marcuse, was particularly concerned with what he saw as the subtly but perniciously despotic and totalitarian nature of modern capitalism, which, under the guise of liberal democracies, promoted a stultifying consumerism, conformity, complacency, and analytical passivity. Robert Witkin (1998: 35, 45) summarizes Adorno's views:

> In the face of these social developments, the continuing affirmation, in bourgeois ideology, of the reconciliation of the individual and society [as in the metaphorical narrative of sonata form] loses truth-value even as a formative ideal. Its survival as ideology served the negative purpose of disguising the totalitarian nature of the conformist pressure in modern society by making it appear to be the reconciliation between individual and society that was promised by an earlier bourgeois society . . . . Classical tonality, no less than linear perspective or the conventions of the absolute drama, was integral to bourgeois ideology. As ideology, it offered an *image* of reconciliation. In an antagonistic society constructed for the exploitation of nature, all social relations bear the scars of that antagonism and no identity is pos-

sible between the oppressive force of society and the spiritual needs of the individual. In that sense, bourgeois art is false and partakes in the construction of illusion and not truth.

For Adorno, the mindless, mechanistic use of standardized song form in commercial popular music epitomized the conformism, commodification, and decline of critical faculties and human agency in the new political and economic order. He also regarded the neoclassicist revival of sonata form in art music as equally specious and false.[6] In general, Adorno's argument is at once insightful, provocative, and problematic in several ways. Not the least of its contradictions is the sense in which modernity—especially as depicted by writers like Sartre, Marshall Berman (1983), and in many ways Marx himself—is characterized by a fundamental condition of freedom rather than totalitarianism.

If Adorno's thought will remain controversial, what seems self-evident is that the spread of a new musical aesthetic—as represented, for example, in the rediscovery of ostinato-based forms—represents some kind of popular disaffection with or ambivalence toward bourgeois aesthetics, classical bourgeois ideology, and modernity in general. While Marothy's attempt to locate this development in a progressive proletarian consciousness seems untenable, other writers have more convincingly linked this new sensibility to issues of sensuality and ethnic (or racial) identity. Paul Gilroy's *The Black Atlantic*, for example, links the new musical aesthetic in a particularly nuanced and insightful way to a cross-cultural nexus of Afro-American alienation and aesthetics. Echoing Marothy's stressing of the class rather than strictly racial groundings of early jazz's aesthetic, Gilroy is careful to foreground the seminal nature of the Afro-American musical contribution without essentializing racial difference. Further, as he and other contemporaries suggest, central to the emergent aesthetic is a new spirit of sensuality that seeks to liberate the body from the demands of capitalist work and control. In a manner again reminiscent of Marothy, Gilroy perceptively illustrates how the Afro-American architects of this sensibility and musical aesthetic were able to draw on the raw materials of existing, pre-modern images, symbols, and artistic practices. These would naturally include the ostinato-based, collective-variative musical forms, from ring shouts to responsorial work songs. These idioms survived long enough to be available for creative rearticulation into blues, rhythm 'n' blues, rock 'n' roll, and other idioms on down to rap and interethnic syncretisms like British-Punjabi *bhangra*.

As Gilroy, George Lipsitz (1994), and others have stressed, the new musical sensibilities can be seen to reflect a critique of modernity and of capitalism, but not in the form of a headlong confrontation from an external, liberated zone (whether geographical, social, or attitudinal). Rather, they constitute *immanent* critiques largely from *within* modern capitalism itself. As such their strictly political significance—that is, as a challenge to the

global capitalist world order—is arguably nil. Nor can they be unproblematically linked to a specific class configuration, such as the bourgeoisie or the
underclass. It would thus seem that in the New World Order, with class
struggle at a stalemate, these aspects of sociomusical evolution have tended
to be conditioned primarily by features other than class-based sensibilities.

Conclusions

As Adorno articulately lamented, the inherently abstract nature of entities like
musical form renders problematic any attempt to ground them in material history, generally atrophying one or the other of the elements of the term "sociology of music." Given the narrowly positivist approach of sociology during the
mid-twentieth century, even the most plausible of sociomusical hypotheses

> enter a twilight zone as soon as, under empirical rules of the game, they are
> shown the bill and asked for incontrovertible proof that Beethoven's music
> really had something to do with humanity and the bourgeois emancipation
> movement, or Debussy's with the sense of impressionism and with the phi-
> losophy of Bergson. (Adorno [1962] 1976: 195)

With socialism defunct and global class struggle stalled, mainstream academics are perhaps more likely than ever to be skeptical of attempts to ground
phenomena like formal musical structures in socioeconomic contexts. Yet it
should be reiterated that for all its uses and abuses, the greatest strength and
overriding emphasis of Marxist theory—whether regarding economics or
culture—have always been in formulating a framework for the critical analysis of capitalism rather than providing a blueprint for a utopian socialism. If
mainstream musicologists have shown little interest in pursuing structural
links between class history and aesthetics—including specific features of
musical aesthetics—then they effectively abandon the field to others who
remain intrigued by the explanatory power of holistic cultural theories
informed by Marxism.

   One alternative, thus, is to pursue a formalism that would regard the
emergence of a coherent aesthetic (e.g., demanding the logical conformity of
parts of the whole) as a purely technical development whose clear parallels to
broader socioeconomic evolution are in the nature of a fantastic coincidence.
The obvious limitations of this approach should not of course inspire us to
suspend critical faculties and endorse patently implausible theories. At the
same time, political developments (such as the demise of socialism) should
not blind us to such phenomena as the overwhelming correspondence, and
evident causal relation, between the rise of capitalism and that of a bourgeois
aesthetic which prescribes a particular approach to musical form. In addition,
as I have suggested, in a period when class consciousness and class-based
political struggles are at a relative nadir, and when a single economic system

(global capitalism) seems destined to triumph indefinitely, it is entirely possible that other social factors may play more important roles in conditioning musical aesthetics. It is in this sense that the best of cultural studies approaches incorporate the most heuristic aspects of neo-Marxist thought, while supplementing them with considerations of gender, ethnicity, and other relevant themes.

Notes

1. In this sense, for example, Cervantes's episodic *Don Quixote* is conservative, although in its content (the ironic treatment of its protagonist) it constitutes a key landmark in the emergence of literary modernism. By contrast, most of the dramas of a contemporary, Shakespeare, are premodern in their fascination with royalty but reflect a distinctly bourgeois sensibility in their tightly knit formal structures, which are essential to dramatic motion and character development.
2. See Hauser 1957: II for further discussion of this development. Accordingly, during this period painters, freed from the collective guilds, came to sign their own works and be renowned as master artists rather than mere craftsmen.
3. From the popular *ghazal* "Dil hi to hai na sang o khisht"; see Matthews and Shackle 1972: 124.
4. "Por ti abandoné a mis niños, mi marecita de mi alma se me murió, ahora te vas y me abandonas, castigo te mando Dios" (traditional *soleares*).
5. As *son* and salsa developed out of rumba, they transformed the initial litany-like *canto* section into a closed song, typically in 32-bar AABA form; the second section, the *montuno*, remains ostinato-based. The pop *ghazal* and Mexican *huapango* discussed effectively grafted structured, closed song format onto strophic patterns (see Manuel 1985).
6. As Witkin illustrates (1998: 43–45), Adorno's perspective parallels that of Lukacs regarding literature, although Lukacs affirmed the novel's ability to expose rather than mask the contradictions in bourgeois society.

References

Adorno, Theodor. 1976. *Introduction to the Sociology of Music*. New York: Seabury. (Originally published in German in 1962).

Berman, Marshall. 1983. *All That Is Solid Melts into Air*. London: Verso.

Cone, Edward. 1989. "Three Ways of Reading a Detective Story—or a Brahms Intermezzo." In *Music: A View from Delft*, edited by Robert Morgan. Chicago: University of Chicago Press.

Feldman, Martha. 1995. "Magic Mirrors and the *Seria* Stage: Thoughts toward a Ritual View." *Journal of the American Musicological Society* 48(3): 423–89.

Giddens, Anthony. 1992. *The Transformation of Intimacy: Sexuality, Love, and Eroticism in Modern Societies*. Palo Alto, Calif.: Stanford University Press.

Gilroy, Paul. 1993. *The Black Atlantic: Modernity and Double Consciousness*. Cambridge, Mass.: Harvard University Press.

Hauser, Arnold. 1957. *The Social History of Art*, Vol. 2. New York: Vintage.

Leppert, Richard, and Susan McClary, eds. 1987. *Music and Society: The Politics of Composition, Performance and Reception.* Cambridge: Cambridge University Press.

Lipsitz, George. 1994. *Dangerous Crossroads: Popular Music, Postmodernism and the Poetics of Place.* New York: Verso.

Lomax, Alan. 1968. *Folk Song Style and Culture.* Washington, D.C.: American Association for the Advancement of Science.

Manuel, Peter. 1985. "Formal Structure in Popular Music as Reflection of Socio-Economic Change." *International Review of the Aesthetics and Sociology of Music* 16: 163–80.

Marothy, Janos. 1974. *Music and the Bourgeois, Music and the Proletarian.* Translated by Eva Rona. Budapest: Akademiai Kiado.

Marx, Karl. 1964. *Pre-capitalist Economic Formations.* London: Lawrence and Wishart.

Matthews, D. J., and C. Shackle. 1972. *An Anthology of Classical Urdu Love Lyrics: Text and Translations.* Delhi: Oxford University Press.

Maus, Fred. 1997. "Narrative, Drama, and Emotion in Instrumental Music." *Journal of Aesthetics and Art Criticism* 55(3): 293–302.

McClary, Susan. 1986. "A Musical Dialectic from the Enlightenment: Mozart's Piano Concerto in G Major, K 453, Movement 2." *Cultural Critique* 4: 129–69.

McLuhan, Marshall. 1962. *The Gutenberg Galaxy.* Toronto: Toronto University Press.

Meyer, Leonard. 1967. *Music, the Arts, and Ideas.* Chicago: University of Chicago Press.

Middleton, Richard. 1990. *Studying Popular Music.* Milton Keynes (U.K.): Open University Press.

Nettl, Bruno. 1956. *Music in Primitive Culture.* Cambridge, Mass.: Harvard University Press.

Newcomb, Anthony. 1984. "Once More 'Between Absolute and Program Music': Schumann's Second Symphony." *Nineteenth-Century Music* 7: 233–50.

———. 1987. "Schumann and Late Eighteenth-Century Narrative Strategies." *Nineteenth-Century Music* 11: 164–74.

Pedelty, Mark. 1999. "The Bolero: The Birth, Life, and Decline of Mexican Modernity." *Latin American Music Review* 20(1): 30–58.

Shepherd, John. 1977. "The Musical Coding of Ideologies." In *Whose Music? A Sociology of Musical Languages,* edited by John Shepherd, Philip Verder, Graham Vulliamy, and Trevor Wishart, 69–124. London: Latimer New Dimensions Ltd.

Temperley, Nicholas. 1991. Letter to the editor. *Ethnomusicology* 35/3 (fall 1991): 399–400.

Treitler, Leo. 1989. *Music and the Historical Imagination.* Cambridge, Mass.: Harvard University Press.

Witkin, Robert. 1998. *Adorno on Music.* London: Routledge.

4

The Hip-Hop Sublime as a Form of Commodification

ADAM KRIMS

To historicize as a Marxist is to historicize as a totality, and one of the signal differences between a Marxism worthy of the name and more so-called vulgar versions is the willingness on the part of the former to historicize itself. Much of the Marxism in the initial version of the present essay, after all, is most profoundly an end-of-the-twentieth-century Marxism, not only in the objects it describes but also in the relative (but emphatically not ultimate) autonomy it grants to superstructural forces. But even more curious, and worth remarking, is the existence of this volume itself, whose contextualization in the so-called return to Marxism in the humanities offers, it would seem, some illuminating perspectives on music studies in general.

Music studies in anglophone academia, of course, have never entirely lacked Marxist contributions. David Morley (1993) must certainly be invoked in this context; and while predominantly anti-Marxist in its rejection of totality and economic determination, cultural studies has certainly entailed some remnants of Marxian notions, for example in the work of Reebee Garofolo, George Lipsitz, and many others (whom I would want to signal, nevertheless, as not fully Marxist, if in the latter term one wants to preserve some notion of totality and determination by the relations of production). But Marxism in musicology and music theory itself, even the burgeoning field of popular(-music) musicology, has been remarkably lacking, even conspicuously so. Of course, as has been remarked in so many different places, social engagement on the whole within the field of musicology has long been sporadic, and seems to have prospered only since the advent of the "New Musicology." And furthermore, the early theoretical sources of the New Musicology were themselves strongly anti-Marxist: as examples one could cite the feminisms borrowed by Susan McClary, Gary Tomlinson's borrowings from Foucault, and the post-structuralist literary theory that inform the work of Lawrence Kramer and many others.[1] While extremely diverse, all these intellectual sources of New Musicology share a heritage in the kinds of postmodern literary and cultural theory that announced major breaks with Marxist theoretical traditions, sometimes (as in the case of Foucault) with more vehement insistence than principled explicitness.

I was thus not particularly sanguine about the birth of a Marxist movement in music studies when I arrived at the University of Alberta in 1993, armed with a few books by Marx or on Marxism and finding an environment (like most others) in which little or nothing about Marx was known or examined. Although Henry Klumpenhouwer was enthusiastically receptive and arguably is now among the best-informed Marxists in any music department, it was nevertheless two years before interest at the University of Alberta was sufficiently widespread and forceful that a panel (later converted to a paper session) was proposed to the American Musicological Society for the 1996 Baltimore convention. The mixture of enthusiasm, curiosity, and consternation that the session met was, frankly, better than the reception I had anticipated.

While some I encountered at the time questioned the wisdom of my introducing Marxism to the work of three already established scholars—I was only just finishing graduate school at the time and had published very little—I am prepared to plead *res ipsa loquetur* while pointing to the existence of this volume. My own contribution to that panel, and Klumpenhouwer's, can reasonably be labeled "Marxist" (and much of our subsequent work has remained so), and all the contributions from that Baltimore session at least engaged the work of Marx in ways that can only be described as productive; and the old Cold War stereotype of Marxism as narrow and dogmatic (often propogated by scholars who quite clearly have little familiarity with actual Marxist scholarship) can be effectively countered by the contributions of Qureshi and Gramit, whose own writings have taken new directions from their encounter with Marxism without necessarily losing their initial non-Marxist grounding. I hope that the contents of this volume, which owes its existence to that session in 1996, could be marshaled to argue that if I did indeed corrupt some minds, then corruption is, just the same, not necessarily a bad thing.

But on the other hand, it would be Pollyannish to pretend that Marxism now has a solid foothold in music studies, in which it remains a marginal (I will not say "discourse") theoretical approach. Even in the most "progressive" music graduate and undergraduate programs, where some background is offered in the postmodern theories, the Marxist tradition in and against which many of them work is examined only obliquely, if at all; and the same can be observed of some of the publications that engage Stuart Hall without the Grundrisse, or Derrida, for that matter, without the Communist Manifesto. All this is not to mention Marxism as a living and continuing tradition, whose revival in the humanities over the last twenty years or so (and continuing vitality in the social sciences, from David Harvey to Mike Featherstone) would seem to suggest a particular relevance to the present. The days when knowledge of Marxist traditions is required for music scholars probably lie far in the future (if indeed they ever arrive at all), and perhaps all the more so because Marxism is tremendously hard to do well in the humanities: one can map relations of production with some help from economic and sociological sources, and one can just as easily observe developments in musical culture, but relating the two worlds with any finesse and plausibility is an elusive and intellectually demanding task. The following, my first public attempt at such a project, is only partially satisfactory to me now quite a few years later, and it is disturbingly silent on some important levels of mediation. Some of it is fixed up, but that particular flaw still awaits more pointed work on urban geography for serious amelioration.

The "Hip-Hop Sublime"

I hesitated to include the phrase "hip-hop sublime" in the title of this essay because of the somewhat twisted history of that phrase. The present study is an extended version of the paper "Hip-Hop and the Commodification of Black Poverty" that I delivered at the 1996 convention of the American Musicological Society in Baltimore. At that time, I had assumed that the striking point of my paper would be the deep perversity of the economic process I was describing, by which poverty itself becomes a source of surplus value (specifically, relative surplus value) for a certain commodity, namely rap music. To my surprise, though, the paper was remembered (if at all) because of the phrase "hip-hop sublime," and even years afterward I heard reference to the "hip-hop sublime" paper. Through the years, I eventually learned to be a bit less stubborn and a bit more, to put it nicely, dialogic, and to feature those things to which others seem to respond: so, in a sense, this *is* now "that hip-hop sublime paper," indeed. I have even advanced one step further, discussing the "hip-hop sublime" in my rap book (Krims 2000) and after a turn to researching urban geography (Krims forthcoming); perhaps after this, I need to hang it up.

But I think that it is worth revisiting the issue once more, not just because not everybody heard it the first time, but because of the massive growth, even since 1996, of the rap and hip-hop music industry, a commercial success story with parameters that were not imaginable even those few years ago. Although a good deal has changed in rap music, partially by way of enabling that broadened audience, I would argue that the fundamental cultural processes to be described here remain basically intact.

The basic argument to be advanced here is that the "ghettocentricity" (Kelley [1994]) of rap music may turn out to be a late twentieth-century mutation of some processes described in the Marxist tradition. Although the focus of the argument is on African-American hip-hop music, I want at the same time to recognize that rap has now become a much more widespread phenomenon and that its cultural inscriptions have now been profoundly internationalized. I will first focus on generalizations about surplus value and commodification in hip-hop; I then would like to focus on a musico-poetic process that seems to exemplify commodification in sound.

Music's role in constructing authenticity has been widely remarked, and, as Paul Gilroy (1993) points out, it has long been especially prominent in African-American culture. And "realness" has always been closely associated with the ghetto in hip-hop representations, just as authenticity in the blues has long been associated with black rural (usually southeastern) life.[2] But there is a major difference between blues and rap authenticities: the different *mode* of its poverty and the way this mode is projected mark hip-hop as a specific product of late, or multinational, capitalism. There were, of course, inner-city black ghettos in the monopoly phase of capitalism; but the "ghetto" projected in hip-hop culture is generally the dangerous, decaying place that arose in the wake of the deindustrialization and urban gentrification of the 1970s.[3]

"Ghettocentricity" in rap music, then, describes a particular economic/ historical moment, one possible only in contemporary cultural production. How, then, may we theorize the symbolic deployment of specifically postindustrial poverty in the promotion of the world's best-selling musical form? Certainly, trusted cultural theories such as scopophilia and "consuming the exotic" may be invoked here, and appropriately so. "Signifyin' " and other specifically African-American cultural theories are also pertinent, as I have argued before (1996a) in connection with Ice Cube; but earlier black musics had never focused so intensely on the ghetto as a locus of authenticity. The intensity of that focus can be posited as symptomatic of a broader process, one that entails new and important relationships among commodification, surplus value, and rap music.

Authenticity in rap is related to a circumstance of poverty that is mainly, if not entirely, separated from the older ideology of rural (precapitalist) attachment to a prelapsarian state of nature. Hip-hop's poverty signals a condition well known to be endemic to capitalist social organization—a permanent urban underclass, often ethnically marked.[4] The videos signal their urbanness in widely recognized ways—quick shots of cityscapes, lyrics focusing on urban geography, inner-city streets, subways, buses, housing projects, abandoned buildings, and so on. Detached from earlier images of the precapitalist "state of nature," representations of late-capitalist ghetto geography are thus deployed symbolically, to become an aesthetic libidinal object: the hip-hop song, the hip-hop video. It is this deployment of poverty as a use value for the production of new capital—especially, though not only, record company profits, which are in turn profits of large entertainment conglomerates—that brings us to the new mutation in surplus value.

Surplus value in Marxist economics is the difference between the exchange value of a worker's labor and the wage value of her labor; in other words, it is the part of the manufactured product's value that is appropriated by the owner of the means of production.[5] In traditional contexts, it is used to pinpoint the source of profit that sustains the capitalist and ensures his or her social domination. The use value could well (and in artistic contexts necessarily does) include the symbolic logic of the product; and the work of Lukacs, Benjamin, Adorno, Jameson, and many others examines the relationships of these use values to the figural structures of art.

In the present case, the figural structure in question is precisely the second term in our equation: commodity fetish. Marx defines *commodity fetish* as the mistaking of an object for a social relation, or vice versa. Its involvement with the music industry is widely discussed, and properly so, but one might well speculate that hip-hop and rap music intensify the dynamic. The process can be described as follows: the commodified image of the ghetto forms a libidinal object. This, in turn, leads—and here is the trick—to a surplus value generated precisely from the commodification of a *lack of value*. In other words, the music industry has found a way to refold some of the most abject results of world economic production, through a direct transformation, to the most fabulous multibillion-dollar wealth. It is this *refolding*—like the rolling into a circle of a sheet of paper picturing an economic spectrum—that constitutes hip-hop's own mutation in the workings of surplus value. The fragmented ends of the economic spectrum are rolled together—without, of course, materially changing the living conditions at either end. The Marxist observer and full-throated apologist for capitalism alike must at least admire the breathtaking efficiency of the process, by which even the decimated byproducts of capitalist production can be recycled and turned into robust economic activity. So the ghetto produces a new use value; it becomes, through the commodification just described, a safe, portable image for pleasurable consumption. Through representation, profit is produced that exceeds the value of the crumbling material structures and infrastructures, and that exceeds, of course, the congealed value of the workers' labors, be they rappers, DJs, sound technicians, or record company executives.

The refolding of commodified poverty works on a number of different levels. In the video realm, these include anything from camera motion to geographical and architectural signifiers, to the artists' dominating gestures toward the camera. In the realm of sound recording, we may of course include the most commonly invoked topics of rap songs and the repeated injunctions to "represent" and "keep it real." However, to trace our "refolding" on the level of what we sometimes (perhaps carelessly) call "the music itself" poses a particular challenge. But it is, in my view, crucial to do just that; for, as Martin Stokes (1994) points out, if music has socializing effects, then it has those effects in particular ways using specifically patterned sounds. And mapping those sounds—that is to say, music analysis, though not necessarily in its most aestheticized form—is crucial to the study of music's social effects. What, then, could be the specific mechanics of representation here, the poetics that constitute marketable "authenticity"? I would like to highlight one possible answer, an aesthetic practice that I call the "hip-hop sublime."

The hip-hop sublime is my description of a particular process, created by particular musical practices and mainly associated with the genre known as "reality rap"—the kind of rap that is most often said to give a "true picture" of ghetto life. A sensory understanding of the hip-hop sublime could only come from listening to relevant excerpts, since it involves the deployment of musical strategies beyond the reach of standard music-theory language; a listen-through of the following songs would certainly suffice: "Can It Be All So Simple" from Raekwon (1995); "Shook Ones, Pt. II" from Mobb Deep (1995); and "Fairytalez" from Gravediggaz (1997). For the present discussion, though, some description should suffice to make the relevant point, so let us focus on the Raekwon songs. Several things are notable there. Possibly most recognizable is the quotation from Gladys Knight's version of "The Way We Were," here recontextualized harmonically and semantically. Rather than referring to a nostalgia for a past love affair, "Could it be that it was all so simple then?" now refers to two historical registers, namely the narrator's description of his easier life in "Job Corps," and the 1970s world invoked by the sampled music. (In connection with this, it is worth recalling the general revival of 1970s nostalgia of the past five or so years, often representing something of a fallen Golden Age for American black culture).

But the particular musical treatment of the sampled excerpt is equally telling. It is imbricated in a dense combination of musical layers;[6] all of them maintain the familiar duple regularity, but in the domain of pitch they comprise a sharply dissonant combination, even by the standards of jazz, or soul, harmony. In fact, the layers are not even "in tune," so to speak: they are separated by intervals that can be measured only in terms of fractions of well-tempered semitones. The result is that no pitch combination may form conventionally representable relationships with the others; musical layers pile up, defying aural representability for musically socialized Western listeners.[7] This is what produces what I call the "hip-hop sublime."

The "detuning" of musical layers just described is a widely used technique of hip-hop musical production, as is dissonant harmonic combination, even within compatibly tuned layers. And its association with "reality rap" and descriptions of ghetto life suggests that the failure of representation itself becomes a figure for inner-city life. Such a reference is not established by a secret language or any mysterious process, but rather by the consistency with which the hip-hop sublime is associated with the genre of "reality rap" and the topics that describe African-American urban devastation (as it does in all the songs named above). And a crucial point here is that the music projects the ghetto not merely as an uncomfortable or dynamic place; it is, in fact, projected as radically unrepresentable in itself, defeating both conceptual boundaries and unifying descriptions. I want to add quickly here that I do not necessarily say this in order to celebrate the finally "postmodern" character of hip-hop; on the contrary, I am more concerned to examine how the hip-hop sublime is itself in some respects subsumed by a market economy that values exactly this representation of ghetto life.

The hip-hop sublime must be contextualized. First of all, I am not claiming that all rap music instantiates this aesthetic. There are genres in rap music, and my exposition applies principally to so-called "reality" rap; I privilege "reality" rap because of the special claim to authenticity that its name implies. In contrast, so-called "mack," or "pimp," rap, including artists such as Too $hort, relies more on what are often called "smoother" R&B sounds for its musical support.[8] At the same time, it is interesting to notice that the poverty of the ghetto is far less highlighted thematically in mack rap; rather, the lavish income and lifestyle of pimping is flaunted in the most conspicuous possible manner. In fact, it would perhaps make more sense to say that the poverty of the ghetto is very much present in mack rap, as what Fredric Jameson might call the "absent center":[9] it is precisely the devastating trap of poverty that produces a proud, transgressive wealth as its determinate negation. Mack rap, then, may act as the dysfunctional utopia of the ghetto dystopia, commodifying some kind of eternal 1970s against that decade's funk and R&B musical backdrops.

Why, if I am correct, has the hip-hop sublime become a chosen representation of ghetto reality and authenticity? The question brings us back to the notion of commodity fetish, which, according to Marx, both results from and reinforces the more general tendency in capitalist societies to mystify social origins. The marketing of hip-hop paraphernalia is an obvious example of commodified authenticity: debates rage among hip-hop fans, for example, about which lines of clothing should or should not be consumed.[10] Although some of the debates center on overtly political aspects of the manufacturers, attention is often focused, particularly in marketing strategies, to projecting "authentic" ghetto "essences." But more important for us, rap fans debate, as do rap artists, what sounds and musical styles are "real" and "represent."[11] This suggests that the musical styles themselves are commodified, in the properly Marxian sense of the word: the "layering" procedures and the construction of the "beat" are themselves considered to embody social conditions. In short, the "hip-hop sublime" functions by the mystifying dynamics of the commodifty fetish.

If the hip-hop sublime is assumed by consumers to embody ghetto reality, then what is its social function? It is probably most plausible to argue that there is an overdetermination going on here. For one thing, consumers of rap music (a plurality of whom are white and middle class) are able to enjoy a closely controlled experience of social danger: the oft-remarked desire to consume the exotic may here be mixed with the enjoyment of violence so prevalent in American popular culture. But at the same time, the very sublimity of the layering techniques—that it to say, the unrepresentability that it implies—may be performing an important socio-economic function. For if ghetto life is ultimately unrepresentable, then to describe it and to describe its terrible economic determinations and human consequences is presumably to miss some great "depth" that the hip-hop sublime would then supposedly capture. What I am getting at is the possibility that the hip-hop sublime, and more generally the commodification of black poverty in rap music, may be a means of *mystifying* the social conditions of inner-city African Americans. Such a function would stem not only from the standard and mystificatory properties of the commodity, properties already well theorized in the Western Marxist tradition (albeit with deviations from Marx's own notions of base and superstructure which I would not necessarily endorse);[12] it would also stem from particularities of music. For if much of the project of so-called "new" (or, perhaps better put, postmodern) musicology is to unravel music's effects, then one might infer, conversely, a certain special power to music, an ability to bypass the listener's critical faculty. In the realm of popular music studies, of course, much ink has been spilled concerning the music's relation to the consciousnesses of listeners, and it can probably safely be said that what Jody Berland (1998: 138) calls the "populist optimism of cultural studies" retains a dominant status today.[13] And consequently, my insinuation of such a passive and one-way role for the listener may be taken as somewhat scandalous in this context: is there not room for the inflection of consumers, for the trumping of the hip-hop sublime's mystification, for the deflecting of the social processes set in motion by the producers and presumably encoded in sound? To such questions, the answer must be: of course, there are consumer inflections, critical responses, and all of those other social processes that complicate the circuits of production and consumption. And to be sure, the present study takes its cue from a particular emphasis that could not be called the whole story, by any means.

But at the same time, I want to avoid the danger of too fragmented a reading, in which the tremendous power of mass circulation is slighted in favor of a cheerful localization. One can most forcefully observe, in mass media and specialized fan literature, in conversations with fans and interviews with artists, that the hip-hop sublime—minus the label, which is my own—is indeed taken by many as an index of "hardness."[14] Whatever its fortunes in the tangled circuits of consumption, reinflection, and reproduction, the hip-hop sublime maintains the traces of what is being described here: a mystification reinforced as a source of pleasure, with a compelling beat.

But the hip-hop sublime may reach even further into contemporary life. Fredric Jameson's important discussion in his essay "Pleasure: A Political Issue" (1988: 61–74) will help to illustrate.[15] Jameson's picture of postmodern culture in general and postmodern theory in particular owes a great deal to Lyotard's expositions; and accordingly, he characterizes postmodern culture as (among other things) invoking various subjective "intensities." He also follows much post-structuralist work in seeing the "intensities" as largely replacing older aesthetics of beauty with those of the sublime.[16] This applies not only to MTV or architecture but to such theoretical formulations as Barthes's *jouissance* and Deleuze and Guattari's "ideal schizophrenic." Jameson describes the postmodern sublime as ultimately being an attempt to figure the unfigurable network of multinational capital:

> The immense culture of the simulacrum whose experience, whether we like it or not, constitutes a whole series of daily ecstasies and punctual fits of *jouissance* or schizophrenic dissolution . . . may appropriately, one would think, be interpreted as so many unconscious points of contact with that equally unfigurable and unimaginable thing, the multinational apparatus, the great suprapersonal system of a late capitalist technology. (1988: 73)

What implications could this idea have in the present context? Would the hip-hop sublime be just another case of the postmodern sublime?

I would like to say no, it's more than just a case in point, for two reasons. For one thing, as Tricia Rose (1994) reminds us, hip-hop music to a great extent has always been *about* technology, specifically about its reinterpretation and appropriation in the hands of subaltern classes. And if rap music is largely about technology on the level of, say, sampling and layering, then the hip-hop sublime may constitute a second inscription of post-industrial life on a more abstract level, suggesting both its omnipresence and its unrepresentability. The double inscription may even help to reinscribe a technological object-world that rap music works to subvert.

The second reason the hip-hop sublime enjoys special status is that the social conditions projected are not simply any part of the late capitalist mode of production, but a particularly significant part. Here we are reminded that Edmund Burke's formulation of the sublime, which has been so influential in postmodern theory, "takes its object as the pretext and the occasion for the intuition through it and beyond it of sheer unfigurable force itself, sheer power, that which stuns the imagination in the most literal sense (cited in Jameson 1991: 72)." Burke goes on to describe the fear of being smashed by the "unfigurable" power. Hip-hop's representations of a fantasmatic ghetto situates the listener (or in the case of videos, the viewer) in precisely the geographical and social location from which capital's smashing power is most visible. In other words, the hip-hop sublime presents a view from the bottom—America's underclass—at the massive, unfigurable but menacing force of world capital.

So hip-hop's own sublime may not only augment and localize the intensity of a generalized postmodern sublime; it may also help contemporary subjects to figure imaginatively and pleasurably one of our society's most disturbing processes—the maintenance of an underclass. It would be no wonder, then, that rap music is often cited, albeit for different reasons and among other descriptions, as a supremely postmodern popular music. We might also wonder whether the effect just described might help to account for the widespread impression that hip-hop soundscapes are menacing and aggressive, quite apart from the lyrical content. The menace is perhaps that of the ghetto's location (even the fantasized ghetto's location) within the means of production of a society fascinated by the spectre of its own underclass.

It is something of a commonplace in much popular music studies, especially that informed by cultural studies, to regard the discussion of music, especially music that is often publicly denigrated, as an act of validation. There is thus something of a danger that the insistently critical stance I have taken toward rap music in this study could be taken as a condemnation, since I am not quick here to celebrate the music's liberatory potential. In fact, the reader who finds such an issue pressing might be interested to know that I find rap music by far the most interesting and enjoyable music being composed today. But the point here is to probe certain aspects of representation that accompany both pleasure and whatever counter-hegemonic forces one might find in rap music. It should also be clear that by locating ideology in hip-hop's poetics, I am not thereby declaring it somehow "false." Instead, I would endorse Slavoj Žižek's notion that ideology does not provide a distorted view of a true reality but rather a true view of a distorted reality. If rap music indeed points toward our own distorted reality, then my discussion here is in fact very much in the best spirit of hip-hop culture.

Afternote

In something of a twist, the musical poetics and images of rap music have changed since I first formulated and presented the hip-hop sublime. Certainly, more scholarly attention needs to be paid to the "Big Willy style" which characterizes so much successful recent rap music (e.g., in the music of Puff Daddy and the No Limit family, to be sure, but also much of the output of Nas, Ice Cube, Dr. Dre, and other artists formerly not affiliated with the Big Willy personage). The musical (and visual) poetics by which urban African-American poverty is sold to the American public can never remain static, and above all it is crucial to measure the cultural changes that have accompanied the long economic "recovery" of the mid- to late 1990s. The commercial viability of urban social tragedy would seem to vary at least in part with broader economic fortunes, mediated by certain socially disseminated images of urban life. So the commodification of black poverty—and one should not assume that it is absent from "Big-Willy-ism," by any means—itself suffers the slings and arrows of economic fortune, but it never disappears. As rap music has now become the best-selling musical genre, the project of tracking its representations remains simultaneously crucial and near impossible: quicker than one can theorize, styles change, images mutate, last year's cutting-edge DJ and MC is "played out." The hip-hop sublime is still around and carries, I would argue, precisely the force I have outlined, but its relative position in the genre system of rap music is shifting. Although rap music arguably moves a little quicker than most of the rest of the popular-music world, such a predicament can still be generalized to some extent as a problem of theorizing capital itself. After all, much of the neoliberalism sweeping the world is a matter of the speed of capital, and the extent to which the latter outpaces any national or regional attempt to control its flows and consequences. To be, as Lenin enjoins, "as radical as reality itself" (quoted in Marcu 1927) approaches the point of impossibility, as the mobility and flexibility of capital continually revolutionize the environment we set out to map. It can at least be said that a serious engagement with Marx, and updated models of capitalism itself, will provide some of the necessary tools.

In a certain sense, the relation of Marxism to music studies is among the less interesting questions one could pose at this point: I have been doing it for a while (with Henry Klumpenhouwer, perhaps the only other person in a music department who explicitly claims the label "Marxist"), but so far there is not much of a field to discuss. Certainly, it is worth at least remarking in passing that the little work within musicology/music theory that bears even an oblique relation to Marxism tends toward "critical" rather than "analytic" work (Paddison 1993, for example). My hope is that this study suggests a different take on Marxism.

But it is probably appropriate to reflect on the existence of this volume, which if not unthinkable, would certainly have been unlikely a mere five years ago. It is, as mentioned, an outgrowth (considerably expanded, of course) of that paper session at the 1996 conference of the American Musicological Society, in itself an event that seemed to surprise a good many people in the field, as much because of the fact of its comprising all professors from the University of Alberta as because of its content (or perhaps more precisely, because of the conjunction of those facts). Indeed, I had little notion of such a development when I arrived in Edmonton in 1993, then only having initially concluded that the problematics in Marxism might most meaningfully address the sorts of questions I was starting to ask of music. At that time, my work engaged substantially postmodern theory, but this was not the case for the other researchers I encountered at the University of Alberta; nevertheless, though of the other researchers only Henry Klumpenhouwer could reasonably be said to adopt Marxist frameworks, some aspects of Marx's ideas were embraced more widely and enthusiastically than I could have imagined. Hence my delighted surprise when the suggestion of an AMS panel was embraced and supported.

In retrospect, I should perhaps not have been surprised, and the antidotal perspective to my surprise is instructive in the wider context of music studies. For what had occurred (in a striking parallel to uneven development) was bridging from traditional musicological methodologies to the social engagement of Marxism, a process that to some extent bypassed some of the postmodern methodologies and perspectives that were by 1996 already prevalent in music studies. For I do not consider it an overstatement that the seeds of postmodern studies in the humanities—from figures such as (the post-structuralist) Roland Barthes to Michel Foucault and the recently de-Marxified Mikhail Bakhtin—are profoundly anti-Marxist, even if the jabs at Marxism are referenced mainly obliquely in terms such as "totalizing" and "deterministic." Although jabs at totalizing and (presumed) economic determinism can only distantly be related to traditional musicology, it could well be expected that postmodern theory's relentless rejection of stable conceptual categories might pose its own obstacles for the embrace of Marxism. This could be so even in the case of Marxist researchers such as Fredric Jameson and David Harvey, whose work substantially engages certain insights from postmodern theory within larger Marxist frameworks. But the flip side of the current historical situation is that a good many of the central problematics of classical Marxism—class analysis, trajectories of history dependent on forces and relations of production—may well be adaptable to traditional (i.e., non-postmodern) musicology. This is especially the case because many of the scientific realist (not naive empiricist) principles specifically of analytical Marxism intersect not only with venerable historiographic issues in musicology but also with debates between "traditional" and "new" musicologists.[17] And at the same time, I hope to have illustrated in the foregoing analysis of rap music that a music-theory Marxism can engage meaningfully with, and even develop in new directions, cultural explanations from postmodern theory.

All of this is to say that Marxism, once understood instead of caricatured, holds some promise, if not to bridge, then at least meaningfully to contextualize the gaps between older and more recent (and postmodern) methodologies in both musicology and music theory.[18] If the hit-and-run blows from some postmodern theory and the Cold War caricatures of Marxism (and sloppy conflations with Stalinism) can be overcome by ambitious intellectuals in music studies, then Marxism may well prove fertile terrain in music studies in the future. [In that case, my initial (and to some extent continuing) surprise that the transport of a few Marxist books to Edmonton in 1993 should result first in a panel, then a book, could be transformed into something of a confirmation that the time for Marxism in music studies has come.]

Notes

1. I have already argued (Krims 1998) that the specifically deconstructive aspects of literary theory in music studies can, in fact, lead away from an engagement with social analysis.

2. Das EFX's "The Real Hip-Hop," Wu-Tang Clan's "Clan in Da Front," KRS-One's "Represent the Real Hip-Hop," Ice Cube's "True to the Game," and Nas's "Represent" are only a few of many hip-hop songs that foreground a claim to "realness."

3. And, interestingly, in films such as Spike Lee's *Crooklyn* and video clips such as Snoop Doggy Dogg's "What's My Name?" the pre-mid-1970s ghetto is itself projected as a utopian space in which a subculture and community remained whole despite poverty and segregation. The current trend in hip-hop to sample and/or imitate the styles of 1970s music can be seen as referencing this image of earlier ghetto life.

4. Arrested Development should be mentioned here as an important, albeit short-lived, exception, seeming to represent an attempt to project images of rural community with a softened sound.

5. Marx discusses surplus value in *Theories of Surplus Value* (1960) and various places in *Capital*. As Ernest Mandel (1978) puts it, surplus value is *the goal of the capitalist production process* (italics Mandel's).

6. Rose (1994) mentions "layering" as one of the fundamental musical procedures in rap music.

7. The unrepresentable combination of layers should be separated from the African-American musical tradition of expressive pitch bending. Pitch bending assumes a fairly constant and unified referential tuning, from which departures are then expressively marked elements. In the case of the sublime being described here, each layer is unified in the same way within itself; but the layers remain statically at their own pitch levels, never allowing for a referential tuning.

8. "Mack," or "pimp," rap stems from a tradition of pimp poetry (described in Cross 1993) and details, often in a bragging manner, the exploits of pimps, and/or sexually aggressive and successful men.

9. Jameson theorizes that late capitalism and its object-world are simultaneously all-pervasive in contemporary life and unrepresentable as a totality. Nevertheless, we are condemned to *attempts* to figure the late capitalist world system, attempts whose results must always be partial and allegorical. Capitalism thus serves as an "absent center" in the sense that it is a pervasive fact to which we respond, and yet it is never completely representable. Jameson (1992: 1–5) gives a succinct and eloquent summary of this view.

10. Letters to the editors of magazines such as *The Source* and *RapPages* are good written witnesses to these debates. Still, there are quite a few subcultures of hip-hop in which, I believe, the relations between artistic production and commodification are, if not innocent, then certainly substantially different from those described here.

11. I discuss the meanings of the word "represent" in hip-hop culture, especially in its intransitive form, in Krims (1998). It is interesting to note, as well, how frequently the debates about musical styles come to be gendered, with the feminine-coded styles associated either with romance, sex, or social betrayal ("selling out"), while the masculine-coded styles are associated with strength, reality, and social resistance. Rose (1994), Gilroy (1995), hooks (1995), and many others discuss related gender issues.

12. The attempts of Western Marxists to overcome the base/superstructure dichotomy are examined in Backhaus 1992.

13. Lipsitz (1994) provides a useful illustration of that optimisim, and furthermore one that bears an explicit relation to Marxism. Rose (1994) manifests a similar optimism with respect to hip-hop.

14. I illustrate something like this in Krims (2000): 43–44.

15. Jameson then elaborated this position in Jameson 1990.

16. Lyotard 1994 provides some of the seminal ideas in the postmodern validation of the sublime.

17. Analytical Marxism is defined and explained in Wright 1994: 178–99, including the relevance of scientific realism to the contemporary construction of Marxism.

18. In Krims (2000), I elaborate this point specifically with respect to music theory.

References

Backhaus, Hans-Georg. 1992. "Between Philosophy and Science: Marxian Social Economy as Critical Theory." In *Open Marxism, Volume I: Dialectics and History*, edited by Werner Bonefield, Richard Gunn, and Kosmas Psychopedis, 54–92. London: Pluto Press.

Berland, Jody. 1998. "Locating Listening: Technological Space, Popular Music, and Canadian Mediations." In *The Place of Music*, edited by Andrew Leyshon, David Matless, and George Revill, 129–50. New York: Guilford Press.

Cross, Brian. 1993. *It's Not about a Salary: Race, Rap, and Resistance in Los Angeles*. London: Verso.

George, Nelson. 1992. *Buppies, B-Boys, Baps, and Bohos: Notes on Post-Soul Black Culture*. New York: Harper Collins.

Gilroy, Paul. 1993. *The Black Atlantic*. Cambridge, Mass.: Harvard University Press.

Gravediggaz. 1997. *The Pick, the Sickle, and the Shovel*. Gee Street 32501.

Harvey, David. 1989. *The Condition of Postmodernity: An Enquiry into the Origins of Cultural Change*. New York: Blackwell.

hooks, bell. 1995. *Outlaw Culture: Resisting Representations*. London: Routledge.

Jameson, Fredric. 1991. *Postmodernism, or, the Cultural Logic of Late Capitalism*. Durham, N.C.: Duke University Press.

———. 1992. *The Geopolitical Aesthetic: Cinema and Space in the World System*. Bloomington: Indiana University Press.

Kelley, Robin D. G. 1994. "Kickin' Reality, Kickin' Ballistics: The Cultural Politics of Gangsta Rap in Postindustrial Los Angeles." In *Race Rebels: Culture, Politics and the Black Working Class*, 183–227. New York: Free Press.

Klumpenhouwer, Henry. 1998. "Commentary: Music Theory, Dialectics, and Post-Structuralism." In *Music/Ideology: Resisting the Aesthetic*, edited by Adam Krims. New York: Gordon and Breach International.

Krims, Adam. 1996a. "Black, White, and Dialogics in an Ice Cube Song." Paper delivered to the First Annual Conference on Popular Music and Culture, Drake University, March.

———. 1996b. "Hip-Hop and the Commodification of Black Poverty." Paper delivered to the annual conference of the American Musicological Society, Baltimore, November.

———. 1997. "Some Structuralist and Post-Structuralist Models for Music Theory." Ph.D. dissertation, Harvard University.

———. 1998. " 'Represent': A Nexus of Signification in Rap Music." In *Musical Signification between Rhetoric and Pragmatics*, edited by Gino Stefani and Luca Marconi. Bologna: University Press of Bologna.

———. 2000. *Rap Music and the Poetics of Identity*. Cambridge: Cambridge University Press.

———. Forthcoming. "Marxist Music Analysis without Adorno: Popular Music and Urban Geography," in Allan Moore, ed., *Analysing Popular Music*. Cambridge: Cambridge University Press.

Lipsitz, George. 1994. *Dangerous Crossroads: Popular Music, Postmodernism, and the Poetics of Place*. London: Verso.

Lyotard, Jean-François. 1994. "The Sublime and the Avant-Garde." In *The Polity Reader in Cultural Theory*. Cambridge: Polity.

Mandel, Ernest L. 1978. Introduction to Karl Marx, *Capital*. London: Penguin.

Marcu, Valeriu. 1927. *Lenin: 30 Jahre Russland*. Leipzig: List.

Marx, Karl. 1960. *Theories of Surplus Value*. Moscow: Progress Publishers.

Mobb Deep. 1995. *The Infamous*. Loud/RCA 66480.

Morley, David. 1993. "Active Audience Theory, Pendulums and Pitfalls," *Journal of Communications* vol 45/4: 13–19.

Paddison, Max. 1993. *Adorno's Aesthetics of Music*. New York: Cambridge University Press.

Raekwon. 1995. *Only Built 4 Cuban Linx*. RCA 66663.

Rose, Tricia. 1994. *Black Noise: Rap Music and Black Culture in Contemporary America.* Hanover, N. H.: University Press of New England.

Stokes, Martin, ed. 1994. *Ethnicity, Identity, and Music: The Musical Construction of Place*. Oxford: Berg Press.

Wright, Erik Olin. 1994. Interrogating Inequality: Essays on Class Analysis, Socialism, and Marxism. London and New York: Verso.

Žižek, Slavoj. 1994. *The Metastases of Enjoyment: Six Essays on Woman and Causality*. London: Verso.

PART III

Relations of Production

5

Mode of Production and Musical Production: Is Hindustani Music Feudal?

REGULA BURCKHARDT QURESHI

Until the early twentieth century hereditary musicians were the sole guardians and exponents of art music in northern India; it was their exclusive purview to deliver music to patrons in a feudally based economy. Over the years I have been privileged to know and learn from many members of this remarkable professional community. As a participant in their oral world, I was taught about music and how to be a musician. In the process, they showed me a world marked by feudal associations. Many older musicians recalled courtly patronage and corresponding musical practices: making music under feudal patronage was a way of life. It was their vivid and detailed experiences of that still-recent past that made me realize how enmeshed their spontaneously improvised music and its personal transmission were with feudal patronage, and how thoroughly they were challenged by the bourgeois transformation of musical life, despite overt government efforts to preserve their art.

Above all I learned about patrons and patronage through the perspectives and strategies of musicians acting as their own agents within the constraints of their particular situation. But I also saw the realities of exploitative feudal service relations that left many musicians living in a state of dependence for mere subsistence. The contradictions between musical mastery and social inequality eventually directed my interest in Hindustani music to the conditions of its production. To anchor this exploration in the real lives of musicians, and to give the reader a sense of individual difference as well as patterns of shared experience, I begin this study with personal accounts of two fine musicians: singer Nasiruddin Khan (alias Gore Khan) and sarangi player Bahadur Khan.

Nasiruddin Khan, Alias Gore Khan (Dehli)

Gore Khan (*gora* means fair; he also had green eyes) was a singer of the Qawwal Bachche community from Sikandarabad/Hapur (near Delhi) who ended his career as a senior *Qawwal* at Delhi's Nizamuddin Auliya shrine, where I learned from him during 1975–76. Respected for his knowledge of music and poetry, he loved to talk to me of his youth as a classical singer taught by the famous court musician Altaf Husain, who hailed from the same community[1] (Khan, B., 1976).

In the old days singers used to visit different courts for special celebrations, like the two Eid festivals at the Muslim nawabs, and Holi Dassehra at the Hindu rajas. I went often. Our patrons were rulers or their wealthy courtiers, at the courts, or in the smaller princely states. The Mughal emperor had lost power and was banished. But members of the royal family lived here in Delhi. Other people of very good families gave some value to music. The public did not know what art music is. But noble patrons understood music, and the few who didn't had a secretary or a manager who was a connoisseur. Rajas or nawabs would take this person's advice. But, say a noble took a liking to a singer, then he'd value and respect a greater artist, but would favor that singer because he had a special connection to him, and could have him learn special things he wanted.

The raja of Tikamgarh [near Bhopal], I haven't seen a better patron of music. He sang so well in tune, and with so much sophistication. I went there last in 1947; he sang as tunefully as a good professional singer. He had only two loves: hunting tigers and listening to music. In 1930, I went to Tikamgarh with my teacher [ustad] Altaf Husain Khan. The manager there gave us a house and we could either get cooked food or cook ourselves, with foodstuffs supplied. We chose the latter, so we could eat the foods we liked. After all there was nothing else we had to do. Every "artist" knows cooking, we learn it. Your teacher taught that first thing, in the old times. Along with music instruction we got cooking instruction too, so that when we would go to strange places, we will be able to cook and eat our own food—not have to be dependent on handouts from others. At 20, I was still very deferential, and I did not smoke waterpipe or cigarette before my ustad. *Those students who drank didn't before their* ustads, *only on the sly. Today it's the opposite, no one obeys his* ustad *anymore.*

Well, we stayed at Tikamgarh for several days and had a very enjoyable time making music; it was the Holi festival. After performing we were granted leave by the raja and then received a very big reward, two to three hundred rupees. At that time there was no permanent court musician, but later Altaf Husain, my teacher, stayed in Tikamgarh for a very long time. Other states also had court musicians, like Fayyaz Khan at Baroda. And some of my own relatives were engaged in Hyderabad, some in Mysore and Rampur.

Once I started singing well, I went to visit a court near Ahmedabad on my own, Dhaulkha ruled by Nawab Sardar Sher Mian, a very outstanding

*and wealthy man. He called me his brother. If I didn't visit there at least
once a year on some special occasion, his letter came to ask me to go. I
would go and he would make me stay for two months. He sent a money
order to my home and gave me a receipt, to feed my family while I was
away. I called him lord [sarkar]. He treated me with great consideration,
giving me a room with bedding, a sitting platform and a carpet, a bolster
pillow, a tambura, harmonium, tabla, a box with betel leaf, and the water
pipe. For his night program, he used to listen to music for six hours a day.
He died in 1964.*

Bahadur Khan (Lucknow)

Bahadur Khan belongs to the Kalavant community in the former princely
state of Banda (Uttar Pradesh). Following his father and uncle, he enjoyed
court patronage in his youth but has long been employed at the State Dance
Academy in Lucknow, where he first taught me in 1984 and where we meet
whenever I visit the city (Khan, B. 1992).[2]

*Among musicians we say: "Don't give an eye to the blind." My uncle, Lallu
Khan, served the raja of Raigarh [Madhya Pradesh]. Once the famous
Akhtari Bai [Begum Akhtar] was invited there. This was when she was in
her youthful prime. When Lallu Khan was challenged to accompany her, he
exclaimed: "I am Lallu Khan, she better watch her sur [tonic, intonation]."
In the performance he played in fighting style [larant]. He guided her further away from the tonic Sa in each interlude, cleverly modulating the tonic
one step up to Re, then another to Ga, first returning to the basic tone to Sa,
then one step up to Re, then another to Ga, and she followed him each time.
Then he put down his instrument, and now she was lost. And now he
showed her the real tonic Sa—she was defeated. The maharaja gave him a
big reward!*

*Lallu Khan returned to Banda when he was old. He raised and trained
me, because he had no son. He was very strict and broke his bow beating
me many times. As a boy my head was shaved so that I would stay in the
house and practice. When my marriage was held, I and my friend, we were
young and well trained; so we said, "Now we will be fettered by household
matters, so let's run off." We lived our life away from Banda, but our families stayed there. That was the life then.*

*But the musical environment in Banda changed once the princely
states were finished off, after 1947. Musicians of that generation had no
inclination toward "service" [wage employment]. My father was engaged
at the court of Maihar. After accession the sons of the raja wanted to keep
my father on but he declined, since no more music was being made.*

Music has for centuries been the jewel of Indian courtly splendor.
Twentieth-century Indian nationalism transformed it into a powerful and
pervasive icon of bourgeois culture, and today Indian music has attained an

unequaled global presence. Throughout these developments, exclusive hereditary lineages of musicians have continued to transmit and perform their art according to their oral tradition, sustained by ideals of feudal patronage and its aesthetic of connoisseurship and improvisation.

This essay posits that the concept of mode of production can become a tool to explore the production and reproduction of Hindustani elite music by service professionals in the feudal colonial economy and society of northern India. The aim is to explore how court patronage and hereditary transmission are implicated in the way professional musicians have shaped Hindustani music. My particular concern is the contradictory yet symbiotic relationship between the feudal exploitation of musicians and the feudal nurturing of their highly professionalized art. Crisscrossing this contradiction is the conundrum of feudalism and the transformation of a music that was exclusively produced and patronized into a national icon of public culture. Outside their own oral milieu, musicians have also been the least audible voice in the discourse that has shaped the history of their music.

The central concept of relations will serve to situate socially marginalized producers in the context of the productive forces of both feudal and postfeudal Indian society. In particular, relations of production can deal with unequal relations by focusing on the interclass dynamic between actors as an indispensible part of accessing their respective role in production, both economic and cultural. It offers a way to connect material and cultural, social and economic dimensions of production within a perspective that could engage both system and agency—at least potentially so. To activate these connections in relation to feudal music-making in India requires a pragmatic adaptation of the mode of production concept, as I attempt to extend it in three directions: from capitalism to feudalism, from material to musical production, and from universalized Europe to particularized India. For mode of production, like all theories, is not a neutral tool. It needs to be detached from its position as a Western hegemonic narrative, especially where the researcher in the Indian "field" is herself inevitably implicated in an exploitative symbiosis between patrons and musicians. The practical corollary is to consider social impact, including the ethics of making exploitation explicit on behalf of others.

The topical questions that drive this exploration are simple: What does the production and reproduction of Hindustani music consist of under feudal patronage? How did this particular music function as part of a particular feudally based economy and social order that productively combined coercion and exploitation with paternalism (Bayly 1983). And how did these social relations of musical production result in the practice later termed art music? In sum, what can we learn about Hindustani musical practices by knowing more about its feudal conditions of production?

Perspectives and Sources on Court Patronage

Feudalism is widely celebrated for its patronage of art music and closely identified with its genesis. In India, the environment of courtly patronage is well documented as crucial to a professionally produced and aesthetically constituted music. Considered a historical moment of significance, the development of art music under courtly patronage has received much attention in the scholarship on European and Asian high cultures. What distinguishes this development in India is the fact that courtly patronage extended well into the mid-twentieth century. Participants in feudal musical culture are thus still alive to report their own experience, adding a critical context to textual sources and a significant dimension of ethnographic authority.

In his seminal book on Indian art and civilization, Ananda Coomaraswami (1948: 46) presents a succinct statement about Indian music and its social conditions of production:

> The art music of India exists only under cultivated patronage, and in its own intimate environment. It is the chamber-music of an aristocratic society, where the patron retains musicians for his own entertainment and for the pleasure of the circle of his friends, or it is temple music, where the musician is the servant of God. The public concert is unknown, and the livelihood of the artist does not depend upon his ability and will to amuse the crowd. In other words, the musician is protected. Under these circumstances he is under no temptation to be anything but a musician; his education begins in infancy, and his art remains a vocation. Musical cultivation of the listener does not consist in "everybody doing it," instead, "the listener must respond with an art of his own."

That was in 1929 when feudal courts were still thriving under British colonial "protection." Meanwhile, the metropolitan movement to democratize music was already under way. By the time Daniel Neuman wrote his landmark study on the musical milieu of Delhi fifty years later, the same music had become a centerpiece of Indian national culture, thriving under state, public, and bourgeois patronage. At the same time, a certain nostalgia persisted among performers as well as connoisseurs, for a

> remembered past . . . in which the nobility were men of high learning and deep sensitivity; men who apprenticed themselves to their own musicians and called them masters, where music contests could destroy in a single night a reputation built over four decades of hard work, and award to the victor his weight in gold and jewels. This was a world where listeners were a rare and delicate species, having the leisure to cultivate an art from early

youth, to mature with age into true connoisseurs; a world, in short, where musicians of excellence flourished, being, as they were, measured only by listeners of excellence. (Neuman [1979] 1991: 21)

Feudal patronage, however, was more than a cultural practice; it was a social and economic arrangement, and one that many musicians have recalled succinctly and wistfully. In 1983, sarangi player Yaqub Husain (ca 1920–85), spoke of his family's patron, then employed at Lucknow's Bhatkhande Music College:

In the time of the princely states, our daily bread [*rozgar*] came from the ta'alluqdar princes. We performed for their soirees [*mahfils*], their wedding celebrations [*shadi biah*], or just for their pleasure. And we were also in their service. My maternal grandfather, Ali Jan Sahib, used to go to the Raja Sahib Mahmudabad when the raja was in the mood for music, he sat and listened for a while. When my grandfather came back home, he could take it easy for months, eating and enjoying himself without a care in the world.

But feudal musicians were not only nurtured. As socially devalued hereditary specialists they were exploited within profoundly unequal relations of patronage. Such recollections, too, are available, though they are less enthusiastically offered. One famous instance is the poetry—and fate—of Hafeez Jalandhari, who was himself a court poet. In his 1929 epic poem "Raqqasa" (the singing/dancing girl) he so effectively expressed and disseminated the plight of a court musician that the prince threatened his life, and the musician was cast out of the realm (Jalandhari 1948).

The social degradation under which hereditary musicians practiced their mastery has continued well past the abolition of feudal courts in independent India. I first confronted the realities of exploitative feudal service relations in a landed Sufi shrine establishment[3] when a visiting *qawwali* party started singing at a Sufi saint's anniversary after patiently awaiting their turn to benefit from the assembled audience. The hosting Sufi patron was displeased with their choice of song, summarily stopped them, and I shall never forget the abject submission with which the singer bowed before the sheikh, not daring to extend his hand to pick up the few rupees offered that were to be his only earnings for the day. Degrading practices have also continued vis-à-vis classical musicians, even under bourgeois patronage. In 1969 my sarangi teacher could no more eat at a bourgeois table than share a meal with a prince (Qureshi 2000), and in 1975 the audible presence of professional musicians nearly got us evicted from the house of a well-to-do businessman in New Delhi. As late as 1994, at a conference on sarangi music the musicians were collectively seated on the floor to address the audience, while middle-class experts spoke standing behind a lectern. And, of course, in the radio stations and academies that have replaced feudal patronage, hereditary musicians have occupied a separate and unequal social as well as economic position.

The crass reality is that hereditary professional musicians have historically formed part of the low social category of hereditary profession. Feted as artists with "court jewel" stature, yet exploited as servants, musicians are represented in literary and scholarly writings in either of the two roles, but mostly the first one. From imperial court chronicles to later historical interpretations, Indian (as well as Western) writings have dealt with feudal patronage of the arts in cultural terms, addressing courtly culture as a self-contained milieu, and thereby essentially limiting their consideration of feudalism to the superstructural realm. Their locus of identification is noble patrons and their outstanding artists; their emphasis is on cultural production generated by paternalism and beneficence (Hasan 1983; Sharar 1975: 615; Newcomb 1980). Musicians in their oral accounts also tend to dwell on their artistic achievements and benefits of patronage, thereby enhancing their own valuation along with that of their patrons.

Outside the magic circle of art and music, however, there is a considerable contemporary literature concerned with economic exploitation and subalternity and their continued presence in contemporary India (Frykenberg 1969; Prakash 1990; Raychaudhuri and Habib 1982; Guha 1982–1987). Writings on economic history deal with material production and productive relations; they focus on primary producers in the agricultural and, to some extent, artisan domain. Subaltern studies also encompass anthropological studies located primarily in villages and in some lower-class urban communities (Kessinger 1974; Gould 1964; D. Kumar and Desai 1982). Musicians, too, are sometimes considered as members of subaltern communities with their own perspective on their situation (Neuman [1979] 1991; Kippen 1988; Qureshi [1986] 1995; Thompson 1992), but these works tend to lack the critical perspective of postorientalist historiography (Prakash 1991; Chakrabarty 2000). Most sophisticated in this respect is Gyan Prakash's (1990) consideration of bonded labor, including its transformation into the freedom of the market under colonial rule.

Considering these literatures in relation to musical production offers a set of perspectives that include a court culture, landed economy, laboring communities, elite cultural production, and the subalternity of dependence through service relations with elite patrons. What creates the focus of this exploration, however, is my personal experience with discipleship and patronage of Hindustani music since the mid-1960s. What erstwhile feudal musicians and patrons have told me is particularly crucial because the world of Indian music-making has been entirely oral. The challenge is to submit this diverse historical and ethnographic domain to analytical simplification without losing sight of individual and cultural uniqueness.

Mode of Production, an Anthropological Perspective

Marx's concept of mode of production as used by anthropologists starts from the dual premise that material production is essential to the reproduction of all societies and that it requires participation in social relationships in which individual subjects are implicated. The central concept is relations of production comprising the social allocation of production, that is, the relationships among those who produce (labor), those who control what it takes to create the product (means of production), and those who appropriate the product (surplus). Social relationships involved in maintaining the productive arrangements can be articulated as social rules like those manifest in kinship and class structures, in laws of property and ownership, or as religious and cultural rules or "ideology." The premise is that the dominant mode of production in a society has social and cultural implications that come into play in both social organization and in what Clifford Geertz (1973a, 1976, 1973b) comprehensively terms "cultural systems." As an interactive concept, social relations of production offers a way of connecting cultural premises and practices not only with social structure but with processes of material, economic production on which survival is predicated for all members of the society.

Marx derived the concept of mode of production from capitalist production, which is predicated on the alienation of the laborer from the means of production and on the fact that the surplus value that labor produces for the owner of the means of production is embodied in the commodity. Commodified surplus value implies not only use value, but the conversion of use value into exchange value. When applying these premises beyond commodity production, the focus is on surplus labor and its appropriation as a necessary element in all possible modes of production (Hindess and Hirst 1975: 10). Relations of production define specific appropriations of surplus labor. Thus mode of production theory particularly addresses social inequality and structures of power as they are linked to the exploitation of direct producers through controls over their labor, the means of production with which they work, and what they produce, including music.

Is Music Production?

In capitalist society commodification has been an obvious starting point for mode-of-production perspectives on music as a commodity in recorded form, as Manuel's (1993) study of audiocassette production demonstrates most effectively (see also Qureshi 1999). The challenge here is to address the production of live music, in which the product cannot be separated from the process of production; furthermore, because live music is consumed in performance, it has use value but no exchange value. Following Marx (1960: 168, 398), music has therefore been relegated either to unproductive "service" or exempted from productive relations as an essentially autonomous artistic creation (Lukacs 1971; Adorno 1978; Jameson 1971). Thus the piano is subject to economic relations of production as an item of manufacture, but it is exempt from them as a tool of performance, along with the musician who plays it. For while the piano maker's labor has exchange value, the player's labor has only use value, for it is beyond materiality (Marx 1973: 305–306n). Nevertheless, value does accrue to the patron of music in the form of "cultural capital," a suggestive concept that usefully evokes a non-material value created through appropriated labor (Bourdieu 1993; Guillory 1993). The concept of cultural capital also points to the function of producing cultural value (ideology) within the nexus of material value production. Relations of musical production (of value) can then be considered with reference to productive relations of the dominant mode of production; the common focus is labor, its value and its mode of appropriation. The idea is to interpose— rather than juxtapose—the productive forces and relations of high culture with the entire society's modes of production.

What Is Feudal?

Marx (1962) and others after him (see Katz 1989) have approached feudal production primarily as a precursor to capitalist production. It therefore remained for scholars of noncapitalist societies to theorize fully the feudal mode in its own terms (Hindess and Hirst 1975).[4] Forces include means and labor (i.e., land and farming). Unlike the capitalist subsumption of labor through capital's control of the means of production, feudal labor is not, in and of itself, alienated, for the direct laborer (peasant) of feudal (agricultural) production remains the occupant and de facto "possessor" of the means of production (land). To make the conditions of feudal exploitation possible requires the noneconomic form of control over land through what Marx (1962: 771) terms a "property relationship that must simultaneously appear as a direct relation of lordship and servitude."

Feudal relations of production, then, include two crucial elements of control that together create a particular complex of exploitation. The first is the appropriation of surplus labor in a form controlled by the landowner. The producer or cultivator has to turn over the product of his labor beyond what he needs to subsist and reproduce himself; he is unable to realize the value of the surplus himself. The second element is the right of exclusion of the cultivator from his means of production; that is, his access and use of the land is controlled by the appropriating landowner through property and ownership based on a conception of landed property as monopoly possession: land is not for sale.

The feudal economy creates and reproduces a division of classes that form the social base of the feudal state. What Hindess and Hirst (1975) term "ideological social relations" form part of "the conditions of existence" of the mode of production overall. For feudalism these conditions include the separation of producing and appropriating classes, conceptions of lordship and servitude, but also of patron and client joined in a network of vertical ties and obligations (Marx 1962: 774). Ideological cultural norms prominently include the misrepresentation of property relations, resulting in the devaluation of labor and the mystification of the value it produces, since it is owning land, not laboring, that results in surplus wealth. Accordingly, production is represented as the fruit of property, not of labor (Bloch 1975: 222). This mystification of labor value needs to be especially underscored in the face of contradictory experiences among the vast majority of producers whose productive contribution is so denied.

In Search of Feudal India

Marxist writers have attempted to universalize European instances of feudalism in the historical materialist rise of capitalism. In order to gain a certain distance from a "waiting room of history" perspective on Third World economic history (Chakrabarty 2000), I shall refrain here from drawing attention to European parallels. The intent is, following postorientalist historians Gyan Prakash (1990, 1992) and Dipesh Chakrabarty (2000), to "metropolitanize India," that is, to historicize and situate feudalism and music by speaking from within, and in terms of, Indian practices.

India has, since independence, become a capitalized and industrialized economy. But for centuries Indian wealth has been based on agricultural surplus produced by peasant cultivators and appropriated as well as (re)distributed by land-controlling nonproducers that continued even under British rule as a form of capitalist predation for raw materials. Viewing Indian feudalism through a mode-of-production lens is complicated by colonial history and by a complex class structure that reflected multiple levels and types of control over surplus appropriation. Furthermore, regionally different social structures and cultural production were linked to differential articulation of modes of production in different regional economies—feudal, mercantile, capitalist. But until the twentieth century the feudal mode predominated even if not all productive relations of feudalism were present—a condition already considered by Marx (1960: 395) in the context of capitalism. Furthermore, commodity production of a diverse and specialized kind has been part of the same basic system of appropriating surplus labor, often involving land controllers, with trade monopolized, reinforcing land-based power structure (Raychaudhuri and Habib 1982; Kessinger 1974).

It is in northern India, especially the Indo-Gangetic plain with its center between Delhi and Benares, that land revenue remained the major and stable source of surplus until independence, supporting a landed aristocracy and an

agrarian bureaucracy. In fact, merchant capital based on cash crops and tex-
tile production actually declined in this region, once railways canceled the
region's preeminence in river transportation (Stokes 1975). In this region
where land revenue constituted half of provincial revenues until 1940, feudal
landowners were protected throughout British rule, both directly and in the
form of princely states that also extended to western and southern regions
(Metcalf 1969; Frykenberg 1969; Stokes 1982).

Also for centuries, landed wealth has constituted the major source of
patronage for music (Hoey 1888–89; Imam 1959–60; Sharar 1975; Wade
1997; Erdman 1985). In particular, the rulers of princely states were a prime
locus of musical patronage, retaining musicians in their permanent service
and, more often, as visitors on special occasions when music was required.

Extensive research in economic history,[5] complemented by historical
microstudies, especially of the Subaltern Studies Group (Guha 1982–87),
more than adequately show how historically entrenched production arrangements underlie social arrangements of domination and hierarchy. Shaped and
legitimized by ideological discourse that is entrenched in Hindu as well as
Sufi Muslim notions of spiritual hierarchy, this is a social system of great
complexity and conceptual beauty. At the same time it articulates exploitative
relations of production; it is, in Maurice Bloch's (1975) words, a "legitimate
order of inequality."

In concrete terms, two special characteristics of these social arrangements have been sustained by the high amount of agricultural surplus. One is
the proliferation of appropriators imposing themselves on an existing feudal
base, creating a set of dependency relationships. The other is the large social
component of service professionals, dependents who received a share of the
surplus in return for service to the appropriators. The mode of appropriation
involved various intermediaries, mainly local gentry and revenue collectors,
who had shares in the surplus. At the princely courts and the salons of minor
nobles, this surplus was spent on retainers, on tokens of royal status, such
as objects of manufacture and buildings and, of course, music. According to
C. A. Bayly (1983), 30 percent of the surplus in eighteenth-century northern
India was spent on rituals and festivals that would be shared with the public,
for example by the raja of Benares and the kings of Awadh (see also N.
Kumar 1988).

Powerful social and cultural norms articulate these relations of production; they in effect constitute a hegemony of differentiated surplus control. At
the center of these norms is the denial of the role of the producer and the
legitimization of the appropriator. Given that relations of exploitation are
controlled by the appropriating class of patrons, how are these norms played
out by producers of music? And how do producers of music claim agency
while working within the restricted yet flexible norms of practice? Finally,
how does the musical performance embody feudal relations of production?

Musical Patronage as Feudal Relations of Production

Indian feudal relations were predicated upon the categorical dominance of appropriators over producers, whether agricultural or musical. Like other skilled and unskilled workers, musicians could expect their labor to earn only enough to reproduce themselves—that is, enough to survive and train their successors. The importance of cooking skills for musicians and the all-out effort of musicians to find sustaining patrons are responses to this condition of earning.

As has already been noted, the crucial target of feudal control was land and the ability to exclude the producer from the means of agricultural production. Despite the nonmateriality of musical production, there is a suggestive quasi-equivalent: the venue of performance, including audience, over which noble patrons exercised similar control, as the Sufi patron's expulsion of a *qawwali* performer made starkly real. An important aspect of controlling both land and venue as productive means is their immobility; this value is affirmed by the habitus of landed gentry to stay on their property and attend musical events only in their own establishment. In the words of the late Umar Ansari, a Lucknow landowner: "A man of property does not move from one place to another." Hosting a performance for a glamorous audience was thus a superb enactment of ownership and status.

The crux of this dual control is to deny the productive value of labor while exalting nonlabor as the condition of wealth; this appropriators and feudal patrons achieve most effectively by not doing work, but having it done by their inferiors, including musicians. Knowing how to "take work" (*kam lena*) embeds laboring in a give-and-take relationship and is a diagnostic of patron status even today. Just as taking work requires that work be offered by someone else, listening to music requires that someone else perform it. Thus musicians not only live the social devaluation of their labor, they perform it, together with and for the benefit of their patrons.

The feudal separation of producers by controllers/appropriators has been socially and spatially entrenched so that musicians, along with other producers, have formed part of a labor-performing category that was clearly set off from the true leisure class of feudal lords. Socially, an overarching two-tier class structure subordinated all kinds of workers, whether their labor produced commodities like kashmir shawls (used as royal tokens to courtiers), or immaterial service like music. Their collective designation was "low people" (*chhote log*), people "low class/caste" (*chhoti zat*), or even "degraded" (*azlal*)—in contrast with the nonlaboring "people of quality" (*achchhe log*), people "of high class/caste" (*badi zat*), or "exalted" (*sharif*). However, within the labor class professional specialists, including musicians, had a better social and caste status than generic laborers (*kamin*); they belonged to the "apprentice professions" (*shagird pesha*) that contributed their skills to the economy of surplus consumption by the appropriator class who patronized them.

Spatially, musicians lived in designated areas well apart from their patrons, but they also had to be within reach so that they could be summoned for a performance at the patron's wish; thus in a marginal way they were part of their patrons' entourage. I heard about the significance of these ancestral quarters from several of my teachers; some are still inhabited by their families, in housing near the great Mughal palaces in Delhi and Lahore, as well as near the nawab's palace in the smaller realms of Banda (in Uttar Pradesh, [Bahadur Khan 1992]) and Sikar (in Rajasthan [Sultan Khan 1993]), while musicians serving the nawab of Rampur were quartered in the nearby town of Muradabad (Hamid Husain 1969).

Feudal separation and exclusion are, however, only one side of the feudal story in India. The other side are bonds of reciprocity and cultural links that are deeply feudal too. Special ties between landowners and laborers were in effect all year long and extended across generations. They consisted of designated "shares" of surplus and gifts. Remuneration was a gift to the person, not a reward for an amount of labor performed. It was given in return for labor offered as needed (Prakash 1990: 32). Professional specialists were part of these ritualized relations of service or *jajmani* (Bayly 1983: 56; Gould 1964); they were sustained by an ideology of a strong valuation of inequality, associating dominance with dispensing power and benevolence, and dependence with receiving security and nurturing. The two were linked together in active relations of submission in return for benefaction. Put in another way, the pervasive notion was that benefaction, not production, generates reward, and that labor is essentially an offering to superiors.

At the highest levels of appropriation, kingship legitimized its force through benign royal patronage and the conspicuous consumption (use value) of luxury objects, from architecture to clothing, and of aestheticized practices from eating a meal to listening to music. This included public festivals and ritual feasting, for which some eighteenth-century rulers spent up to 30 percent of their incomes (Bayly 1983: 59–60). Professional specialist labor could be exploited at a distance from patrons for this production, with the exception of musicians whose production required being in the presence of their patron. Uniquely Indian, and enshrined in the Hindu exaltation of music and its instruments, is the inclusion of musicians—professional specialists—among the most highly valued experts of the realm. The most exalted among such court musicians was Tansen, whom Mughal Emperor Akbar chose as one of his legendary Nine Court Jewels (*nauratan*), along with poets, historians, financial and government experts, and philosophers. The practice of cultivating musicians at courts was continued by both Hindu and Muslim rulers, notwithstanding the low valuation of music in Islam. The implication of this unique social elevation of professional specialists as court artist was enormous, to the point of musicians becoming ministers at the courts of both Delhi and Lucknow in the mid-nineteenth century.[6] While British colonial control put a stop to "fiddlers and drummers" in government, the conspicuous presence of musicians at courts continued.

The Musician as Feudal Producer

The feudal starting point for musicians has been their exclusive hereditary identity as musical specialists who cultivated and transmitted their inherited oral knowledge and skill within their families in order to provide for the musical needs of noble patrons, with the expectation of partaking of their surplus in the form of hospitable subsistence and a generous reward. Also inherited was the right to work for patrons with whom one had an established patronage tie and by whom one could expect to be well fed and generously rewarded. How central these ties were to the producer's survival can be seen from the way musical as well as agricultural producers configured their origin or ancestry in relation to their patrons. Like *kamia* cultivators from Bihar, Hindu *dhari* musicians from Rajasthan claimed descent from a landlord who also had performed labor, on a special occasion. The *kamia's* ancestor had performed agricultural labor when needed, while the *dhari's* Rajput ancestor had provided the music necessary for the birthday ritual of Lord Rama (Nahata 1961). Invoking royal as well as musical association, classical Muslim *mirasi* musicians traced their musical ancestry to King David through his disciple, *Hakim Fisa Ghoris* (Pythagoras), while *qawwali* musicians identified their ancestry with imperial court poet and Sufi, Amir Khusrau, who raised and taught the first "boys" (*bachche*) of the *qawwali* community. The name of their lineage, *qawwal bachche* invokes this ancestry along with a claim to paternal sustenance from Sufis.

Both lineage and paternalism are relevant to feudal relations of production and have their echo among appropriators. Even an appropriator famous for his ruthlessness would designate his cultivators as his children (Bayly 1983: 45). And children/disciples of a court musician could claim a right to be favored by the same patron. Paternalism, both across and within lineages of producers as well as appropriators, ensured the reproduction of these feudal relations of production, but only as long as the lineages and productive functions of both classes remained distinct. Thus musicians could not control or inherit means of production regardless of ancestral claims. There is a widespread, though sporadic memory among musicians of having received villages from their patron, but their professions clearly prevented them from claiming that income (Sultan Khan in Sikar, Shabbir Husain in Mewa, Allah Rakha in Jammu). As producers they had no right to surplus, and even their claim to inherit patronage was predicated on professional competence, as is eloquently confirmed by court records (Erdman 1985).

The musicians' control remained confined to the domain of their professional skill and its production: family and community. Families (*khandan*) have been patrilineal but also part of bilateral kinship networks embedded within the wider socioprofessional endogamous community or *bradri* (brotherhood). The *bradri* has provided marriage partners and also class solidarity through professional links and strategies, and even a trade lingo of Urdu in coded form, thereby protecting the collective musical inheritance (*miras*) from outsiders. The *bradri* extended across, and musically "covered," a region within prerailway traveling distance and remained a regional-residential domain even for its widely dispersed members who would travel home at least during the Islamic holiday of Muharram, when no music is made (Sultan Khan, Nazim Ali Khan, Bahadur Khan, and others). For individual musicians, *bradri* solidarity and pride of identity as members of the "nation" of musicians (*qaum*, literally: nation or hereditary, bounded social group) effectively reinforce the identity of a joint professional monopoly, keeping out competing outsiders and controlling musical quality internally through contests and adjudication by *bradri* elders (*panch*). Musicans described such recitals, and I have attended one of them, of all the students in the *bradri,* starting with the youngest boys and ending in a contest between more advanced youths (Faruq Ahmad 1969).

Why were *bradri* membership and solidarity so important? Musicians are produced to gain patronage. But permanent and even occasional court patronage that could also support the family at home came only to relatively few outstanding individuals. The performers spent much of their adult lives away, living in or traveling between courts and wealthy estates or landed Sufi shrines. But their families, starting with the musician's own household, stayed within the home community. Children were trained by retired or nonperforming relatives, and musicians returned and eventually retired there, since patronage was rarely permanent. Marriages were arranged with *bradri* members, including relatives (for Muslims).

The major focus for both family and community was to reproduce artists, outstanding individual performers, masters through a mode of producing music that meshed with the productive system of the larger society. Training was discipular and personal, imparted orally from *ustad* to student, and the tools of production—musical knowledge, performance skills, instruments—were tightly controlled by the master. Reminiscent of the feudal controller-producer relationship, training was marked by the master's coercive control, especially through beatings, but also by support and rewards (Husain 1969; B. Khan 1984; S. Khan 1984; N. Khan 1984). The crux of this training was practicing (*riyaz*): learning how to labor (Thompson 1992). In notable contrast to the appropriators' devaluation of labor, the labor of practicing was supported with a ritual association that legitimized it as something more elevated than labor. The concept of *riyaz* is clearly derived

from Muslim, especially Sufi, devotional exercises (*riyazat*), and its practice
is most recommended at similar times: after predawn (*fajr*) and night (*'isha*)
prayers, and during a 40-day seclusion (*chilla*) (Neuman [1979] 1991).

Central to the process of transmission is the concept and ritual of discipleship (Silver 1976, 1984; Menon 1973; Neuman [1979] 1991), which articulates a paternal commitment in return for filial submission. Discipleship
meant lifelong allegiance, since in productive terms it offered the student
access to the means of musical competence in return for a share of the surplus he would gain later as a producer of music. Understandably, teachers
were reluctant to accept or fully train outside students from whom lifelong
loyalty could not be expected and who would create damaging competition
to the master's own offspring. Hence the oral process of reproducing productive skills has tended to remain internal to the hereditary musicians' kin
group or to die altogether.[7]

In the end, this very traditional, coercive hereditary training produced a
cadre of well-trained specialists. What is astonishing is that it also produced,
and continues to produce, highly creative individual artists of remarkable cal-
iber, capable of setting new standards—then among feudal elites, and today
across the world. Can it be the very feudal conditions of musical production
and reproduction that have made this possible? This exploration suggests
looking at several such conditions, among them the 24-hour immersion in the
musical language; the arbitrary and quasi-feudal domination by, and uncon-
ditional imitation of, one's master; the open-ended duration of training made
possible by subsistence provided by feudal rewards; and finally, the resulting
amalgam of rigid training and freedom to create.

The Performance as Feudal Relations of Production

"Feudal" performances can be considered as a use value, as a form of conspicuous consumption, and thus as an addition to surplus cultural capital. At
the root of the uniqueness of musicians among hereditary producers is their
dual participation in feudal relations of production: as laborers, and as producers of an elite art performance that articulates and transcends that laboring role. How this duality was played out in performance can only be
suggested here, based mostly on earlier reminiscences by both musicians and
patrons, and on my own experience with the late feudal milieu in northern
India. The crux is a shared aesthetic, articulated through a poetics of music
that is as much socially as culturally referenced.

Two aspects of feudal relations of production were "performed" by
hereditary professional musicians for, and with, their feudal patrons. The first
aspect is the relationship of feudal controller and producer, which was acted
out literally in staging the performance by the patron controlling the means
of venue and audience, with the performer providing the labor of producing

the music in return for subsistence and rewards given by the patron at his pleasure. Thus, with the music began the performance of that fundamental diagnostic of feudal status: namely, having labor performed by others, here aesthetically realized in the complementary partnership of performer and listener (as Coomarswami (1948: 46) states so succinctly).

The second aspect is the relationship of musical producer and controller that was acted out in the performance itself. The actual production of music requires a consumer of the product and an arena for its consumption; thus the value of labor, including the labor of practicing, is not realized until the moment of performance. The event of the musical performance offered a shared moment of consumption, which means entering into a personal relationship with the product and directly recovering its use value. Paraphrasing Jean Beaudrillard (1975: 97), the event is a moment of strong psychological and social charge, exactly because it avoids exchange value. Musicians as well as patrons have quite explicitly identified the musical experience as a shared meal, literally "food for the soul" (*ruhani ghiza*), but this was a meal created jointly by host and cook. Musicians, not patrons, presented established ragas or genres to be judged; they also dished up musical innovations to be tasted and accepted into the preferred repertoire by patrons. Patrons responded in ways that were aesthetically coded, but as listeners; they would not perform themselves, even when they were competent to do so. As a service, the art musician's product was no different from other feudal personal services (e.g., those by a barber or cook). What was different was the construction and content of the product. Unlike the cook, the musician was inseparable from what he produced, as the only servant who shared the feudal salon as a full participant in the most elite events. What he uttered musically was of course subject to control, but that was an arbitrary control of the person, not of the music as such. The musicians were in charge of the musical rules, and there was no separate canon of musical works, since ragas and song compositions were inherited individually and transmitted orally.

As a performance of elite art, the musical work was created in a spontaneous process of negotiation between performer and listeners. From the choice of stylistic, melodic, and rhythmic frameworks to the details of ornamentation, performers would propose and listeners dispose (or counterpropose), whether through approval, indifference, or displeasure. To build a performance in this spontaneous way required connoisseurship on the part of the patron or his listening partners, but the onus was ultimately on the musician to know not only his music but the predilections and preferences of his exalted audience. Then he had to have the creativity and flexibility to pull the right registers, to demonstrate the special skills and formulas of his lineage, but also to dwell and expand on what his listeners found pleasing. This was a process not so much of "improvisation" (a term unknown to Hindi or Urdu) but simply of "singing and playing" (the traditional term for "music") so as to create a fine performance. In other words, the basis of that "improvisation" turns out to be social, an insight confirmed by numerous accounts of feudal musicians and patrons.

While providing service as agent of the music, the musician was also a master, the master of his product. Delivered with spontaneous ease, this was musical production that transcended the labor of practicing. In the process of performing he, the servant, could take on the ways of patrons. The art music ensemble offered a replication of the feudal power hierarchy of which the lead musician was a highly dependent partner. Musically, he was in control of a hierarchical performance structure of soloist over accompanist, singer over instrumentalist, melodic over rhythmic accompanist. In improvising, the master performed the arbitrariness of the power holder; he could play with and even contest the feudal relations of dominance and subordination, all the while affirming the courtly pyramid of lead musician, support singer, instrumental accompanists, melodic over rhythmic focus, pedigreed over newly introduced repertoire. Labor was replaced by inspiration, mastery could act out the master.

Indulging in inversions of status, whether intimate or carnivalesque, was aesthetically pleasing and safe, given the socially entrenched difference between patrons and musicians. This entrenched social distance easily permitted patrons to turn their musicians into putative "generals" and "colonels" wearing uniforms and medals, like the legendary Fayyaz Khan, whose special title was "Moon of Music" (*Aftab-e-Musiqi*), and the famous vocal duo Ali Muhammad and Fateh Ali Khan, who were known (in Urdu) as *Jarnail Qarnail* ("General and Colonel"). Patrons used their musicians as combatants in status contests to compete for cultural capital, especially with a musician representing another feudal lord. Musicians, in turn, made the combat their own, using their victories and those of their forebears to stock their own professional "capital," as Bahadur Khan's account of Lallu Khan illustrates. Clearly, musicians identified with the aestheticizing which they performed for and with their patrons.

Above all, musicians, according to their own statements, valued and aspired to the personal musical relationships that musical performance entailed. Some court musicians even became teachers of their patrons, creating a more formalized version of inverted mastery and even the kind of fraternal bond between patron and musician recounted by Gore Khan. Focus on the person beyond the music and on the relationship beyond the performance event also characterized the economic rewards for music, which varied with the effect of music on the audience and, above all, with the noble patron's mood or his desire to display public largesse. Whether the musician performed one or five songs, for five minutes or five days, it was the person who got rewarded; hence individual performers, though servants, could, like a higher-class retainer, risk potentially rewarding creative liberties. This was made possible especially because feudal rewards were given over and above generous subsistence, which was itself a sign of respect for the person of the performer (as well as a signature for the patron's noblesse oblige status). In feudal terms, links to individuals with power were the means to attain rewards.

But feudal performances were also aborted, performers' work rejected, and they themselves put in their servile place or dismissed from feudal venues altogether. Apart from petitions to court officials (Erdman 1985), the Jalandhari poem, and my own, nearly postfeudal observations, I have hardly seen such scenarios mentioned, perhaps because doing so would be acknowledging a "cultural deficit" (pace Guillory) damaging to both patrons and musicians. In fact, the musicians I have known and read about have had little to say about even the obviously negative aspects of feudal service, while stories of its blessings are told and retold among hereditary musicians, especially to their students. Their accounts of the feudal past, as well as what they continue to practice in their families, has given me a differentiated and expanded sense of what feudal patronage could mean in relation to the survival of a musical practice and of the community of its practitioners. For hereditary musicians, feudal patronage may not be ideal, but it may well have been indispensable for sustaining the hereditary and professional productive arrangements of their music.

Concluding Questions

The goal of this chapter has been to interrogate the Hindustani music-making process through the prism of feudal relations of production, on the premise that it may help render concrete the social nature of this music, which, like land or products, is the result of social and economic relationships. I have tried to convey the kind of approach to insight that I have gained from engaging with mode of production theory, particularly when dealing with a musical practice that has substantial links to a predominantly noncapitalist society. Using a feudal hypothesis for Hindustani music as a "theory for practice" does point to relevant parallels and enmeshments with feudal productive relations, but it also highlights differences between musical and material production.

The problematic of addressing these differences involves raising questions about the very use of concepts of material production to which the notion of producing "cultural capital" is but a partial answer. Is music a form of production or simply a service? If performing music can be considered labor that produces surplus value, if only in the form of cultural capital (though Marx disdainfully dismisses that option), then what kind of labor is practicing, the "real work" of producing music, and what kind of means are musical skills? And, in the absence of a material product, how can surplus labor be appropriated, and in the absence of surplus appropriation, what motivates the exploitation of musical labor?

Interestingly, these questions take on a different hue when considered in relation to the larger context of feudal rather than capitalist productive relations from which mainstream Marxist theory is derived. The basis of appropriating surplus labor in feudal (agricultural) production is coercive power rather the alienation of labor in the commodity; this means that feudal production and musical production share basically similar productive relations that govern all kinds of products and services produced by low-class labor for high-class appropriators. What they have in common is the simple exploitation of the "surplus value that always inheres in labor," and the corollary of paternalist redistributive ties which make the appropriator a giver and the producer a taker, thus perversely inverting the economic reality of production.

Ethnographically, this exploration is deliberately set within the post-railway feudal antecedents of independent India; hence the elaborate social hierarchy, with its socially entrenched hereditary professional specialization of music. As the most important and most recent feudal-imperial economy of the nineteenth and twentieth centuries, India offers a richly suggestive feudal basis for a new look at European music in relation to its feudal-absolutist contexts of production and productive relations. Proposing an India-centered look at Europe is also a move toward the postcolonial goal of what Dipesh Chakrabarty (2000) calls "provincializing Europe."

Ultimately, this consideration of feudalism is of course primarily relevant to the post-feudal production of Hindustani music itself, especially in other parts of India, and nationally since Indian independence. To keep the feudal focus as clear as possible, I have kept out of the picture both the very prominent quasi-feudal patronage of and by courtesans contemporary with the last century of feudalism, and the nationalist bourgeois institutions of later twentieth-century patronage, with its attendant social revolution and its reactive feudal musical nostalgia. With this exposé on feudal music-making I hope to have created a starting point for addressing these complex subsequent developments of Hindustani music-making in a productively different light.

In the end, I return to the primary focus that underlies this academic exercise: the musicians who taught and shared their histories with me. My main effort has been to do justice to the work of hereditary musicians in India and to highlight the multiply referenced cultural and historical value that they alone embody. And I return with due humility to the impossible challenge of making this kind of work productively relevant for them. I consider it a beginning to create a public focus on hereditary musicians as agents by demonstrating *how*, not only *that*, patronage is vital to their way of making Hindustani music. My goal is to strengthen already existing initiatives in

India to sustain such patronage, so that hereditary musicians can continue to make a life-giving difference to this music beyond the more predictable sounds of bourgeois institutions.

For Gore Khan and Bahadur Khan, whose accounts helped launch this exploration, it is already too late. Gore Khan died in 1985 in Delhi, focused on religious devotion. He had moved out of the *bradri* support system and suffered poverty to educate his son and daughters, who became successful professionals and have no connection with music. Bahadur Khan is retired from the U.P. State Dance Academy and still lives in Lucknow. His son works in a shoe factory in Kanpur, and his wife has moved there. Banda and Kalavant music are dead. Bahadur Khan continues to visit the academy and sits on a chair on the lawn, hoping that someone will see him and offer him a gig. This is where I hope to find him next year and offer him some quasi-feudal patronage, starting with a meal at the hotel and an affectionate conversation, like Gore Khan and his music-loving patron.

Notes

Support for this research by the Social Sciences and Humanities Research Council of Canada is gratefully acknowledged. Parts of this paper were presented at the Annual Meeting of the Association for Asian Studies held in San Diego in March 2000. Thanks for stimulating comments go to discussant Bonnie Wade and to Michael Asch, Daniel Neuman, Martha Feldman, Brenda Dalen, and Keri Zwicker. I am most grateful for the generous teaching of the late Nasiruddin Gore Khan, Yaqub Khan, Hamid Husain, Nazim Ali Khan, Faruq Ahmad, Shabbir Husain, and Umar Ansari, and of Bahadur Khan, Sultan Khan, Sabri Khan, Allah Rakha, and Khaliq Ahmad.

1. Italics are used throughout this chapter to indicate primary, oral source materials. This conversation (in Urdu) took place on January 20, 1976. The translation is my own.
2. This conversation (in Urdu) took place on November 28, 1992. The translation is my own.
3. Nearly all major Sufi shrines are permanently endowed with land holdings.
4. Applications of the mode-of-production model to surplus-producing precapitalist societies are by Perry Anderson (1974) and Maurice Bloch (1975). In this context, it needs to be emphasized that Marx's own concept of an "Indian" mode of production, based on nineteenth-century Indological constructs, has long been invalidated by later scholarship. The seminal critique is by Daniel Thorner (1966); see also Hindess and Hirst (1975).
5. Often enriched by a Marxist theoretical orientation, economic histories contain extensive documentation on production and surplus appropriation generated by imperial and colonial interests. A good basic source is *The Cambridge Economic History of India* (1982).
6. Documented for both the Lucknow court of Wajid Ali Shah and the Delhi court of Jahandar Shah (Sleeman 1858; Hoey 1888/89; Miner 1993).

7. Hence also the resistance of musicians to having their musical knowledge converted into writing, most notably by the great musical reformer Pandit Bhatkhande in the 1920s (Y. Khan 1984; Nayar 1989).

References

Adorno, Theodor. 1978. "Freudian Theory and the Pattern of Fascist Propaganda." In *The Essential Frankfurt School Reader,* edited by Andrew Arato and Eike Gebhardt, 118–37. New York: Urizen Books.

Allah, Rakha. 1993. Conversation with the author. Edmonton, Canada.

Anderson, Perry. 1974. *Lineages of the Absolute State.* London: NLB.

Ansari, Umar. 1992. Conversation with the author. Lucknow.

Bayly, C. 1983. *Rulers, Townsmen, and Bazaars: North Indian Society in the Age of British Expansion, 1770–1870.* Cambridge: Cambridge University Press.

Beaudrillard, Jean. 1975. *Mirror of Production.* St. Louis: Telos Press.

Bloch, Maurice. 1975. "Property and the End of Affinity." In *Marxist Analyses and Social Anthropology,* edited by Maurice Bloch, 203–22. London: Malaby Press.

Bourdieu, Pierre. 1993. "The Field of Cultural Production." In *The Field of Cultural Production: Essays on Art and Literature,* edited by Randal Johnson, 29–73. Cambridge: Polity Press.

Chakrabarty, Dipesh. 2000. *Provincializing Europe: Postcolonial Thought and Historical Difference.* Princeton, N.J.: Princeton University Press.

Coomaraswamy, Ananda K. 1948. *The Dance of Shiva: Fourteen Indian Essays.* New Delhi: Asia Publishing House. (first published 1929)

Erdman, Joan L. 1985. *Patrons and Performers in Rajasthan: The Subtle Tradition.* Delhi: Chanakya Publications.

Frykenberg, Robert Eric. 1969. *Land Control and Social Structure in Indian History.* Madison: University of Wisconsin Press.

Geertz, Clifford. 1973a. "Ideology as a Cultural System," in *The Interpretation of Cultures.* New York: Basic Books, 193–233.

———. 1973b. "Religion as a Cultural System," in *The Interpretation of Cultures.* New York: Basic Books, 87–125.

———. 1976. "Art as a Cultural System." *Modern Language Notes* 6/3: 1473–99.

Gould, Harold. 1964. "A Jajmani System of North India: Its Structure, Magnitude and Meaning." *Ethnology* 3: 12–41.

Guha, Ranajit. 1982–87. *Subaltern Studies: Writings on South Asian History and Society.* Delhi: Oxford University Press.

Guillory, John. 1993. *Cultural Capital: The Problem of Literary Canon Formation.* Chicago: University of Chicago Press.

Habib, Irfan. 1963. *The Agrarian System of Mughal India (1556–1707).* Bombay: Asia Publishing House.

Hasan, Amir. 1983. *Palace Culture of Lucknow.* Delhi: B.R. Publishing Corporation.

Hindess, Barry, and Hirst, Paul Q. 1975. *Pre-Capitalist Modes of Production.* London: Routledge and Kegan.

Hoey, William. 1888/89. *Memoirs of Delhi and Faizábád : Being a Translation of the Tārīkh Farahbakhsh, from the Original Persian.* 2 Vols. By Muhammad Faiz-

Bakhsh. Allahabad, India: Government Press, Northwestern provinces and Oudh.

Husain, Hamid. 1969. Conversation with the author. Karachi.

Husain, Shabbir. 1984. Conversation with the author. Delhi.

Husain, Yaqub. 1983. Conversation with the author. Lucknow.

Imam, Hakim Mohammad Karam. 1959–60. "Ma'danu'l-Musiqi,' translated in part by Govind Vidyarthia," under the title "Melody through the Centuries," *Sangeet Natak Akademi Bulletin* 11/12: 6–14, 13–26, 30, 49.

Jalandhari, Hafeez. 1948. "Raqqasa." In *Nuqush Literary Annual*. Lahore, Pakistan: Ferozesons.

Jameson, Fredric. 1971. *Marxism and Form: Twentieth-Century Dialectical Theories of Literature*. Princeton, N.J.: Princeton University Press.

Katz, Claudio J. 1989. *From Feudalism to Capitalism: Marxian Theories of Class Struggle and Social Change*. Westport, Conn.: Greenwood Press.

Kessinger, Tom G. 1974. *Vilyatpur, 1848–1968: Social and Economic Change in a North Indian Village*. Berkeley: University of California Press.

Khan, Bahadur. 1984. Conversation with the author. Lucknow. Translation from Urdu by the author.

———. 1992. Conversation with the author. Lucknow January 20. Translation from Urdu by the author.

Khan, Faruq Ahmad. 1969. Conversation with the author. Karachi, Pakistan. Translation from Urdu by the author.

Khan, Gore (Nasiruddin). 1976. Conversation with the author. Delhi November 28. Translation from Urdu by the author.

Khan, Nazim Ali. 1985. Conversation with the author. Lahore, Pakistan. Translation from Urdu by the author.

Kahn, Sabri. 1984. Conversation with the author. Delhi. Translation from Urdu by the author.

Khan, Sultan. 1993. Conversation with the author. Edmonton, Canada. Translation from Urdu by the author.

Khan, Yaqub. 1984. Conversation with the author. Lucknow. Translation from Urdu by the author.

Kippen, James. 1988. *The Tabla of Lucknow: A Cultural Analysis of a Musical Tradition*. Cambridge: Cambridge University Press.

Kumar, Dharma, and Meghnad Desai, eds. 1982. *The Cambridge Economic History of India*, Vol. 2. Cambridge: Cambridge University Press.

Kumar, Nita. 1988. *The Artisans of Banaras: Popular Culture and Identity, 1880–1986*. Princeton, N.J.: Princeton University Press.

Lukacs, Gyorgy. 1971. *History and Class Consciousness: Studies in Marxist Press*. Translated by Rodney Livingstone. London: Merlin Press.

Manuel, Peter. 1993. *Cassette Culture: Popular Music and Technology in Northern India*. Chicago: University of Chicago Press.

Marx, Karl. 1960. *Theories of Surplus Value*, Part 1. Vol. 4 of *Capital*. Moscow: Foreign Languages Publishing House.

Marx, Karl. 1962. *Capital*. Vol. 3 Moscow: Foreign Languages Publishing House.

Marx, Karl. 1973. *Grundrisse: Foundations of the Critique of Political Economy (Rough Draft)*. Translated by Martin Nicolaus. London: Allen Lane.

Menon, Raghava R. 1973. *Discovering Indian Music*. Turnbridge Wells, Kent: Abacus Press.

Metcalf, Thomas. 1969. "From Raja to Landlord: The Odh Talukdars 1850–1870." In *Land Control and Social Structure in Indian History,* edited by R. Frykenberg, 123–41. Madison: University of Wisconsin Press.

Miner, Allyn. 1993. *Sitar and Sarod in the 18th and 19th Centuries*. Intercultural Music Studies, Vol. 5. Noetzel Edition, edited by Max Peter Baumann. Berlin: Florian.

Mir Hassan Ali, Mrs. B. 1917. Conversation. In *Observations on the Mussulmans of India: Descriptive of Their Manners, Customs, Habits, and Religious Opinions.* 2nd ed by W. Crooke. London: Clarendon Press.

Nahata, Agarchand. 1961."Rajasthan ki gane-bajanewali qaumen aur dhadhi (Musician Communities of Rajasthan and the Dhadhi)." *Sangeet*, October 27–28.

Nayar, Sobhana. 1989. *Bhatkhande's Contribution to Music: A Historical Perspective*. Bombay: Popular Prakashan.

Neuman, Daniel M. [1979] 1991. *The Life of Music in North India*. Chicago: Chicago University Press.

Newcomb, Anthony. 1980. *The Madrigal at Ferrara 1579–1597*. Princeton, N.J.: Princeton University Press.

Olmsted, Anthony. 1993. "The Capitalization of Music in London, 1660–1800." M.A. thesis, University of Alberta.

Parikh, Arvind, ed. 1994. *Seminar on Sarangi*. Conference proceedings. Bombay: Sangeet Research Academy.

Prakash, Gyan. 1990. *Bonded Histories: Genealogies of Labor Servitude in Colonial India*. Cambridge and New York: Cambridge University Press.

———. 1991. "Writing Post-Orientalist Histories of the Third World: Perspectives from Indian Historiography." *Comparative Study of Society and History* 32/2: 383–408.

———. 1992. "Can the 'Subaltern' Ride? A Reply to O'Hanlon and Washbrook." *Society for Comparative Study in Society and History* 34/1: 168–84.

Qureshi, Regula Burckhardt. [1986] 1995. *Sufi Music of Pakistan: Sound, Context, and Meaning in Qawwali*. Chicago: University of Chicago Press.

———. 1999. "His Master's Voice: Qawwali and 'Gramophone Culture' in South Asia." *Popular Music* 18/1: 63–98.

———. 2000. "Confronting the Social: Mode of Production and the Sublime for (Indian) Art Music." *Ethnomusicology* 44/1: 15–38.

Raychaudhuri, Tapan, and Irfan Habib, eds. 1982. *The Cambridge Economic History of India,* Vol. 1. Cambridge: Cambridge University Press.

Sharar, Abdul Halim. [1913–20] 1975. *Lucknow: The Last Phase of an Oriental Culture*. Translated and edited by E. S. Harcourt and Fakhir Hussain. London: Paul Elek. (UNESCO: Indian Series).

Silver, Brian. 1976. "On Becoming an Ustad: Six Life-Sketches in the Evolution of a Gharana." *Asian Music* 7/2:27–58.

———. 1984. "The Adab of Musicians." In *Moral Conduct and Authority*, edited by B. Metcalf. Berkeley: University of California Press.

Sleeman, W. H. 1858. *A Journey through the Kingdom of Oude in 1849–1850*. London: Richard Bentley.

Spivak, Gayatri C. 1988. "Can the Subaltern Speak?" In *Marxism and the Interpretation of Culture*, edited by C. Nelson and L. Grossberg, 271–313. Urbana: University of Illinois Press.

Stokes, Eric. 1975. "The Structure of Landholding in Uttar Pradesh, 1860–1948." *Indian Economic and Social History Review* 12/2: 113–32.

———. 1982. "Agrarian Relations: Northern and Central India." In *The Cambridge Economic History of India,* Vol. 2, edited by Dharma Kumar and Meghnad Desai. Cambridge: Cambridge University Press.

Terray, Emmanuel. 1975. "Classes and Class Consciousness in the Abron Kingdom of Gyaman." In *Marxist Analyses and Social Anthropology*, edited by Maurice Bloch, 85–136. London: Malaby Press Limited.

Thompson, Gordon R. 1992. "The Carans of Gujarat: Caste Identity, Music, and Cultural Change." *Ethnomusiology* 35/3: 381–91.

Thorner, Daniel. 1966. "Marx on India and the Asiatic Mode of Production." *Contributions to Indian Sociology* 9 (September): 33–66.

Wade, Bonnie C. 1997. *Imaging Music.* Chicago: Chicago University Press.

Willis, Paul E. 1981. *Learning to Labor: How Working Class Kids Get Working Class Jobs.* New York: Columbia University Press.

The Capitalization of Musical Production: The Conceptual and Spatial Development of London's Public Concerts, 1660–1750

ANTHONY A. OLMSTED

Tracking the impact of large-scale changes in the economic foundations of a society is a daunting task in the best of times. When faced with history as an added facet to understanding the operation of an economic system, the analysis becomes even more difficult. In the case of London's long and rocky transition to a capitalist mode of production during the seventeenth century, it is well worth an attempt to make some sense of the impact that such broad changes in the productive relations of the society had on specific areas of cultural endeavor. The changes in the fundamental economic and cultural organization of London and surrounding areas have been well documented (Corrigan and Sayer 1985). However, I would like to take the analysis one step further and offer some sense of the impact that these changes had on what many economists regard as a peripheral or secondary economic activity—musical performance.

For purposes of illustration, I will focus on only one type of musical activity that in many respects exemplifies the growing capitalist ideas of the time. The "invention" of the public concert—presenting a musical performance for sale to any who could afford it—happened at effectively the same time as the new capitalism began to sweep England after the restoration of Charles II to the throne in 1660.[1] The growth of the public concert offers a perfect case to illustrate the impact of the capitalist mode of production on an activity that, prior to the Commonwealth, had been solidly feudal in organization (Woodfill 1953). The development of the concept of presenting a musical "object" for sale to those who wish to purchase it, without restricting admission on a class or membership basis, was quite revolutionary.

There has been remarkable consensus about both the time and the spaces, locations, and organizational details surrounding the arrival of public concerts in seventeenth-century London (see Elkin 1955; Hyde 1985; Scott 1936, 1937). As the popularity of this type of musical presentation increased

106

into the eighteenth century, so too did the complexity of relations surrounding its organization and performance, leaving us with ever greater amounts of detailed evidence—witness McVeigh's (1993) record of more than 5,000 performances in London between 1750 and 1800. In the end, however, we are left to ponder a pair of questions that has not yet been addressed in the literature interested in the early decades of English public concerts: Why did such concerts happen at all, and What are the specifics of the relations between music and the economy that made the concerts possible?

Ehrlich (1976) was the first to identify these two related issues in his "Economic History and Music" for the Proceedings of the Royal Musical Association. With respect to the origination and growth of public concerts, Ehrlich made the following observation: "There is no shortage of material, raw and processed—on institutions, including orchestras and concert societies, theatres and concert halls, repertoire. . . . What appears to be lacking is convincing explanations of why it all happened" (1976: 193). This is, indeed, a fundamental question—one that in historical hindsight may or may not be satisfactorily addressed. However, a broader approach to this question was suggested by economic historian R. H. Tawney and was recognized by Ehrlich to be the second of the key approaches to the intersection of economics and music: "Apart from a few commonplaces, we know at present next to nothing of the relations, if such exist, between the artistic achievements of an epoch and the character of its economic life" (cited in Ehrlich 1976: 188).

Fortunately, a number of works have in recent years addressed issues very much in line with Tawney's observations: work ranging from Milhous 1984 and Milhous and Hume 1993 on the economics of opera production in seventeenth- and eighteenth-century London, Fenlon 1987 and Brook 1975 on early English publishing, to a range of contemporary work on a variety of issues concerning broadly economic approaches to music including Shore 1983, Mabry 1990, Olmsted 1999, and Qureshi 2000. However, in an effort to unite both Tawney and Ehrlich's concerns in a manner that has little precedent, I will draw on earlier work (Olmsted 1993) to address the rise of public concerts in London within the context of the rapid rise of capitalized productive relations in the seventeenth century.

In line with the theme of this volume, the basic organizational principle of this essay will be the foundations of the mode of production itself. The most elaborate and influential theoretical writings on the subject are clearly those of Karl Marx, particularly in *Capital* (1963). In recent years, the concept of mode of production has been well described by a variety of authors in addition to Marx: Bennholdt-Thomsen (1982), Soiffer and Howe (1982), and Wolpe (1980). However, for two reasons, I prefer the formulation utilized by Laclau (1971, 1985) and summarized by Scott (1976). First, it offers a brevity in its basic structure that will work very well for an exploratory essay such as this. Second, and more important, it is a formulation that has shown

real analytical value by illuminating changing productive relations in both
specific political situations, as well as in my own analysis (1999) of Folkways Records. The formulation identifies four sets of relations that must be
described in order to specify a given mode of production: (1) a determinate
type of ownership of the means of production; (2) a determinate form of
appropriation of the economic surplus; (3) a determinate degree of development of the division of labor; and (4) a determinate level of development of
the productive forces.

The key elements of these four facets of economic organization are the
relations of production and the forces of production. The relations of production are just that: the relationships that individuals must enter into in order to
produce the items necessary for the operation of the economy. The forces of
production are most often conceived of as a combination of the means of production—the technological/material base of production—and the basic organization of production, which work together to motivate the production and
reproduction of the social formation (Friedman 1974: 445). Of course, understanding the lived material and social relations essential to production will then
lead to the elucidation of the political, legal, and subsequently ideological precepts that order those relations. As Marx and Engels (1947: 13–15) state:

> The fact is . . . definite individuals who are productively active in a definite
> way enter into these definite social and political relations. Empirical obser-
> vation must in each separate instance bring out empirically, and without any
> mystification and speculation, the connection of the social and political
> structure with production. . . . [I]t is the real living individuals themselves,
> as they are in actual life. . . .

To address these issues, this essay will begin with a more specific discussion of the object of our consideration, the public concert. Clarification of
the exact parameters of a public concert are important as they vary within the
literature, potentially affecting the conclusions that one might reach about
the origins and meaning of these performances. In discussing the rise of public concerts, the text itself is organized to illustrate the impact on such concerts of the introduction of highly capitalized relations and forces of
production. The sections that follow will then consider each of the points
from the delineation of a mode of production in their turn. Each section will
direct itself primarily to highlighting the intersection points between the economic changes of the time and what was occurring in the early concerts. The
use of various parts of a mode of production to organize the discussion will
help to highlight a variety of factors that played into the creation of the earliest musical commodities.

Finally, the essay will close with a discussion of the importance of a
mode-of-production approach to illustrating cultural phenomena, particu-

larly music. I will argue that the rise of public concerts was largely a result of a combination of the influences of existing productive relations that supported music-making prior to the Interregnum. However, these forces were ultimately disrupted by the violent upheaval of the time, and musicians, faced with the additional burden of highly prejudicial legislation, had little option but to seek out new performance opportunities in the changing marketplace of post-Restoration London. Fortunately, the new capitalist relations of the time supported such endeavors, and the public concert was born as a commodity available to a wide range of consumers.

For brevity and clarity of illustration, this paper will be neither a theoretical excursus nor a historiography. There will be much that could be discussed on both fronts that will necessarily be omitted. Nonetheless, focusing attention on the mode of production within which a social phenomenon develops (in this case, a specific type of musical presentation) can highlight features of its organization and interrelationships that would not ordinarily be considered if one were simply examining the phenomenon itself. In this respect, using a mode-of-production approach not only ties activities into the economic infrastructure of a social formation but forces the analyst to consider wider forces that may, or may not, affect the conditions under which an event takes place.

In order to consider best the object of this analysis, I believe the most suitable definition of a public concert is the performance of instrumental or vocal music for an audience whose attendance is restricted only to the payment of admission on a per-event basis. This is a very specific definition in terms of historical identification, as will be seen below. However, the importance of such specificity is clear when one considers the definition of a concert offered by McVeigh (1993: xiv), for example, who writes that a concert

> is interpreted rather loosely to incorporate public subscription series, benefits, oratorios and performances at the pleasure gardens, as well as meetings of orchestral societies and private or court concerts. But glee clubs and other convivial groups have been excluded from detailed discussion, and no attempt has been made to cover all those myriad occasions in eighteenth-century London when music played an ancillary part—from odes to anniversary dinners through elaborate church services to wind-bands playing on Thames barges.

I will foreshadow a later discussion by suggesting that one of the weaknesses of McVeigh's definition is the variety of productive relationships that it allows, particularly the range of relationships between performers and audience members. The development of a performance event at which attendance is not restricted in an extraeconomic fashion—private and court performances almost certainly would have been so—obscures the impact that the public concert had on existing relations of production. In contrast, to ignore 'ancillary' music is to overlook opportunities for performance that would have supported many working musicians.

In other words, private court or salon performances assume a different type of performer/audience relationship than would a subscription concert series, and both would be very different from a single admission concert. In each case, the relationship between performer and audience becomes more explicitly economic and less dependent on fostering the social connections that may be necessary to support a patron-type relationship. Consequently, I would suggest that, in fact, such everyday concerts are more in keeping with the spirit behind the formation of the public concert tradition outlined below than many of the high-profile performances that more commonly endure for the historian. Indeed, looseness of definition also contributes to conclusions about eighteenth-century musical life that do not do the common musician much justice in terms of their ability to manage new developments in the relations and forces of production of the new musical economy.

Currently, there are two dissenting opinions concerning who deserves the honor of having presented the first public concert. The earlier of the two is a single reference to a public concert organized by singer/composer Ben Wallington, held at the Mitre Inn (unknown location—several Mitre Inns existed in London) in 1664 (Young 1980: 616). Beyond this, there is no mention of Wallington. The more commonly accepted event, however, was arranged by John Banister the elder, reported to have held the first public concert in a room of his house (the "Musick School") on 30 December 1672.[2] As Hyde (1985: 174) declared: "To John Banister of London belongs the honor of arranging the first series of concerts for the general public at which payment was accepted." A noted musician in his own right, Banister had been a court musician since 1660 and was made chief of His Majesty's violins in 1663. Unfortunately for Banister, he suggested that English violinists were better than the French (of whom Charles II had grown very fond during exile) and was dismissed from court service in 1667 (Elkin 1955: 19–20; Harley 1968: 135), after which he became something of a concert impresario.

Banister's concerts began every afternoon at four o'clock as advertised in the *London Gazette*. As the concerts' popularity grew, larger accommodations were needed, and, according to contemporary Roger North (in Forsyth 1985: 26), Banister relocated:

> to a large room in Whitefriars, neer [*sic*] to the Temple back gate, and made a large raised box for the musicians, whose modesty required curtaines. The room was rounded with seats and small tables ale-house fashion. 1s. was the price and call for what you pleased. There was very good musick [*sic*], for Banister found the means to procure the best hands in town.

In 1673, he moved to Chandos Street, Covent Garden; in 1675, his "Academy" moved to Lincoln's Inn Field; and in 1678 he moved his concerts to a house on Essex Street off the Strand (Young 1965: 35). With each of these locations, Banister's concerts appear to reinforce the prevailing pattern for the giving of such concerts. Through a modest setting, reasonable cost of admission, and relative informality of presentation, Banister offered a new protocol for the presentation and consumption of instrumental and vocal music.

The emphasis on instrumental and vocal music over the developing English and foreign opera in defining public concerts is deliberate and necessary. While both foreign and English opera would initially appear to fulfill the definition of a public concert, both opera and masques are distinguished by the existence of a strong dramatic element that includes the use of costumes and scenery for dramatic effect (Lindenberger 1984; Price 1989). For example, the performance of William D'Avenant's *The Siege of Rhodes* in 1656, commonly regarded as the first English opera, had to disguise itself from Puritan censure. To do so, "the acts were called 'entries' and the whole spectacle was known not as an opera . . . but as 'A Representation by the art of Prospective in Scenes and the Story sung in Recitative Musick' " (Grout 1988: 155). Thus, there was a clear recognition that masques and operas were entertainments fundamentally different from the simple presentation of music.

More pragmatically, there was not much opera available in London after the Restoration. Prior to 1700, only a handful of English "semi-operas" were presented along with traditional theater at Dorset Garden: *The Tempest* (1674), *Psyche* (1675), *Circe* (1677), *Albion and Albanius* (1685), *The Prophetess* (1690), *King Arthur* (1691), and *Fairy Queen* (1692). As for why there were so few presentations, Milhous (1984: 568) concludes that "not much is known about the cost of these pieces, except that they were ferociously expensive." These semi-operas were presented by the theater companies in addition to their regular seasons. The Duke's Company was able to pay out its dividends in 1675–77 because of its "solid if unspectacular profits from the ordinary plays it offered up to two hundred days each season" (Milhous 1984: 569). Fully sung Italian opera was not introduced to London until *Arsinoë* and *Camilla* were translated and performed at Drury Lane in 1705 and 1706, respectively (Milhous 1984: 571).

Aside from being an identifiably different genre from opera, the public concert is of great interest because it began to present itself as the convergence of three existing social practices into a form that was uniquely capitalist. First, public attendance of theatrical presentations in the late sixteenth and early seventeenth centuries foreshadowed many of the patterns of consumption that emerged with the performance of musical entertainments in the 1660s. Second, the negotiation of status among the increasingly differentiated economic classes that began to emerge in the capital expansion in the seventeenth century clearly affected the meaning of public consumption. As a result, new public events were required that could satisfy such desires in a manner appropriate to the standing of the consumers. Public concerts provided a relatively inexpensive, highly visible means of fulfilling such consumptive desires. Finally, the tradition of music-making at the community level provided a resource pool from which to draw both talent and consumers as the production of public concerts expanded, filling different venues with a familiar kind of musical entertainment. The convergence of these existing traditions with the catalyst of the generalized capital expansion of the period brought forth public concerts as a newly available and affordable mode of cultural expression.

The first of these social practices centered upon paying money to gain admission to a "presented" entertainment that existed in pre-defined spatial and temporal conditions. The idea of paying money to attend an entertainment in a specific venue had strong foundations more than a century before the first public concerts, in public theaters where plays were presented for a paying audience. London theaters played an important part in setting a precedent for the consumption patterns of public musical entertainment. Virtually all of the productive relations necessary to present a public concert would have been present in these early theatrical productions.

The Theatre was one of the first playhouses, erected in 1576 immediately outside the London city limit by James Burbage. It could accommodate a large number of patrons, so the admission prices could be kept low— between one penny and sixpence[3] (Rea 1990: 539). Public theaters (figure 1) were large open-air theaters intended as a "mass entertainment enterprise" with an estimated capacity of up to 3,000 patrons (Oates and Baumol 1972: 141). These theaters were quite financially successful as the falling real wages of the time were to the advantage of labor-intensive theater. It was estimated that a play could begin to profit with a run of only two weeks (Oates and Baumol 1972: 151–52). Such public plays thus set the precedent

Figure 1. Periods of activity of public theaters in London, 1575–1642. (Adapted from Oates & Baumol 1972: 148.)

Name	Date
The Theatre[a]	c. 1576–c. 1599
First Globe	c. 1599–c. 1613
Second Globe	c. 1613–1642
The Curtain	c. 1577–c. 1626
Crosskeys Inn	c. 1579–c. 1595
Newington Butts	c. 1580–c. 1595
The Rose	1587–c. 1616
The Swan	1595–c. 1621
First Fortune	1600–c. 1621
Second Fortune	c. 1622–1642
Red Bull	c. 1605–1642
Hope	1616–c. 1632

[a]Indentations indicate formation of subsequent theaters in the same location.

for practicability and profitability. By targeting the middle ranks of the social ladder, the public theaters could provide an affordable entertainment to a larger audience. Furthermore, the immediate exchange relationship between those presenting the show and the audience was being cemented in the consumer consciousness.[4]

The second line of convergence that played a role in the growth of concerts was the peculiar social necessity of status consumption. The reasons such practices abound in society will not be reviewed here (see McCracken 1988). Suffice it to say, public concerts could offer a commodity for the middle classes to consume as a public entertainment that provided them with the necessary amount of social acknowledgment of their status. But social classes were no longer predicated specifically on social position and obligation, as had been prevalent in the feudal structures prior to the 1640s (Ashley 1961). Indeed, as wealth became increasingly important, social divisions were beginning to show themselves as built upon access to economic resources. This is demonstrated by the number of authors—including several contemporary observers—that have suggested a variety of economic classes in the seventeenth and eighteenth centuries, ranging from one (Laslett, in Neale 1981: 71) to three (Rose 1981: 256), five (Neale 1981: 133; Nelson [1763], in Leppert 1988: 25–26), and seven (Defoe [1709] and Massie [1756], in Corfield 1987).

A review of the details of each formulation is not necessary here. However, what is clearly indicated is the evidence for, and importance of, recognizing the growing differences in income and wealth throughout the population. Ultimately, most models (with the exception of Laslett's "single class"—the ruling land owners) reflect the distinction among the aristocratic landowners, a merchant/petite-bourgeoisie middle class, and a working class or classes. The importance of recognizing such economic distinctions arises from the growing importance of the middle classes in the economic activity of the time. The aristocracy was highly stressed financially by its involvement in the Civil War, with many aristocratic households depleting their economic reserves. The merchant classes, on the other hand, were beginning to reap the benefits of a confident and expanding domestic market in England and to realize a great deal of wealth from continued British expansion abroad (Barber 1975; Ehrenberg 1928; Hannay 1926).

The huge increases in merchant income and the concurrent loss of much of the aristocratic wealth through the Interregnum created a great deal of tension between the two groups (Stone 1984). As a consequence, the economic power of the middling classes began to grow rapidly. Economic data of the eighteenth century, implied in part from parish tax lists (Schwarz 1982), broadly suggest that in London proper, a median family income of £50 a year was necessary to begin participating in a non-subsistence consumer economy (Eversley, in Lemire 1990: 70n). Putting this figure against additional demographic data by Schwarz (1982) and Brewer (1980), it can be conservatively concluded that 20 to 25 percent of the population of London could have participated in a non-subsistence consumer economy by the end of the eighteenth century.

Though this figure may appear low, based on London population estimates from Wrigley (1987: 133), a London population of 575,000 in 1700 would

Figure 2. London public houses where music is known to have been performed, 1648–1731.

Name	Date	Location
Black Horse	1648	Aldersgate St. (Black Horse Court?)
'Blew Bell'[a]	1658	London Wall
Mitre[b]	c. 1659–60	Fleet Street
Mitre[c]	c. 1664	Wapping
Mitre	c. 1664	London House Yard (St. Paul's Churchyard)
Music House[d]	c. 1665	Stepney
Black Swan	c. 1670s[e]	Bishopsgate
The Two Golden Balls[f]	c. 1689	Bow Street
Queen's Head[g]	1691	Paternoster Row
King's Head	Pre–c. 1700	Gray's Inn (north of Lincoln's Inn Fields)
Castle Tavern	c. 1700	Paternoster Row, St. Paul's, Cheapside
Crown and Anchor Tavern	1710 (1726)	Arundel Street in the Strand
The Two Golden Balls[h]	pre-1719	Great Hart Street, James St., Long Acre
Devil Tavern	1731	possibly Temple Bar, West Fleet St.[i]

Source: Compiled from Elkin 1955; Hyde 1985; Young 1965; Tilmouth 1957; Scott 1936, 1937.

[a]Harley (1968: 139) notes a contemporary observer refers to a visit to the "Blue Balls," which John Banister also frequented. This may or may not be the same place.
[b]"There were a great many 'Mitre' taverns in old London, so called because built on land belonging to a bishop or abbot" (Elkin 1955: 15). The Mitre is also known as the "sign of the spiritual helmet" (Hyde 1985: 69). See also Endell 1968.
[c]Harley (1968: 136) notes that this Mitre may have been in a place called Music House Court.
[d]Scott (1936) gives strong evidence that this music house, whose sign was the head of Charles II, was not the same place as the King's Head. Maurice Greene began concerts in 1731 after quitting the Academy of Ancient Music (Young 1965: 75).
[e]There is a reference to Samuel Pepys having attended, therefore it was in existence sometime between the 1660s and 1680s (Hyde 1985: 70).
[f]It is unknown whether this is a previous location or a separate establishment from the Two Golden Balls in Great Hart Street.
[g]Previously Crosskeys, it was reputedly changed to Queen's Head on the accession of Queen Elizabeth. The conflict in dating the names may be an error, or may indicate a second location of the same name. The Queen's Head is mentioned in relation to music in a 1691 tract, *The Last Search after Claret* (Hyde 1985: 73).
[h]It was also used as a painting auction gallery, similar to the Vendu (Tilmouth 1957: 15).
[i]There is a mention of a Devil Tavern at Temple Bar in the late seventeenth century, but it is not referred to in connection with music until 1731 (Scott 1937: 379).

have yielded a consumer population approaching 150,000 citizens. Assuming this number includes children, it is still representative of a significant consumer base from which to draw. Such figures also clearly support the notion that the majority of London residents were participating in some type of monetary economy, even if income levels did not allow for their participation in non-subsistence consumption. The developing economy also supported a new group of consumers eager to show their economic strength: a group able to challenge the beleaguered aristocracy in the pursuit of taste (Weber 1975).

The third line of convergence grew out of the tradition of music-making at the community level, in what were known as public houses—a range of establishments that included inns, taverns serving wealthier clientele, and the local ale-houses. Figure 2 is a compilation of some of the public houses where music performance has been documented.

The difficulty in dating such events is obvious; the dates given through-out are those of the earliest documented references to music performance. There very likely was music performed at most of these locations (and undoubtedly many others) before the first references to it were recorded. With music commonly associated with public houses, this list can only be considered suggestive of the London area.[5] Indeed, there is almost a sense that it is remarkable that references to music-making in public houses were made at all as it was such a commonplace occurrence. However, there is no solid evidence that this was the case. Taverns and ale-houses in particular were, in fact, some of the only public places music could be heard during the Interregnum, despite a Parliamentary edict to the contrary (Scott 1936: 448). The penalties for performing in public without a patron were swift and severe before and during the 1640s and 1650s. The importance of public music-making can be found in the fact that music continued to be performed at the Black Horse and the Blew Bell during the 1650s, despite London's impor-tance as a center of Puritan activity.

The larger question at hand, of course, is what forces may have prompted the synthesis of admission practices, status consumption, and com-munity music-making? The impetus for such convergence appears to be twofold. First, the disruptions of the Civil War and the Cromwellian Parlia-ment were significant, to say the least. Upheaval in all areas of English life was profound, from the sweeping political changes to the impact of Puri-tanism on the moral conduct of the population. More important, "the monar-chy, the House of Lords, the Anglican Church, and the administrative and judicial apparatus of the Prerogative Courts all came toppling down together," forcing England and its musicians into an important economic and political rebuilding phase after the Restoration of Charles II to the throne in 1660 (Stone 1980).

Second, such upheaval laid England, London in particular, open to trans-formation. The expansion of wage labor relations to encompass the growing capitalist relations quite firmly set the groundwork for the emergence of a range of new productive networks. These networks responded to the new circumstances that post-Restoration London offered. In particular, the combination of an increasingly wealthy merchant class and the relative security of Charles II's reign opened the door for the populace to explore entertainment options. As Tilmouth (1957: 13) suggests, "it cannot be denied that his [Charles II's] hedonistic inclinations set a pattern of behavior which was only too readily followed by London society." It is out of this rich mix of change and opportunity that the connection between the general changes in London's economic life and the growth of public concerts can be made.

The key element in the spread of capitalism into the London landscape in the seventeenth century was the separation of the owner of the means of production from the labor used to create the product. Marx (1963: 668) was quite clear in asserting that within capital, the owner of the tools, machinery and raw materials required to produce an item was separate from the laborer.

> The capitalist system pre-supposes the complete separation of the labourers from all property in the means by which they can realise their labour. As soon as capitalist production is once on its own legs, it not only maintains this separation, but reproduces it on a continually extending scale. The process, therefore, that clears the way for the capitalist system, can be none other than the process which takes away from the labourer the possession of his means of production; a process that transforms, on the one hand, the social means of subsistence and of production into capital, on the other, the immediate producers into wage-labourers.

With more and more peasants being forced off their land in the countryside, greater numbers of individuals came to London and other cities to find a venue to sell their labor (Marx 1963). Musicians were no different in their efforts to find employment. Prior to the Interregnum, there were few musicians who were able to secure dependable incomes practicing their craft—those associated with the King's Musick, a few waits in London, and those connected to the households of noblemen and gentlemen. In fact, "As a rule musicians [had] to depend on casual employment, on an uncertain, irregular succession of odd jobs given to them by many employers" (Woodfill 1953: 3). Indeed, some might suggest the situation is not much different today. However, in early-seventeenth-century London, competition for the "odd jobs" became even more pointed, in part because of London's economic importance. As Woodfill (1953: 4–5) notes,

> London sheltered during much of the year the royal musicians, household musicians accompanying their patrons to court, and many of the hungry minstrels and musical vagabonds of the rest of England and the continent, and most of them competed with London's own citizens. Custom and law

allowed the retained musicians to come to London, and the impossibility of forming a strong organization, in large measure because of the deficiencies of the local government, admitted the rest.

However, it was at this point that musicians came to hold a slightly more advantageous position with respect to their ability to create a product. For musicians, their instruments are their tools for performance—their means of production. As a result, musicians were able to continue to produce their "products" using their own tools, not requiring the capital of another. Thus, to a certain extent, the competition for employment was not necessarily a competition for existing capital—musicians brought with them everything they needed to perform their service.[6] Given that we can fairly assume that most musicians did own their instruments, then the defining parameters of the new public performance event become physical. Musicians required a venue within which they could structure the presentation of their musical products.

We can begin to see, then, the nature of the growing exploitation of existing space by musicians in order to generate income for themselves by selling their "products"—the performance. The use of venues as indicators for performance activities is important for two reasons. First, as mentioned above, if one is to charge admission to consume a particular object or commodity, particularly a sonic commodity in a performance, then delineating the space in which such a commodity will be delivered becomes central. Second, from an analytical point of view, the existence and reported usage of venues provides us with physical evidence to use in the reconstruction of a peculiar kind of labor—labor that does not result in a durable object. Thus the increasing evidence of use of venues for the purposes of performance strengthens the argument for the expansion of this particular kind of presentation.

The evidence for this use of existing venues can be found in three areas: the use of existing public houses, the use of existing rooms in houses or other buildings, and the use of pleasure gardens for performances. Music does have considerable advantages over theatrical works in this context. Not only is music a far more portable entertainment, but it is also less formal with respect to who has access to repertoire. The long traditions of music in the home and church make it a familiar pastime. Coupled with the age-old link between music and drinking (see, e.g., Hackwood 1985), it seems only appropriate that to a great extent, much of the public concert tradition grew out of the public houses of the day. This is also the type of performance that scholars have traditionally defined as having produced the first "public concert."

Whether it was Wallington or Banister who actually presented the first public concert, two elements are particularly important. First, both reports occur very shortly after the return of Charles II to the throne and the return of a degree of political stability to London. This is clearly important as it represents a diverting of energies and incomes toward pursuits other than conflict. The second element is that both events are said to have occurred either in a public house in Wallington's case or in "ale-house fashion" in a large, existing room in Banister's case. Banister's example is particularly telling in that he quickly went from being a favored court musician to being unemployed and thus was forced to arrange an alternative form of performance to offer to the public.

What is clear, however, is that something very similar to public concerts likely occurred in the decade or so preceding these first accounts. The evidence for this is the reporting of the performance of music in a variety of public houses in London from 1648 (see figure 2). These venues offered up exactly what the musicians of the day required—a venue that would bring some order to the nature of the performances, but in which performers were not limited to being strictly wage labor by the owner of the venue. As in Banister's case, it was a direct economic relationship between the audience and the musicians. It is reasonable to suggest that the musicians could still be considered wage laborers in this type of situation. However, I would argue that it is not until the venues become more specifically directed to presenting musical performances that the issue of venue ownership becomes a significant one. In fact, it is fair to suggest that with public houses, the performance of music represented a mutually beneficial arrangement between musician and venue owner, as the customers drawn in or held by the performance of music would benefit the owner, while the patrons there for refreshments would provide a potential audience base from which to solicit payment for a performance.

The use of existing rooms in London was also important to the early establishment of a different set of productive relations—relations that expanded the notion of traditional performance venues to include virtually any large room that could accommodate musicians and an audience. This is clearly evident in the venues listed in Figure 3. A couple of these venues are worthy of mention, not so much because of the room itself, but because of the organization behind the presentation of music in the first place. The most notable of the early concert clubs began in 1678 with the Small-Coal Man's Musick Club, which took place in a room over a shop in Alyesbury Street that had been fitted with a small organ. The Small-Coal Man was Thomas Britton (1644–1714), a seller of small-coal who had a passion for music, books, and knowledge in general. His enthusiasm for the arts attracted some of the finest performers and well-heeled audiences in London (Young 1980: 617). The concerts presented there were initially free of charge, but Britton eventually began charging 10 shillings per year subscription, with coffee available for a penny a cup (Forsyth 1985: 27).

A second location of great interest to concertgoers was the York Buildings,[7] located between the west end of the Strand and the Thames, which proved to be a hive of musical activity. The York Buildings Room (also

Figure 3. Music rooms and music clubs known to be active, 1672–c. 1738, listed chronologically from first reference. (Compiled from Elkin 1955; Harley 1968; Scott 1937; Forsyth 1985.)

Name	Date(s)	Location
"Musick-School"	December 30, 1672	Dogwell Court, Lombard St., Whitefriars
Small-Coal Man's Musick Club	1678	Aylesbury St., Clerkenwell
Villiers-St. Room (a.k.a. York Buildings Room)	1680–March 28, 1734[a]	East Villiers St., off the Strand
Dancing school	c. November, 1685	Walbrook
Vendu	1689	Next to Bedford-gate in Charles St. Covent Garden
Large room	c. January 1693	Freeman's Yard, Cornhill
Hickford's Room	December 6, 1697– c. 1738	Between Panton and James Streets
Hickford's Great Room[b]	c. 1738–c. 1780	No. 41 Brewer Street

[a]Scott (1937) gives this date. Elkin (1955: 37) notes the performance of *Esther an Oratorio* on July 20, 1732, "appears to be the last event worth recording in the history of the York Buildings concert room."
[b]Burney noted in 1744 that "the only subscription concert at the west end of the town at this time, was at Hickford's room or dancing school, in Brewers-street" (Elkin: 45). It measured 15.2 × 9.1 × 6.7m high, with a coved ceiling and a platform at one end. By mid-century it was *the* place to attend concerts.

known as the Villiers Street Room) has been called the "first room specially designed for commercial concert giving" with the date of first reference 28 March 1680 (Harley 1968: 147). However, there may have been performances there as early as 1678 under a license to Thomas Mace. Mace was one of the first to promote the idea of building a room specifically for the presentation of musical concerts in 1676. There is no evidence Mace actually constructed the room; instead, he settled for a license to hold musical performances, issued in 1678. Though it is reported that the likes of Purcell and a variety of British and foreign virtuosi performed at the York Buildings under Mace, there is no evidence that such performances occurred prior to the date given by Harley (Young 1980: 616; Tilmouth 1957: 14).

A closely related category of performance event was the growing practice of benefit concerts that occurred at the York Buildings and other venues. One of the first recorded instances of the phrase "For the benefit of . . ." appeared in concert notices in January 1698. Such events were usually for the benefit of the person(s) who gave the concert, as the notice from the 6 January 1698 issue of *Flying Post* indicates (Scott 1937: 387):

> In *York Buildings*, On Monday the 10th of this instant *January*, at the
> request of several Persons of Quality, will be a Concert of Vocal and Instru-
> mental Musick, never performed there before; beginning at the usual hour;
> for the Benefit of Mr. *King* and Mr. *Banister*.

The purposes of benefit concerts are obvious: income and exposure. The income derived would certainly be welcome. More important, this particular type of productive relationship, culminating in a direct exchange of labor for money, could be considered the "purest" form of remuneration for labor. One organizes, promotes, and performs at an event where all net income is gar-nered by the individual(s) involved. Benefit concerts also provide an excel-lent example of the lack of division of labor in the relations of production of the performance event—differentiation that becomes more and more evident as both productive and consumptive relations become entrenched later in the eighteenth century and the scale of such events expands to make such differ-entiation profitable.[8]

Weber (1977) has also identified the importance of benefit concerts later in the eighteenth century in launching a larger performance career. He suggests that as interest in amateur musical training increased through the century, so too did the need for music teachers in bourgeois and aristocratic homes in Lon-don. Not only did such efforts provide a stable income for musicians, it also provided a means of networking to increase exposure among the upper and upper-middle classes.[9] Exploiting the social relationships developed through teaching and private interactions, these benefits "had audiences primarily of the families for which the sponsor had taught or performed, since hiring a musician for such purposes carried with it an obligation to buy tickets to his or her annual concert" (Weber 1977: 8). Although such benefits were largely lim-ited to the musicians' circle of personal relationships (Supicic 1985: 257), the practice was pervasive through the eighteenth century with such notable per-formers as Gasparini, Gottfried Finger, Baptista Drahgi, Margarita de l'Epine, and Nicola Matteis holding benefits (Scott 1937: 387; Tilmouth 1957: 18).

Returning to our discussion of venues, a third, unnamed room was also considered of some importance. Starting as a Bow Street, Covent Garden, concert room, the concerts held there were joined with those held at York Buildings in October 1689. The Bow Street concerts had apparently been regarded highly as they claimed royal patronage through proprietors Robert King and Johann Franck, who had received a royal patent to hold concerts there from William III. In 1691 the concerts moved to Charles Street into a room subsequently referred to as La Vendu or Vendu. By 1691, both the Vendu and the York Buildings were reported to have relatively well-established weekly concerts (Tilmouth 1957: 17).

Although Scott (1937: 381) makes an uncorroborated claim that the Vendu "was expressly built for concerts," given the very short history of public concerts it seems unlikely. To make such an assertion would suggest that there was enough demand and enough likelihood of profit for someone to provide the capital necessary to build a venue specifically for music. If such construction did occur, it would be more than likely that the name of the venue would more accurately reflect its purpose, and that the presence of such rooms in the musical history of London would have significantly more prominence than they appear to have. In either event, these venues provided the next step in the reconfiguration of productive relations in the move out of public houses, where audiences were likely to be whether music was present or not, to a venue where an audience would attend solely for the consumption of a musical performance.

Finally, pleasure gardens provided a third type of venue to be coopted by musicians in order to gain access to payment for performance. From the late seventeenth century the gentry and the landed aristocracy began spending much more time in London and environs during the off-season (May to October) instead of returning to the country (Tilmouth 1957: 23). This dramatically increased the presence of moneyed classes as a potential audience in London. Attending promenades was also a common recreation (Corfield 1990), reflecting quite closely what was available in the pleasure gardens. Weber (1977: 13) notes that a "promenade" usually involved a large-scale orchestral concert, drawing crowds typically between one thousand and three thousand at a shilling per person. Promenades thus provided an important parallel to attending pleasure gardens—essentially parks or open areas that had been cordoned off to supply entertainment to those who paid an admission (figure 4).

Of this collection of pleasure gardens, the most widely regarded and emulated were the Vauxhall Gardens and its rival, the Ranelagh Gardens (Corfield 1990: 136):

> Tree-lined avenues were laid out, with fountains, statuary, lamps, musicians, food stalls and dining booths. Many provincial "Vauxhalls" were named after the famous Spring Gardens of south London, while others aped "Ranelagh", the rival venue at Chelsea, open to great fashionable success in 1742 . . . Entrance fees preserved some social discrimination, but a degree of hurly-burly and popular support was essential for success.

Vauxhall and Ranelagh represented the most fashionable of the pleasure gardens. Vauxhall was free from its opening in 1661, but, in line with Banister's concerts a decade later, "visitors called for what they liked and paid accordingly" (Southgate 1912: 148). In 1736 a per capita admission of one shilling was charged, which remained unchanged to 1792. Ranelagh was considerably more expensive, charging 2/6d. admission, or 5/- on nights when fireworks were presented (Corfield 1990: 163n).

At the other end of the spectrum were gardens that were never visited by "persons of quality." Of Sadler's Wells, an author of a local travel guide in

Figure 4. Pleasure gardens in and near London known to have had music, c. 1659–c. 1745.

Name	Date	Location
Marylebone Gardens	c. 1659–1778	—
Belvedere Tea Gardens	c. 1664–1876	Pentonville Road
Vauxhall Gardens (prev. New Spring Garden)[a]	1661: Music intro. 1667	Lambeth
Islington Spa[b]	c. 1684	Islington
Sadler's Wells[c]	1684–post 1879	Clerkenwell
London Spa	c. 1685–1754	Between Rosomon and Exmouth Streets
Cuper's Gardens	1691–c. 1750	Lambeth
Lambeth Wells[d]	c. 1697–c. 1829	Lambeth
Pancras Wells	c. 1690s	—
Hampstead Wells[e]	August 18, 1701	—
Adam and Eve Tea Gardens	c. 1718–pre 1811	Tottenham Court Road
Lord Cobham's Head	1728–c. 1744	Cold Bath Fields
New Wells	c. 1737–1750	Near London Spa
Marble Hall	1740–1813	Vauxhall
Mulberry Garden	1742–1752	Clerkenwell
Ranelagh Gardens	1742–1805	Chelsea
Sir John Oldcastle Tavern	c. 1744–1746	Faringdon Road
White Conduit House	c. 1745–1849	Penton Street

Compiled from Croft-Murray 1980; Harley 1968.

[a]The proprietor, Tyers, had provided orchestral music and in 1745 added vocal music (Hyde 1985: 183).
[b]Admission for "watering" and entertainment was threepence (Harley 1968: 150).
[c]Pre-1700 music was played from 11A.M. to 1P.M.; admission was a sixpence/person (Young 1965: 42).
[d]Admission was threepence. Harley (1968: 150) A "Post Boy" advertisement of 11 May 1697 stated admission at one shilling.
[e]Admission ranged from one shilling to half-crown for the concert (Harley 1968: 150).

1699 suggests that there is far more than music to draw a crowd: for five Guineas a gentleman known as the "ingurgitating monster" would "swallow a live cock, feathers, spurs, and all." Epsom Wells was not much different. Though it boasted "Eight MUSITIANS [sic] and a TRUMPET" for the amusement of the patrons, "the fact that ladies were not required to pay anything for admission, makes one wonder whether any ladies other than professionals ever frequented the place" (Tilmouth 1957: 27, 24).

The presentation of music at pleasure gardens was important for several reasons. First, and perhaps most important, it was yet another outlet for musicians to exchange their labor for money early in the post-Restoration period, and indeed, briefly during the Interregnum. Such an opportunity was not viewed lightly, for a wide variety of musicians both composed music specifically for the gardens and performed at them regularly through the eighteenth century, including Handel, Mozart, Haydn, Arne, Hook, Arnold, Storace, Boyce, and Dibdin (Southgate 1912: 141). Second, it was another venue in which individuals who clearly had money to spend on entertainment (be it a shilling or much more) could emphasize the connection between direct payment to musicians, or the payment of admission, with the consumption of a musical entertainment. Certainly not all gardens relied heavily on music as part of their promotion. Nevertheless, there was an effort to provide music at a great number of gardens, indicating at least a generalized appreciation for the music itself. Finally, it was another venue for the promotion of the music, getting individuals interested in new pieces, and allowing both composer and performer to benefit from a growing interest in music by the public. Perhaps, as today, someone attending a garden would find a performance particularly appealing and actively seek out the performer and/or composer at another venue, or buy a printed version of the score.

The identification of a determinate form of appropriation of the economic surplus is quite easy within London's new capitalist economy. Within the capitalist mode, the form surplus typically takes is currency. As the feudal mode of production that once prevailed in England transformed into a capitalist economy, the musician in particular was no longer supplying musical entertainments as part of a larger role within a feudal household. In the feudal mode, the extraction of value from the employee by the feudal lord was done through service, either labor in the case of agricultural workers, or through composition and performance in the case of musicians belonging to a feudal household. In the transition of the general economy to a capitalist mode, the extraction of surplus shifts to a monetary form. This is due to the change in the nature of the relationship between employer and employee. Rather than trading value in kind (land for labor, for example) the wage-labor relationship of capital only offers a monetary extraction through the difference between the cost of labor and means of production to the capitalist and the value of the product sold to a consumer willing to pay such a price.

Surplus extraction in a monetary form affected the musicians involved in these early performance activities in a manner that was, to a limited extent, in their favor. In their use of preexisting venues, musicians of the day would have the advantage of having control of their own labor, as well as controlling their own means of production. This reflects the fact that within the performance environment, the musician was often both labor and capital, owning the means of production (instruments) and using such means to create the product (music). Thus, whether the musicians chose to solicit donations for requests or set out advertisements to solicit customers to pay admission, they were largely in control of both the performance and the collection of the surplus.

It should also be noted that in terms of the amount of risk in the capital-ized relationship, the greater the risk, the greater the possibility of larger and larger amounts of surplus that could be extracted. In the first instance, the performer as their own owner and labor, has very little to risk by doing as Banister or Wellington are reported to have done: gather a few people together and "call for what they please" in return for a small sum. In this case, the risk of loss of their capital is very small—they already own their instruments and, especially in a public house, there are certainly few costs incurred that could not be covered by the venue owner through patron con-sumption, rather than extracted out of the performer/audience relationship.

In the case of the impresario, we have already begun to move into a new level of stability and assurance in the social life of the public concert. For an impresario to be successful, capital costs must be established up front, ensur-ing that the performers (labor) and the venue owners (capital) are secured at a set rate. It is then incumbent on the impresario to ensure that the admission paid to attend the event exceeds capital costs. There is, of course, consider-able risk in this process as the impresario is liable for the payment of these capital costs whether the received income meets these costs or not. An excel-lent example is the case of "eager, inexperienced" opera impresario John Vanbrugh, who, in an attempt to capitalize on the perceived demand for Ital-ian opera in 1708, was left "broke in just four months, caught in a predictable bind between high salaries and receipts that were lower than anticipated" (Milhous and Hume 1993: 29). Naturally, if the impresario is successful and the income generated is in excess of the capital costs, a profit is earned and the entire set of productive relations is considered an economic success. Indeed, it is a success within the context of a capitalist mode of production because the impresario was able to successfully exploit the value of the labor expended for a profit.

Finally, there is the case of the venue owner staging performances as a means of extracting surplus from the labor of the performers. In many respects, this is simply an extension of the impresario relationship to include the ownership of the venue. In the early stages of the development of the pub-lic concert, the venues were constructed and used for an alternative purpose: as a public house, a large multipurpose presentation room in a fashionable address, or a pleasure garden where music is simply an added attraction. What could be considered the sign of the final phase of the entrenchment of public concerts in the consumption environment of eighteenth-century Lon-don is the commitment of capital to construct venues *specifically* for the per-formance of musical entertainments.

Opera had been able to accomplish some of this stability through a com-bination of Royal patents, patronage, and the generalized support of the aris-tocracy. Public concerts, however, had been adopted by a range of classes as a suitable pastime that was affordable to the majority of those participating in consumer society (Stone 1984; Weber 1977). By the middle of the eighteenth century, evidence of specifically constructed London-area concert rooms begins to appear (Forsyth 1985). The investment of considerable capital in these rooms marks the establishment of public concerts in the mainstream of musical consumption opportunities. Perhaps more important, commitment to such construction affirmed that the relations of production of musical enter-tainments had solidified to the point where some level of consumption can be predicted. As Todd (1989: 112) points out, "Modes of perception do not change arbitrarily but in response to real socio-economic developments." By the mid-eighteenth century, such modes of perception of the value of public concerts were becoming firmly entrenched.

Although beyond the stated chronology of this discussion, the final stage in the development of the performance venue was the building of large rooms and halls to accommodate the increasingly prodigious audience for instru-mental and vocal concerts. These rooms were to be regarded as music venues in their own right, not as multipurpose rooms where music was a secondary concern. The construction of The Music Room in Oxford in 1748 (despite being outside London), Carlisle House (c. 1765), Pantheon Theater (c. 1772), Tottenham Street Rooms (c. 1772) and the Hanover Square Rooms (c. 1775) marks a definite advancement in the relations of concert production (Young 1980; Forsyth 1985; Hyde 1985). The life of the Pantheon Theater is also instructive in highlighting the differences between opera production and the presentation of concerts. The Pantheon Theater opened on Oxford Street in January 1772 and was considered the crown jewel of London theaters of the time: "Obviously no expense had been spared on its design or decoration and it attracted not only the most famous performers of the day, but also the most glittering audiences which often included the King and Queen" (Hyde 1985: 186). Its designated purpose was for "masquerades, balls, and music, with orchestral concerts every two weeks followed by a ball" (Forsyth 1985: 32).

When the King's Theatre, Haymarket, burned down in 1787, a four-year license was granted to the Pantheon to stage Italian opera while the King's Theatre was being rebuilt. Taking almost four years to be converted for opera production, the Pantheon was ready at about the same time the new King's Theatre was opened. Both produced operas and both lost money until the Pantheon burned down on 14 January 1792 (Forsyth 1985: 34–35). The opera conversion provides a particularly good example of the financial and com-mercial risks of opera production. The time-consuming conversion of the Pantheon demonstrates the technical specificity of opera venues of the time compared to nonstaged performances. However, the fact that the consumer marketplace could not (or would not) support two opera houses further illus-trates the advantage of reconfiguring productive relations in order to exploit the attendance of public concerts. The costs of production were certainly lower, and so the cost of admission could be lower while still maintaining a margin of surplus. As Fischer (1963: 49) pointed out, "Personal patronage was superceded by a free market. . . . The work of art was subjected more and more to the laws of competition."

The development of permanent, dedicated venues for musical performance is strong evidence for the manifestation of the third and fourth components of a productive mode: the development of a division of labor and the development of a certain level of productive forces. It becomes clear that as the productive forces of capital continue to expand, the labor force also evolves to meet the demands of the relationships necessary to push the mode forward.

As public concerts and English society as a whole moved into the mid-eighteenth century, capitalist relations of production continued to entrench themselves as the predominant productive relations of English society. The impact of this development can be seen in the organization of public concerts. Again, the growth of venues specifically constructed for the presentation of musical works highlights this development. These buildings represent the development of the productive forces encapsulating the musical event to such an extent that the public concert is no longer simply a diversion in a public house. The construction of concert rooms for such performances suggests the refinement of the means of production for performances to include direct consideration of the utility of the material conditions of performance. The rooms were built to take into consideration the comfort of the performers and audience, the arrangement of the audience to maximize the acoustical qualities of the room, and ultimately, the choice of materials with which the room is constructed to optimize the spatial and aural parameters of the performance events (Forsyth 1985).

The organization of production itself also began to become more normalized. No longer was the notion of charging an admission for an assortment of musical entertainments an unusual occurrence. By the middle of the eighteenth century, different roles within the range of productive relations were being expanded to better exploit the labor of the musicians. Musicians no longer considered public concerts as one option in a strategy to continue to develop their careers. The public concert soon became the most important means for presenting themselves and new musical material to the public. Public concerts became key income-generating events in the lives of most musicians.

Interestingly, it appears that to a large extent it was musicians from the Continent who were eager to take advantage of the opportunities that the new relations of production presented. Contemporary observer Roger North (in Tilmouth 1957: 14) pointed out early in the eighteenth century that Continental musicians discovered "the Grand secret, that the English would follow Musick & drop their pence freely, of which some advantage hath been taken." Westrup (1941) and Leppert (1988) certainly agree with North: in Leppert's words,

> Music increasingly functioned as entertainment which a (passive) audience paid for and which was increasingly performed by foreign, especially Italian, professionals, who came to England—in what was viewed by the natives as an invasion—seeking their fortune from public performance.[20]

Such an expansion of relations of production to produce public concerts undoubtedly produced considerable spin-off positions to support the increasingly capitalized infrastructure of performance: concert artists, composers, arrangers, teachers, and impresarios all had direct contributions to make to the performance at a public concert. Further afield, however, one could also include publishers, copyists, music dealers, printers, and engravers, to name a few occupations. As Brook (1975: 14) suggests, "What made this era exciting, even revolutionary, was the new freedom of choice brought about by a greatly increased demand for their [musicians'] wares." Weber (1977: 12) is more specific:

> The primacy of sheet music in [virtuosi] fame nonetheless made their concerts more than just the localized gatherings of the eighteenth century. When one went to a concert by Liszt or Thalberg, or even to one by a minor performer playing works by the giants, one went because of the fads which surrounded that music. The functioning of the relationships within the concert's life was now controlled by the larger musical market.

Weber's identification of the large—and increasing—sphere of productive relations that surround the performance event is key to the entrenchment of the public concert within the broader capitalized relations of eighteenth-century London. More specifically, it is the constellation of productive relations that quite rapidly envelop the public performance event that signify the broader expansion of the forces of production. Of course, key to this expansion was not only the creation of larger regional markets for printed music that supported public concerts, but also "the provision of a wider range of commercial and credit facilities so that the latent strengths of the economy can be more expertly, quickly and cheaply mobilized" (Walvin 1987: 151). Not only could the expansion of such economic capacity create more actual surplus that would be expressed in terms of nonsubsistence spending, but the greater the speed of movement of such resources, the greater the expression of presumed wealth, further supporting a wide range of consumable entertainments.

We can now return to consider the challenge put forth by Ehrlich at the beginning of this essay and consider whether a "convincing explanation for why it all happened" has been offered, particularly in reference to the broad economic changes of the time. I would not make such grand claims of the conclusions in this work. Much more important, however, I do believe this essay clearly demonstrates that a mode-of-production approach offers an important alternative for explaining the growth of public concerts in seventeenth and eighteenth century London.

A few readers may disagree with using the basic structure of a mode of production as the starting point to consider public concerts. In many minds, such performance events are musical, not economic. To a limited extent, I would be in agreement. However, there is little doubt that the factors so briefly outlined above—the upheaval of life during the Interregnum, the expansion in patronage from the aristocracy to include the newly moneyed middle classes, and the dramatic reconfiguration of productive relations in all areas of London life, including music—had a very important role to play in laying the foundations for the performance of the first public concert in 1672. In fact, in Banister's case, the organization of the concert had every appearance of being a straightforward exploitation of prevailing economic conditions and opportunities after his dismissal from court.

The tracing of parallel influence between the (re)actions of the larger economic forces in London and the changes in musical performance that led to public concerts has provided some insight into the interaction between larger economic forces and specific changes in both the forces and relations of production. The manner in which the capitalist mode of production extracts surplus through the exploitation of the wage-labor relationship is dramatic. The reconfiguring of relations of production for musicians was central in creating the perception that a performance of instrumental or vocal music was a commodity to buy and sell. There is no doubt that without this new type of productive relationship, public concerts would not have flourished as they did.

As these productive relations developed and became socially accepted, so too did the number and types of employment opportunities that surrounded the concert event. The persistence of the public's willingness to purchase admission to a musical performance allowed for the rapid development of the division of labor surrounding the public concert into a variety of different areas. More important, perhaps, was the concurrent development of the productive forces that supported both the existing relations of production while demanding greater degrees of control over the means of production.

This brief review of the elements of a mode of production has, of course, left out a final consideration of the ownership of the means of production. This is, in part, because there are two additional considerations that need to be taken into account when examining the rise of public concerts: the nature of musicians' ownership of their means of production in a capitalized economy; and the larger question of the role of the superstructure in the functioning of specific sets of productive relations.

In the first instance, the astute reader might be left wondering about the implications of the separation of a musician from their means of production as predicated by capital (Marx 1963). At first glance, the notion of the separation of the means of production from a musician's labor does not ring true for the reasons stated above—that the musician in all likelihood owns the instrument that is played in order for the product (the music) to be created. In this case, the musician would not meet Marx's conditions for participation in the capitalist mode of production. At its logical extreme, this example could also include singers, who quite clearly are the only "owners" of their means of production: the voice. While it would be possible for a violinist or pianist to play on an instrument not his own, it would be absurd to consider a singer applying his labor to produce music through another's voice.

If one attempts to measure the impact of the expansion of the capitalist mode using musicians as the test case, the result would be inconclusive at best, but would likely fail the measure. How then can the rise of public concerts—obviously a reorganization of productive relations among musicians to create a product for sale (a commodity)—be reconciled with the apparent failure of musicians to meet even the most basic of tests for their participation in capitalism? Marx (1960: 395) offers an explanation to account for this apparent double identity of musicians as both noncapitalist and capitalist:

> It is possible that these producers, working with their own means of production, not only reproduce their labour-power but create surplus-value, while their position enables them to appropriate for themselves their own surplus-labour or a part of it (since a part of it is taken away from them in the form of taxes, etc.). And here we come up against a peculiarity that is characteristic of a society in which one definite mode of production predominates, even though not all productive relations have been subordinated to it.

Understanding Marx's position is key to understanding the mechanism of the rise of public concerts. As capitalism expands, it does not necessarily convert all productive relations into exclusively capitalized wage-labor relations. It is clearly much more productive for capital simply to subsume existing productive relations within a larger network of capitalized relations in order to maximize the value of the object produced (Sayer 1987). What we see in the seventeenth century is exactly this process during the formation of public concerts. The method that musicians were using to combine their labor and their means of production was unchanged from centuries before. What the capitalist mode introduced was the mechanism through which the object being created (performance) could be delimited and purchased in a manner different from what was previously possible.

The simple efforts of Banister in the 1670s to organize a slightly different presentation evolved into the highly organized and publicized concerts a century later (McVeigh 1993). It is important to note, however, that the way the music itself was performed did not fundamentally change. The change was in the manner in which the reconfigured relations of production combined with expanded means of production (particularly venues) to extract surplus out of the relations of production that were already present in the creation of music. Musicians, realizing that the Interregnum largely destroyed what few opportunities had existed to secure a livelihood, took advantage of these new, broader relations of production (as did some nonmusicians) to explore alternative configurations and to exploit the new mechanisms for the extraction of surplus value.

One is left wondering, however, to what extent the changes leading up to the creation of the first public concerts made such concerts 'inevitable?' In addressing a question such as this, it becomes necessary to expand our view and examine the role of the superstructure in shaping the development of the force and relations of production that make up the economic infrastructure—in particular, the role that the politico-legal structures played in directing and shaping the possible opportunities for musicians to find employment in the post-Restoration period.

To understand the restrictions—especially legal restrictions—that musicians were under at the time, we must return to the issue of patronage a century prior, to the mid-sixteenth century. Patronage in England was not primarily an economic obligation as was commonly the case on the Continent. As a result, patrons were less likely to foot the bill for the endeavors of members of their households. In the theater community, despite the fact that theaters were largely self-sustaining commercial enterprises, the patron was still an important figure for political and legal protection (Oates and Baumol 1972: 143). For musicians, however, such patronage was critical (Price 1981). As Wainwright (1997: 1) asserts

> It is a truism to state that patronage was of vital importance to English musicians of the seventeenth century. A musician could not operate as an isolated individual at that time: he was utterly reliant upon institutional or noble patronage. An individual's personal advancement could only take place through the assistance of a well-placed and well-disposed patron or sponsor, and the patron-client relationship was an essential part of the social mechanism of the seventeenth century.

The importance of this type of relationship was not simply a question of prestige or security on the part of performers, as much as such restrictions were required by Queen Elizabeth I in an act passed in 1572 (6 Elizabeth c.5, with similar statutes 18 Elizabeth, c.13, and another in 1597). The law stated that (Marx 1963: 687):

> Unlicensed beggars [including "Comon Players in Enterludes & Minstrels"] above 14 years of age are to be severely flogged and branded on the left ear unless some one will take them into service for two years; in case of a repetition of the offence, if they are over 18, they are to be executed, unless some one will take them into service for two years; but for the third offence they are to be executed without mercy as felons.

Such punishments may or may not have been carried out, given that they seem unusually severe. Nonetheless, such legislation would have served its purpose in keeping actors and musicians away from unsanctioned public performance. The statutes continued with the addition of the following provision by James I (Marx 1963: 688):

> Whilst in prison they [beggars] are to be whipped as much and as often as the justices of the peace think fit. . . . Incorrigible and dangerous rogues are to be branded with an R on the left shoulder and set to hard labour, and if they are caught begging again, to be executed without mercy.

It is difficult to comprehend the severity of the punishment in connection with the nature of the offense. Nonetheless, these statutes persisted to the beginning of the Interregnum in 1642 and were carried into eventual consideration by the Cromwellian Parliament. It is at this point that the development of the statutes censuring efforts by performers, especially musicians, to make a living by soliciting payment on the streets reached its most pointed. Consistent with the content of the previous acts, Cromwell's Third Parliament (1656–57) further refined the statute, and

> passed an "Act against vagrants and wandering idle dissolute persons" in which it was ordained that "if any person or persons, commonly called fiddlers or minstrels, shall at any time after the 1st of July be taken playing, fiddling or making music, in any inn, alehouse, or tavern, or shall be taken proffering themselves, or desiring or intreating any person or persons to hear them play or make music, in any of the places aforesaid" they should be adjudged rogues, vagabonds and sturdy beggars, and be punished accordingly. (Scott 1936: 448)

It is perhaps ironic that the Enclosure policies prior to the Restoration, in addition to the edicts of the Cromwellian Parliament, were largely responsible for forcing many musicians out of traditional patronage relations (Woodfill 1953). From the stress on the aristocracy that resulted in the release of musicians from households, to the banning of instrumental music during church services, to the prohibition of finding one's own opportunity in public houses, the Interregnum proved very difficult for musicians. Whether a result of public pressure or simply a recognition of the changing nature of activities or the values of the time, the statutes were not repealed until the beginning of the eighteenth century with 12 Anne, c.23.

Three comments can be made concerning the impact of such restrictive legislation. First, these statutes put patrons in England into an enviable position. Patrons could exploit a performer's need for their protection and at the same time minimize their economic obligation to the performer. Furthermore, in providing such patronage, patrons would not only ensure a supply of performers to enjoy virtually at their command, but could enjoy the prestige and status that would accrue from being the patron of a successful theater company or esteemed composer or performer without the fixed capital expense of doing so. In effect, a traditional feudal relation had, by the late sixteenth century, taken on the appearance of having been transformed into a capitalized, wage-driven, event-specific relationship.

Second, with the foundations of feudal relations already in jeopardy at the beginning of the seventeenth century, the marketplace provided little opportunity for professional musicians. If patronage was hard to come by and offered little by way of financial advantage, and public performance was deemed illegal without patronage, it seems likely that a significant portion of musicians must have sought work outside of England or in other fields. Of course, prevailing opinion was not necessarily in support of the performers; or, as Woodfill (1953: 3) so eloquently states, "Men seldom think music essential: if musicians hunger, let them work at an honest and useful calling." There is little doubt, however, that the legislation severely limited the options that musicians had at the time. As a result, the post-Restoration period must have seemed rich with opportunity for those wishing to perform.

Finally, on a more abstract note, the tenure and eventual repealing of the act appears to parallel the efforts of the politico-legal superstructure to preserve existing productive relations. The demands of the legislation that performers belong to a household continued to reinforce the predominance of feudal relations and the power of the lord of the household over his employees. The efforts to discourage workers from leaving the households (or not belonging to one in the first place) and the punishments meted out to those who attempted to find alternate productive relations for livelihood, further impeded the advancement of the strictly economic relations engendered by capitalism. The fact that the act was repealed at a time when capitalism was really beginning to flourish, and that public concerts grew out of the very venues that the act targeted in stamping out performance, seems to illustrate quite clearly the positive impact for musicians of the infrastructure/superstructure dialectic that was developing so rapidly at the end of the seventeenth century.

This essay has, from its inception, been a work of exploration. Ultimately, the vagaries of history are such that we may never know the details of the earliest public concerts, and as a result may never be able to adequately theorize their origins. However, the breadth of the argument presented here should, at the very least, spawn thought and discussion on the relationship between the dynamics of the transition from a feudal to a capitalist mode of production as the predominant productive mode, and the impact that such a transition might have on the concrete productive relations underlying the public presentation of music. The rather sweeping tone of much of this discussion quite deliberately obscures many of the counterarguments that might exist. Discussions of the feudal/capital transition itself are rife with disagreement (see Hilton 1976), let alone any consensus about the effects of such an economic transition on specific cultural elements.

The restriction of much of the discussion to the seventy or so years after the Restoration may also be a point of contention. Indeed, earlier I noted that the first dedicated concert venues do not appear until 1748 and in Oxford, no less. To ignore such a development would be negligent. However, to ignore the decades prior to such a development would be doubly so. To this end, I would take issue with McVeigh's (1993) contention that the inarguably rich concert life of the latter half of the eighteenth century had more to do with the aristocratic support such events received than with the middle-class adoption of public concerts for their own amusement.

On one point I would agree: the consumption of public concerts was undoubtedly part of the range of entertainments of the upper classes. The success of J. C. Bach and Karl Abel in the 1770s and 1780s would not have been possible without the support of the aristocracy. Nor would we have seen the success of the first concerts by Small-Coal Man Thomas Britton a century before. What I believe is missing from the formulation is the fairly solid evidence that such concerts—while attended by many of the upper class— were priced at a level that was affordable to those of middle-class means. This is particularly true of performances by the likes of Banister or the various pleasure gardens where patrons "called for what they pleased and paid accordingly." To argue that the middle classes were not involved would also be to ignore the dramatic alterations in the productive relations of the musicians of the time. The loss of aristocratic patronage by the few fortunate enough to have had it was hard enough. However, the flood of performers into London through the sixteenth and seventeenth centuries—to such a degree that a letter of patent was issued in 1635 to form the Company of Musicians in a vain attempt to stem the flow (Woodfill 1953)—would simply place too many demands on the upper-class consumer. It would seem to be naive to ignore the income potential in performing to larger numbers of people for a lower cost per admission—taking the first steps toward appealing to a "mass" musical culture (Thirsk 1990; Supicic 1985; Weber 1984).

The interest and potential of a mode-of-production approach to music is amply demonstrated within this volume alone. The inclusion of basic economic processes to the analysis of artistic production of any kind may, at first glance, seem cynical—a disregard for the creative element in such productive arenas. Yet to ignore the necessity of all laborers to require a basic level of subsistence in order to continue to produce would be careless. In this particular case, the rise of public concerts—a type of organization that is still very much an economic force in musical life—illustrates the utility of tracking the capitalization of such productive relations.

There is clearly much more work to do. To better understand the economic basis for artistic and musical production of any kind is not to ignore the creative element that makes such endeavors invaluable for expressing the richness of the cultural life of a society. Indeed, to raise awareness of the impact that economic organization can have on such practices will give us all a better understanding of the pressures that face those in our communities who commit themselves to such creative ventures. More important, such awareness will also help to provide a basis from which to help protect and nurture those who add color and sound to our lives.

Notes

1. The period from approximately 1642 to 1660 is referred to in a number of different ways: the Interregnum (period between the reign of Charles I and Charles II); the Civil War (period of violence between the monarchists and the Puritans led by Oliver Cromwell); along with additional references to the rule of the Cromwellians—the period of the Long Parliament (1650s) or of the Commonwealth. I will use Interregnum or Civil War, depending on which is more appropriate to the context.
2. As a point of interest, Tilmouth (1957: 14n) suggests that the first public concerts on the Continent were the Concert Spirituel in France in 1725.
3. General admission at the public theaters was 1 penny, the best seats at 3 pence, and the Lords seats at 6 or even 12 pence. Private theaters started at 6 pence, up to 1 shilling or 1/6d: "occupants of sixpenny seats were sneered at as 'groundlings' " (Oates and Baumol 1972: 143).
4. It is important to note that despite fairly strong evidence suggesting that the modern rules of admission were firmly in place, as late as 1689 such rules were still being negotiated. While the basic terms of admission were as we understand them, there was a loophole in theater admission that one did not have to pay admission if one did not stay for the entire performance, "a state of affairs that was endlessly abused." The practice of charging admission to public concerts was adopted from the theaters, complete with abuses—so much so that in the 1689 license granted to Robert King to hold concerts (Tilmouth 1957: 19) stated that "all were required 'to forbeare rudely or by force to enter in or abide there during the time of performing ye Musick without observing such Rules & paying such prices as shall be by him sett down'. In enforcing this all the officers 'Civill and Military' were to lend their assistance."
5. Taverns have a very long history in England, dating to the twelfth century. In 1309, 354 taverns were reported operating in London (Clark 1983: 11).

6. Clearly some musicians did not enjoy such portability—organists in particular. Though a relatively infrequent case, organists would still, nonetheless, enjoy control over their own labor power.
7. Because the York Buildings also provided a very fashionable residential address, the York Buildings Room (or Villiers St. Room), was occasionally referred to after the current resident—two known examples are Sir Richard Steele's Great Room and Mr. Topham's Great Room (Scott 1937: 383). Such variations in nomenclature illustrate "how extraordinarily slipshod they were over such terminological matters in the seventeenth century." This provides yet another reason why accurate verification of the actual number of concert rooms in London at this time is so difficult (Scott 1937: 381).
8. It must be added that there is also the possibility of losing money on such a venture if additional costs are incurred (rental fees, materials, advertising) in the course of putting on the benefit. See Milhous and Hume (1993: 78–79), for example.
9. Of course, the reverse was also true—teaching careers were built out of a well-regarded performance career (Sand 1944, for example).

References

Ashley, M. 1961. *England in the Seventeenth Century (1603–1714)*. Baltimore: Penguin.

Barber, W. J. 1975. *British Economic Thought in India, 1600–1858*. Oxford: Clarendon Press.

Bennholdt-Thomsen, Veronika. 1982. "Subsistence Production and Extended Reproduction. A Contribution to the Discussion about Modes of Production." *Journal of Peasant Studies* 9(4): 241–54.

Borsay, P. 1990. "Debate: The Emergence of a Leisure Town: Or an Urban Renaissance?" *Past and Present* 126: 189–96.

Brewer, J. 1980. "English Radicalism in the Age of George III." In *Three British Revolutions: 1641, 1688, 1776*, edited by J. G. A. Pocock, 323–67. Princeton, N.J.: Princeton University Press.

Brook, B. S. 1975. "Piracy and Panacea in the Dissemination of Music in the Late Eighteenth Century." *Proceedings of the Royal Musical Association* 102: 12–36.

Clark, P. 1983. *The English Alehouse: A Social History, 1200–1830*. London: Longman.

Corfield, P. J. 1987. "Class by Name and Number in Eighteenth-Century Britain." *History* 72(234): 38–61.

Corrigan, Phillip, and Derek Sayer. 1985. *The Great Arch: English State Formation as Cultural Revolution*. London: Basil Blackwell.

Ehrenberg, R. 1928. *Capital and Finance in the Age of the Renaissance*. Translated by H. M. Lucas. London: Jonathan Cape.

Ehrlich, C. 1976. "Economic History and Music." *Proceedings of the Royal Musical Association* 103: 188–99.

Elkin, R. 1955. *The Old Concert Rooms of London*. London: Edward Arnold.

Endell, F. 1968. *Old Tavern Signs*. Detroit: Singing Tree Press.

Fenlon, I. 1987. "Production and Distribution of Music in 16th- and 17th-Century European Society." *Acta Musicologica* 59(1): 14–16.

Fischer, E. 1963. *The Necessity of Art: A Marxist Approach.* Translated by A. Bostock. Hammondsworth: Penguin Books.

Forsyth, M. 1985. *Buildings for Music.* Cambridge: MIT Press.

Friedman, Jonathan. 1974. "Marxism, Structuralism, and Vulgar Materialism." *Man* 9(3): 444–70.

Grout, D. J. 1988. *A Short History of Opera.* 3rd. ed. New York: Columbia University Press.

Hackwood, F. W. 1985. *Inns, Ales, and Drinking Customs of Old England.* London: Bracken Books.

Hannay, D. 1926. *The Great Chartered Companies.* London: Williams and Norgate.

Harley, J. 1968. *Music in Purcell's London: The Social Background.* London: Dennis Dobson.

Hilton, R., ed. 1976. *The Transition from Feudalism to Capitalism.* London: NLB.

Hunter, D. 1986. "Music Copyright in Britain to 1800." *Music and Letters* 67(3): 269–82.

Hyde, N. 1985. *Four Faces of British Music.* Worthing: Churchman.

Laclau, Ernesto. 1971. "Feudalism and Capitalism in Latin America." *New Left Review* 67: 19–38.

———. 1985. *Hegemony and Socialist Strategy: Toward a Radical Democratic Politics.* London: Verso.

Lemire, B. 1990. "Reflections on the Character of Consumerism, Popular Fashion and the English Market in the Eighteenth Century." *Material History Bulletin* 31: 65–70.

Leppert, R. 1988. *Music and Image: Domesticity, Ideology and Socio-Cultural Formation in Eighteenth-Century England.* Cambridge: Cambridge University Press.

Lindenberger, H. 1984. *Opera: The Extravagant Art.* Ithaca, N.Y.: Cornell University Press.

Mabry, Donald J. 1990. "The Rise and Fall of Ace Records: A Case Study in the Independent Record Business." *Business History Review* 64: 411–50.

Marx, Karl. 1960. *Theories of Surplus-Value. Vol. 4 of Capital. Part 1.* Moscow: Foreign Languages Publication House.

———. [1887] 1963. *Capital. Vol. 1.* Moscow: Progress Publishers.

Marx, Karl, and Frederick Engels. 1947. *Literature and Art (Selections).* New York: International Press.

McCracken, Grant. 1988. *Culture and Consumption: New Approaches to the Symbolic Character of Consumer Goods and Activities.* Bloomington and Indianapolis: Indiana University Press.

McVeigh, Simon. 1993. *Concert Life in London from Mozart to Haydn.* Cambridge: Cambridge University Press.

Milhous, Judith. 1984. "Opera Finances in London, 1674–1738." *Journal of the American Musicological Society* 36(3): 567–92.

Milhous, Judith, and Robert D. Hume. 1993. "Opera Salaries in Eighteenth-Century London." *Journal of the American Musicological Society* 46(1): 26–83.

Neale, R. S. 1981. *Class in English History, 1680–1850.* Oxford: Basil Blackwell.

Oates, M. I., and W. J. Baumol. 1972. "The Economics of the Theatre in Renaissance London." *Swedish Journal of Economics* 74(1): 139–60.

Olmsted, Anthony. 1993. *The Capitalization of Music in London, 1660–1800.* M.A. thesis. University of Alberta.

————. 1999. *"We Shall Overcome": Economic Stress, Articulation and the Life of Folkways Record and Service Corp., 1948–1969.* Ph.D. diss. University of Alberta.

Price, C. 1989. "English Opera." In *History of Opera,* edited by Stanley Sadie, 38–46. London: Macmillan.

Price, David C. 1981. *Patrons and Musicians of the English Renaissance.* Cambridge: Cambridge University Press.

Qureshi, Regula Burckhardt. 2000. "Confronting the Social: Mode of Production and the Sublime for (Indian) Art Music." *Ethnomusicology* 44(1): 15–38.

Rea, K. G. 1990. "Theatre, The History of Western." *Encyclopaedia Britannica* 28: 531–54.

Richardson, A. E. 1934. *The Old Inns of England.* London: B.T. Batsford.

Rose, M. E. 1981. "Social Changes and the Industrial Revolution." In *Economic History of Britain Since 1700. Vol. 1: 1700–1860,* edited by R. Floud and D. McCloskey, 253–75. Cambridge: Cambridge University Press.

Sands, Mollie. 1944. "The Teaching of Singing in Eighteenth Century England." *Proceedings of the Royal Musical Association* 71: 11–33.

Sayer, Derek. 1987. *The Violence of Abstraction: The Analytical Foundations of Historical Materialism.* London: Basil Blackwell.

Schwarz, L. D. 1982. "Social Class and Social Geography: The Middle Classes in London at the End of the Eighteenth Century." *Social History* 7(1): 167–85.

Scott, C. D. 1976. "Peasants, Proletarianization and the Articulation of Modes of Production: The Case of Sugar Cane Cutters in Northern Peru, 1940–69." *Journal of Peasant Studies* 3(3): 321–41.

Scott, H. A. 1936. "London's Earliest Public Concerts." *Musical Quarterly* 22: 446–57.

————. 1937. "London's First Concert Room." *Music and Letters* 18(4): 379–90.

Shore, Lawrence K. 1983. *The Crossroads of Business and Music: A Study of the Music Industry in the United States and Internationally.* Ph.D. diss. Stanford University.

Soiffer, Stephen M., and Gary N. Howe. 1982. "Patrons, Clients, and the Articulation of Modes of Production: An Examination of the Penetration of Capitalism into Peripheral Agriculture in Northeastern Brazil." *Journal of Peasant Studies* 9(2): 176–206.

Southgate, T. Lea. 1912. "Music at the Public Pleasure Gardens of the Eighteenth Century." *Proceedings of the Royal Musical Association* 39: 141–59.

Stone, L. 1980. "The Results of the English Revolutions of the Seventeenth Century." In *Three English Revolutions: 1641, 1688, 1776,* edited by J. G. A. Pocock, 23–108. Princeton, N.J.: Princeton University Press.

————. 1984. *An Open Elite? England 1540–1880.* Oxford: Clarendon Press.

Supicic, I. 1985. "Early Forms Of Musical Mass Culture." In *Music in the Classical Period: Essays in Honor of Barry S. Brook,* edited by A. W. Atlas, 249–57. New York: Pendragon Press.

Thirsk, J. 1990. "Popular Consumption and the Mass Market in the Sixteenth to Eighteenth Centuries." *Material History Bulletin* 31: 51–58.

Tilmouth, M. 1957. "Some Early London Concerts and Music Clubs, 1670–1720." *Proceedings of the Royal Musical Association* 84: 13–26.

Todd, J. 1989. "Production, Reception, Criticism: Walter Benjamin and the Problem of Meaning in Art." In *Benjamin: Philosophy, History, Aesthetics*, edited by G. Smith, 102–25. Chicago: University of Chicago Press.

Wainwright, Jonathan P. 1997. *Musical Patronage in Seventeenth-Century England: Christopher, First Baron Hatton (1605–1670)*. Aldershot, England: Scholar Press.

Walvin, J. 1984. *English Urban Life, 1776–1851*. London: Hutchinson.

Weber, W. 1975. *Music and the Middle Class*. London: Croom Helm.

———. 1977. "Mass Culture and the Reshaping of European Musical Taste, 1770–1870." *International Review of the Aesthetics and Sociology of Music* 8(1): 5–22.

———. 1984. "The Contemporaneity of Eighteenth-Century Musical Taste." *Musical Quarterly* 70(2): 175–94.

Westrup, J. A. 1941. "Foreign Musicians in Stuart England." *Musical Quarterly* 27(1): 70–89.

Wolpe, Harold, ed. 1980. *Articulation of Modes of Production: Essays from Economy and Society*. London: Routledge and Kegan Paul.

Woodfill, Walter L. 1953. *Musicians in English Society from Elizabeth to Charles I*. Princeton, N.J.: Princeton University Press.

Wrigley, E. A. 1987. *People, Cities, and Wealth: The Transformation of Traditional Society*. Oxford: Basil Blackwell.

Wyn Jones, D. 1983. "Haydn's Music in London in the Period 1760–1790. Part One." *The Haydn Yearbook* 14: 144–72.

Young, P. M. 1965. *The Concert Tradition: From the Middle Ages to the Twentieth Century*. New York: Roy.

———. 1980. "Concert (ii)." *New Grove Dictionary of Music and Musicians*, edited by Stanley Sadie 4: 616–25.

7

Marx, Money, and Musicians

MARTIN STOKES

This chapter concerns the ways in which musicians get paid for producing music. Ethnomusicologists have often, oddly, ignored this topic, no matter how central it might be to the lives of those we study, and no matter how much the discipline of ethnomusicology is committed to understanding music materially. This may be partly due to the general prominence of hermeneutic models that privilege the reading of texts and tend to regard the material struggles of the world of text producers as at best a kind of parallel text to be subordinated to the text itself. Ethnomusicologists are still suscep-tible to disciplinary pressures from Western historical musicology, in which such models are influential, to say the least. Could it also have something to do with the inchoate senses of guilt many (of us) professional academics nur-ture as we contemplate both the grinding struggles of those we write about and, often, lives we ourselves have left behind? Whatever the reasons, ethno-musicologists have not routinely made it their business to discuss the ways in which money circulates in situations of music making.[1]

If we were to do so, we would in the first instance strengthen ethnomusi-cology's claim to be the one subdiscipline that insists on understanding music in the context of real lives and concrete social situations. In the second instance, we might begin to resist the teleological, historicist assumptions about the inevitably dominating "incursion" of money into musical worlds that a simplistic reading of Marx seems to supply. This would be to explore other and more productive ways of reading Marx, whose critical slant on modern culture, in my view, remains persuasive and absolutely undiminished by the collapse of "actually existing Marxism" in Eastern Europe and else-where. More specifically, touching on the subject of this chapter, we might begin to consider relationships between sentiment and commodity form in a rather more sympathetic and productive manner than that habitually associ-ated with Marxian cultural theory. We could thus consider how and when and

where a morally charged aesthetic practice might emerge with due compre-
hension and acknowledgment of the worlds of exchange—of money, labor,
commodity, affect, language, sentiment, and much else—in which musicians
actually move. And this, surely, would provide us with a firmer basis on
which to configure a critically engaged cultural practice than nostalgic or
utopian hermeneutics.

My case studies come from Mediterraneanist ethnography. This literature is particularly useful to my task. Mediterraneanist ethnography has
dwelt critically and at length on the categories of "premodernity," notably
forms of public sentiment and violence that have been considered to reside
within modernity's national and colonial spaces on Europe's fringe. Today,
notions of premodernity are insistently mobilized in relation to movements
for regional autonomy within the European Union, to the traumas of ethnic
violence in Eastern Europe, and to Islamist movements on the Mediterranean's southern and eastern shores. The movement of refugees and labor
migrants from, for example, Morocco, Algeria, former Yugoslavia, and eastern Turkey invest these discussions with a sense of urgency and, increasingly,
crisis in the metropolitan centers of Western Europe. The Mediterranean Sea
connects Europe to, and involves it with, those very Others whose historical,
political, and cultural exclusion defines modern European history, not only
for most Europeans but for those elsewhere who have absorbed their teaching
as a universal standard. Movements across it continue to call Europe and all
we believe it to stand for into question (see in particular Herzfeld 1987).
Questions about modernity and that which we assume to lie outside it thus
have a peculiarly sharp focus in this context.

Payment as Performance

The first example comes from my own fieldwork.[2] In the mid-1980s, I knew
two musicians from the eastern Black Sea province of Trabzon, Turkey,
whose attitudes toward payment, and much else, seemed to be diametrically
opposed. Ibrahim was from a village in the subprovince of Besikdüzü, which
comprised the coastal plane and the lower reaches of Agasar river valley.
When I first got to know him he was in his mid-twenties; he found employment as a singer at the Turkish Radio and Television there. By that stage he
was already probably making more money singing at weddings and in clubs,
and was appearing regularly on television. He was also contemplating marriage to a girl whose family came from Kars, in Eastern Anatolia, and a move
out of his predominantly Black Sea neighborhood to a large apartment block
near his prospective wife's parents.

Necmi was from a village in the subprovince of Salpazarı, higher in the
Agasar valley; he had dropped out of school and was whiling away a year
before military service, living with his mother and sister. At the age of seven-

teen, he epitomized the Black Sea '*delikanlı*', the "mad-blooded" young man. His quick wit, high spirits, and fine voice made him much in demand throughout the summer wedding season, and at music sessions in the summer high pasture festivals. He carried his dead father's gun in his pocket, promising trouble. This he duly delivered when, some years after I had first got to know him, he attended a wedding in a neighboring valley and eloped with a local girl. He made himself scarce in Istanbul, I gathered; I was never able to find him on subsequent visits, evidently with good reason.

From a metropolitan perspective, both were typical *Laz*, Black Sea provincials in the big city, the source of a genre of humor, part mocking and part affectionate. Both were associated with the *kemençe*, a short three-stringed fiddle, whose quick and fidgety music was quite different from the slow monophonic styles dominated by the *saz*, a long-necked lute much promoted in those years by the Turkish Radio and Television (TRT). Oddly enough, neither singer could play the instrument; both had to rely on others to do a job normally done by one person. Both could recognize themselves in terms of the metropolitan *Laz* stereotype. At the same time, both had a keen sense of the ways in which they were different from their Black Sea neighbors. They were descendants of Turkoman settlers in the Black Sea region in the fourteenth century, in this respect quite different from their immediate neighbors, speakers of Laz, Pontic Greek, and the Kurds on the other side of the mountains.[3] Their sense of distinction was maintained by a fairly strict system of endogamy, and through residence in remarkably self-enclosed migrant neighborhoods. Whether in Trabzon, Istanbul, or Stuttgart, Agarsarı had a reputation for remaining aloof.

There were major differences between the two musicians, though. Some of these were musical, relating to the kemençe and the state's national media project. Ibrahim had a kemençe in his backing bands, following TRT. For Ibrahim the kemençe was there primarily for symbolic purposes, an iconic presence in a musical texture whose sound was dominated by the saz. He was, though, preoccupied with ways of bringing the two different aesthetics together. Indeed, he understood his job at the TRT very much in these terms. He would experiment restlessly in his commercial recordings with putting together kemençes in groups of two, three, and more, with attempting to do without the saz in its entirety, with playing kemençe and other regional instruments together. There were enormous difficulties, not the least of which was finding kemençe players who could read musical notation, or were prepared to put up with the kind of work discipline that studio and concert work involved. There were a few younger players in Istanbul and Ankara at that time that could credibly deal with the musical demands of both worlds, but they were few and far between. Ibrahim was thus interested in finding some common stylistic standard that could embrace both the national (saz-dominated) and the regional (kemençe-dominated) style and allow for a process of musical exchange.

Necmi improvised, vocally, to the accompaniment of a single kemençe. He traveled the wedding scene in Agasar's upper valley with his taciturn friend, Mohamed, a superb kemençe player. Necmi was entirely uninterested in the TRT's musical style and had little time for the efforts of singers such as Ibrahim to reconcile the two aesthetics. For Necmi, the saz and the kemençe just played different kinds of music. If he or fellow musicians in the upper valley stopped to think about it, usually at my prompting, they would say that the kemençe was just "too quick" for the saz. One said that the thing about the kemençe was that it had "no notes on it." His companions laughed, assuming a bit of skillful and good-humored mockery, but the point was, on reflection, a good one, and the look on his face told me that he was trying to be serious. The saz has frets; one can identify pitches in musical space and time; it lends itself to transcription in Western musical notation. The kemençe has three strings, which are often played simultaneously, involving a drone and parallel fourths at formidable speed and with much ornamentation. As generations of TRT researchers discovered, this is phenomenally difficult music from which to extract a single melodic line, and almost impossible to transcribe in conventional Western staff notation.

The saz was not unpopular in the upper valley. Indeed, I went to a number of weddings to which a saz player had been invited. Kemençe and saz would alternate, and people simply switched from the one style of dancing to the other. The pleasures associated with each instrument were just "different," from Necmi's perspective. The saz was metropolitan and urbane. One could dance and sing along to recent arabesk hits, for example. It was a public pleasure, but of a somewhat individualistic kind. The kemençe, on the other hand, spoke of localized and communal pleasures associated with the *horon*, the line dance, the *meci* (from Turkish *imece*) work party, for which a good kemençe player was considered a valuable asset, and most notably *muhabbet* gatherings. A muhabbet could take place anywhere, though it involved only men. It would always involve rakı (aniseed liquor), some food, some decent cigarettes, and, of course, a kemençe. Its poetry, largely improvised in dialogue, drew on local stories of brigandage, dense poetic reference to landscape and the rituals associated with it, but also, in a veiled and opaque way, to matters of love and friendship. The ideal muhabbet was one in which sentiment, rakı, and cigarettes circulated freely in response to the kemençe's swaying and energetic rhythms. Necmi, at the age of seventeen, was already an acknowledged master of the muhabbet.

Ibrahim and Necmi accepted money for their music in very different ways, too. The material imperatives that governed their lives were, admittedly, very different. Ibrahim had to deal with life in Istanbul, and brothers and sisters for whom he assumed a large amount of financial responsibility. Necmi had only one sister, a large village house, and a generous insurance policy from Germany to draw on, activated by his father's recent death there.

But the differences between the two could be seen as part of a wider pattern. Ibrahim understood in fine and analytic detail the mechanics of turning music into money in Istanbul. He could weigh the advantages and disadvantages of his TRT post, live performance at weddings and clubs, and his recording career, and would expound on them at length to me as he was, I guessed, figuring them out in his own head. But he also had the explanation of the business logic of the music world down to a fine art. He could patiently sit down with the owners of a new Black Sea club, for instance, and explain to them exactly what kind of evening music programme their money would buy; he would do so in an entirely helpful and comprehensible manner. This was one of many things that made him extremely popular in this world, I suspect. He could also patiently explain to wedding hosts exactly how long he and his musicians were going to perform. Ibrahim's keen sense of abstract labor time was in fact often a source of conflict. Largely this was a consequence of the responsibility he assumed for members of his group, who didn't receive large sums of money for these gigs and had long journeys back home on public transport, with their equipment, to consider. When he performed for free (and paid his musicians out of his own pocket), he did so, usually, to repay a favor already paid to him or to establish a debt with a clearly definable objective.

He also had a very keen sense of music as commodity. He knew exactly what was involved in "collecting" a song, adapting, registering with the TRT, shaping according to the abstract exchange system of TRT folk music style, and laying claim to rights over the tune (not then yet absolutely enshrined by copyright). Ibrahim was not a calculating person, and was not unaware of the moral conundrums that his own rational calculations sometimes involved. For example, I remember him once finishing his performance at a distant relative's wedding in Istanbul absolutely on schedule, to the fury of the relative, who insisted he stay and keep the party going, though it was already late. The matter, as I remember it, was ultimately decided by appeal, on Ibrahim's part, to the Islamist municipality's recent ruling on live music after dark. The situation was not without irony, since Ibrahim was vigorously secular. This argument did at least serve to put the matter beyond further discussion: if he continued, he would be breaking the law, the police would be involved, and so forth. This was a matter of substantial discomfort to him, and he agonized over it for days. Ultimately, though, there was no reason, in his scheme of things, why music and money should not circulate freely, fluidly, and by means of the national media system, in a system of generalized commodity exchange.

Necmi seemed to scorn money, but was far from being indifferent to it. He would regularly boast about how much he had been offered to come and play at a wedding in neighboring villages and elsewhere—payment often in deutschmarks. Discussions of payment with wedding hosts were always veiled in an elaborate language of hospitality and honor; the precise sums involved were a secret, to be revealed precisely and only on occasions such as these, when one could put on a flamboyant performance of disinterest. One such conversation involved a (somewhat older) kemençe-playing friend from the neighboring village, who had been offered a very large sum of money to play at a wedding and had simply not turned up. He hadn't felt like it, he said. Whether or not these musicians actually showed up was a matter of extreme unpredictability and was always treated by hosts as a slight to honor and hospitality, which led to grudges lasting for years. But musicians such as Necmi seemed to delight in being unpredictable, indifferent to cash, and often difficult and demanding guests. It was almost as though this was expected of them, and their cash value went up the more they met this expectation. Necmi's elopement conformed entirely to this unstable logic, constituting the most explicit and shocking challenge to his hosts imaginable. He took the girl rather than cash, committing everybody involved to the structured violence and ferocious emotions of reprisal and counterreprisal. I presume, at least, that he didn't return for his fee.

This cultivated and often beautifully performed indifference to the cash economy extended to his attitude toward the national mass media. The Turkish friend who was traveling with me at the time had contacts in the TRT and was deeply worried by Necmi's reckless ways. This friend had somehow persuaded him and Mohamed, the kemençe player, to meet a kind of TRT talent scout in Giresun, the neighboring provincial capital. Everything was arranged. I think even bus tickets were brought. But Necmi and Mohamed didn't show up. There were probably plenty of reasons, but the opportunity to make a public statement about indifference to the state's media system would have been too good to miss, especially when it involved somebody from Istanbul (working on a degree in folklore at the State Conservatory, no less) and his English friend.

Mass media seemed to live their own, rather unruly, life in the upper valley, and Necmi's indifference was part of a general ethos. A short newspaper article in the national press related an incident in which a fight had broken out between the young men of two villages. One village had been using the local radio stations (just then beginning to be deregulated) to insult the women of the other village and taunt the delikanlılar. At least one person had been killed. In another incident, a song touching on the delicate subject of the famous beauty of the wife of a local man (Necmi's uncle, as it happened) was being played in a café. When the uncle, according to this well-storied account, entered the room, everyone froze. He walked over to the cassette player, unplugged it, walked out of the café with it, put it on a gate post, took his gun out, and blasted it to smithereens. Two extreme responses to the incursion of mass media, one might say, but indicative of the ways in which sound recording and public broadcasting were put to defiantly local use. At all moments in the upper valley, it seemed, the wider, abstract, and more fluid sphere of exchange was rejected in favor of social performances that localized and particularized.

The opposition of these two views of musical exchange could, from a certain perspective, be explained quite simply. The matter was relatively simple, at least for Ibrahim, whose viewpoint owed much to the TRT and to Turkey's modernizing elites. The kemençe would ultimately give way to the saz, or become something more saz-like, just as the local would give way to the national, and eventually the universal. Remote areas would be subordinated to increasingly higher-level ordering principles and more abstract patterns of exchange. Muhabbet, the world of intimate and localized moral sentiment, would disappear as a cultural ordering principle, though something of its spirit could be pleasurably reproduced in commodity exchange and a heightened and nuanced sense of national belonging. This view had tremendous local resonance too. The upper valley was seen, from the lower valley and the provincial capital, as remote and colorful, possessing in abundance something ("folklore") that they had once had in large quantities but had since lost with the gradual introduction of roads, electricity, the national labor market, and the extensive cash cropping of hazelnuts. But that something was always disappearing. Scholars and a local folklore industry attended the highland pasture festivals in force, documenting everything with tremendous anxiety as though it would shortly disappear from sight. Foreign researchers absorbed and reproduced this view in turn, giving it added prestige. Laurence Picken (1975: 325) commented briefly on the increasingly valued currency of the saz in 1975:

> In the coastal towns, the kemençe (box fiddle) is replaced among the settled urban population by the saz (long-necked lute) in its various sizes. A sailor from Akçaabat (Trabzon) for example, with a family shoe-making business to return to after his period of national service, is more likely to play the baglama (saz) than the kemençe.

Music has, it seems, only one possible history in the eastern Black Sea region. A more powerful force, associated with the nation-state and the commodity form, meets with a world of localized sentiments and exchanges. This latter has one historical role, and one only: to figure as difference, soon to be subordinated, disciplined, and administered by the higher and more abstract ordering principles of nation and commodity form. It might "persist," but does so as persistence against the odds, standing outside of history, a form of resistance or opposition whose ordering principles are entirely different. It is not difficult to read the contrast between Ibrahim and Necmi in these terms. Ibrahim came from a world given over to cash-cropping and close ties with national media and communications, very much bound to the modern state project. Necmi came from a world of decidedly premodern sentiments and moral solidarities. One might appear to find a ready source of agreement in Marx.

Marx on Money and Sentiment

"In money matters," Marx's worker said, "sentiment is out of place" (Marx 1976: 363). In this it would appear that he was in general agreement with most modernist thinkers, for whom, for better or worse, modernity and sentiment could not be reconciled. For Marx, there seems to be little doubt about the matter. As money's place expands, sentiment's place diminishes. Victory for the one necessarily entails defeat for the other. Marx's worker continues his address to the capitalist: "You may be a model citizen, perhaps a member of the Society for the Prevention of Cruelty to Animals, and in the odour of sanctity to boot; but the thing that you represent face to face with me has no heart in its breast. That which seems to throb there is my own heart beating. I demand the normal working-day because I, like every other seller, demand the value of my commodity" (364). For both parties involved, the moral sentiments associated with citizenship, religion, and the protection of defenseless creatures have no role to play in this elemental conflict, whose final and only arbiter, Marx reminds us coldly a few sentences later, is brute force. Modernity and social warmth stand firmly opposed.

Since the Romantic period, music has been seen as the most morally compelling form of social warmth. When music served to collectivize, it did so in a way that suggested that the primitive could be recuperated within the modern soul. When it individuated, it did so in a way that enabled people to see their individuated selves reflected in ever-widening circles of morally accountable others. It permitted the kind of sympathetic moral resonance earlier depicted by Hume and Smith, providing a vital counterpoint to the abstractions of Enlightenment political form and an antidote to the cold world of commodity exchange. It is not difficult to understand why "the arts aspired to the condition of music" in nineteenth-century Europe and beyond, and not difficult to understand why music became a secular religion, inevitably debased by its contact with the commodity form. From this perspective music and money do exist in separate moral spheres and are not easily exchanged.

This has generated well-known anxieties in music scholarship too, in which capital and the cash economy are often understood as eroding the bonds of sociality that music plays such an important role in forming. Accounts by ethnomusicologists and others of the transformations of musical life in industrial capitalism have stressed the disenchantment of commoditized musical worlds, especially when these have been engineered in some shape or form by the nation-state. Nostalgia hovers over questions of what music once might have been, and an ungrounded utopianism over the question of what it still could be. Western Marxism's hermeneutic turn has entrenched and institutionalized this tendency. What are the alternatives, though? Is this the only perspective on music that Marx's analysis of the commodity form permits? Does the exchange of money for music point in one historical direction only?

There are two sources to which one might turn to consider this issue in an abstract and theoretical light. One is the tradition of thinking in economic anthropology that is much concerned with the "embeddedness" of economic systems in social and cultural worlds. This tradition draws much from Mauss's influential discussion of the gift. It is concerned with the ways in which exchange produces moral solidarities, and is interested in the kinds of moral force reflected back on, and considered to inhere in, the objects of exchange themselves. In this respect, this view is quite the opposite of Marx's notion of the commodity fetish, whose character it is not only to obscure the social nature of the commodity, but also to cause those involved in its production to think of themselves in individuated thinglike terms too. Economic anthropology has primarily been concerned with understanding the relationship between diverse spheres of exchange, in which specific exchange media (women, cattle, brass rods, yams, and so forth) circulate according to diverse moral imperatives and symbolic logics. (See, for example, Bohannan and Bohannan 1968; Barth 1967; Bloch and Parry 1989.)

It is also much concerned with interpreting processes of change. When money has entered the equation, for example in a colonial context, two assumptions have prevailed. One is that Marx was right: money and the commodity form sweep the kinds of moral particularism associated with spheres of exchange into oblivion. For better or worse, this process is simply a matter of time. The other is that Marx was not so much wrong as culturally and historically limited in his view that money and the commodity form point in one historical direction only. Even in situations of rapacious colonial extraction, many anthropologists have argued, money and the commodity form enter into a dialectic and mutually constitutive relationship with local symbolic systems and spheres of exchange. This process of absorption is a creative and morally restitutive cultural response to forms of incursion marked by greater or lesser degrees of violence. In this view, money does not, morally speaking, have it all its own way. Money might, indeed, be used to structure and organize the very forms of sociality—based on bonds of affect and sentiment—that it is usually held to disrupt (Bloch and Parry 1989). This is a common theme in a number of (Western) Marxian efforts to recuperate the category of culture. The spinning of diverse and socially integrative symbolic logics around the commodity form was also a constant theme in subcultural theory, in which music held a distinctly privileged role. Both general tendencies posit a world dominated by capital, to which Marxian thinking can unproblematically be applied, countered or held in check by forces lying outside of capitalism, which ultimately require some other framework, or at least a supplementary framework, in order to be conceptualized.

Recent critical thinking, however, suggests that Marx's writings on money and the commodity form contain dialectical complexities that are often overlooked, sometimes by Marx himself (see, in particular, Postone 1996). I want to suggest that these complexities can be extremely useful in thinking about the ways in which people exchange money for music. Money is, indeed, a remarkably opaque category in Marx's thinking. First one has to distinguish between the youthful Marx of the (notorious) *On the Jewish Question* from the mature Marx of the *Grundrisse* and, later, *Capital*. In the former, Marx's view of money picked up on the primitivist and racialized hatred of money and trade that has run throughout Western history, much shaped by the medieval church. As he put it in an infamous passage:

> Money is the jealous god of Israel, beside which no other god may exist. Money abases all the gods of mankind and changes them into commodities. Money is the universal and self-sufficient value of all things. It has, there- fore, deprived the whole world, both the human world and nature, of their own proper value. Money is the alienated essence of man's work and exis- tence; this essence dominates him and he worships it. (1978: 50)

In the later works, Marx left the anti-Semitism of *On the Jewish Ques- tion* behind him and came to think of money in more complex historical terms.[4] These complexities emerge clearly in his *Grundrisse* notebooks, as he considers, in a lengthy analysis, how money operates in societies before capitalism. When capitalism emerges, he suggests, money always seems to carry with it something of its precapitalist past. Money has technical proper- ties that make it a significant component of the way in which capitalist soci- ety shapes itself, but the history of money and the history of capital formation come to be seen as two rather different, albeit interrelated, things.

> Money itself, to the extent that it also plays an active role, does so only insofar as it intervenes in this process as itself a highly energetic solvent, and to that extent assists in the creation of the plucked object-less free workers; but certainly not by creating the objective conditions of their exis- tence; rather by helping to speed up their separation from them—their prop- ertylessness. (1978: 271)

At issue, then, is not money per se, but the complex processes by which it is converted to capital. The senses in which money lives a social life con- nected to but also rather separate from capital itself are somewhat obscured in *Capital* by a heavier emphasis on money as fetish. However, in *Capital*, money's "dazzle" seems constantly to exceed its stated function as that "energetic solvent" which creates the "plucked object-less free workers" sep-arated from their own means of production. The riddle it presents is never easily solved. It is hard not to detect a tone of anxiety in Marx's formulation of this riddle and the need to resolve it in the pages of *Capital*. For here is something that lies close to the rational heart of capitalism that doesn't always behave as it should.

This anxiety extends to the commodity form itself, whose structuring not only by money but also by time and labor is not as straightforward a matter as some readings of *Capital* suggest. These complexities are of far-reaching sig-nificance to cultural analysis, and it would be worth emphasizing them briefly before returning to the category of money. Value in commodity exchange requires a common and abstract unit of measurement: abstract labor and abstract time. The value of the commodity, as Marx painstakingly demonstrated, derives from how long somebody takes to produce something according to these abstract criteria. The process of abstraction accompanies a struggle at the heart of capital's developmental process. To increase value, the capitalist must not only reduce the amount of time taken, but also trans-form the *kind* of labor that has gone into the making of a particular product. In this sense, capitalism systematically erodes the criteria on which it bases value (abstract labor and time). It is thus obliged constantly to reach beyond the world that it establishes in order to reconstitute itself.

If, as Marx constantly stressed, the commodity form "thinks us," and provides us with our fundamental categories of thought, the fact that it under-mines these same categories of experience as a basic aspect of its operation has far-reaching consequences. Capital appropriates labor in ways that it itself fashions; as it changes, so too does labor. The "critique from labor" associated with most strands of Western Marxism and with the "dictatorships of the proletariat" in Eastern Europe and elsewhere was based on a totalizing and transhistorical notion of labor. This is a view that one can easily derive from the currents of vitalism which seem to animate so much of what Marx himself had to say on the subject (Chakrabarty 2000: 60–62). In this view, labor was, so to speak, the real and unchanging thing appropriated and chan-neled by the bourgeoisie to its own ends with the help of its own corrosive ideologies. Labor, in this pristine and transhistorical sense, was to be recu-perated in a political act of redistribution. What has been missed was Marx's fundamental point that labor itself is constantly refashioned by capital. One can thus base no coherent notion of the working class as historical subject and agent upon it, since it is every bit as "partial" as the capital to which it is opposed. The notion of class does not, then, provide such a firm handrail in Marxian cultural analysis as one might assume. One must also view the romantic celebration of working-class musical cultures (which sometime emerge by default in the context of critiques of self-serving bourgeois musi-cal ideologies) with considerable caution.

The argument extends to the category of time, with, again, far-reaching consequences for Marxian cultural analysis and ethnomusicology. For if capitalism's abstract clock time was, like abstract labor, riven by a deep and abiding contradiction, the notion of empty, secularized, abstract time through which we habitually think of history and configure both the expansion of capital and resistance to it, must be rethought. Both modernization theory and underdevelopment theory work with a notion of abstract time through which capital's relentless logic is perceived to unfold. In both theories, capital encounters difference and subordinates it to its own demands. This is a process that takes place and can be calibrated in real and observable historical time.

Marx's historicism can seem unilinear, but it is clear from his own writing that he was also attentive to the ways in which the dialectics inherent in capital interrupt the temporal processes that it itself fashions. Chakrabarty has neatly summarized this somewhat underdeveloped aspect of Marx's thinking about history with the notion of type one and type two histories. Type one is the history that capital itself configures as the history inexorably leading up to (and by implication beyond) a particular formation. Type two might be understood as the history that type one selects from; an archive of possibilities generated by capital and by its encounter with difference, which might be constitutive of capital's next moment, but equally might not. Historically speaking, capital produces more than it requires for its own self-reproduction. This "excess," from the point of view of type one histories, comes to appear as traditions, customs, and redundant moral sentiments— leftovers from the past bound for historical oblivion. They are, of course, not only connected to capital's present but also very actively *constitutive* of that present. It is also often the case that history twos come not only to be associated with but also claimed by those who are marginal to capital's current moment of self-actuation. Type one and type two histories engage in a turbulent dialectic, which generate the complex and plural cultural worlds we actually inhabit.

Read sympathetically, Marx himself responds to two well-known tendencies in response to the issue of historical difference that his own writing subsequently generated. On the one hand is a perspective in which difference is encountered and eventually overcome by capital. On the other is a notion of capital, as global fact, creating difference itself according to its own demands and imperatives. In ethnomusicological terms, one might connect the first to Alan Lomax's (1968) influential notions of the "cultural greyout": colorful musical difference eroded by a homogenizing force—in the shape of mass media—that it cannot, in the final analysis, resist. The second would be instantiated by Veit Erlmann's (1993) equally forceful portrayal of capital's global dynamics as regards the World Music industry, in which capital cumulatively fashions a world of musical difference from within. This has the significant advantage of suggesting that we shouldn't immediately equate musical difference with something that either predates its encounter with capital or lies geographically beyond its reach. Both accounts, though, remain firmly lodged in type one history. Neither provides a means of grasping the historical excess that capital itself produces. To read musical worlds in terms of a productive and dialectical relationship between type one and type two histories, as Chakrabarty suggests, would result in a somewhat different picture. And here we might usefully return to the ethnographic literature on the payment of musicians.

Selling Musical Selves

Bernard Lortat-Jacob's various discussions (1994, 1995) of the professionalization of musicians in Morocco, Sardinia, and Romania elaborate a significant and compelling theory. He considers in intricate detail the relationship between communal solidarities structured and organized by music and the commodity logics that impinge on the lives of musicians. For Lortat-Jacob, this is essentially a relationship of opposition. The terms in which he draws this opposition are both stark and dramatically engaging. They range across space, in the first instance, in which Morocco and Romania are diametrically opposed. Communal mechanisms are embedded in music during Berber festivals in the Moroccan Atlas. The community, in a real, tangible, and direct sense, *is* its music. Communal and musical mechanisms are mutually constitutive. This interaction can be seen at work in the Berber *ahwash*, with its balanced reciprocity of male and female voices, its interlocking drums, and the slow process by which the dance gathers momentum and transforms itself into something above and beyond its constituent parts—the very definition of Durkheimian effervescence.

In Romania, by contrast, villagers have lost the capacity to create their own music. The vital task of generating a sense of community through festivity is left in the hands of professional *lautari*, Rom musicians, paid in cash. This is the source of extensive anxiety and a degree of friction between the two groups. The villages, though, seem to be fighting a losing battle, and appear to be well aware of what is entailed by their inability to generate festivity from within. They reconcile themselves to this loss of musical autonomy by turning the participating Rom musicians into exemplary "others" in their own rituals of self-affirmation. In this ritual space, Rom musicians "incarnent un autre façon de vivre, litteralement debordante et fondamentalement musicale" (Lortat-Jacob 1994: 126).

Sardinia sits between the two extremes in this analysis, or, rather, contains both extremes within it. *A tenore* singing and the genres performed in liturgical processions for Holy Week constitute extreme forms of musical solidarity—intimate, physical, tactile. Performance entails magical processes of communal transformation. The quartet singing the liturgical music hears a fifth voice, the quintina, emerge—an acoustic effect of combined overtones, or so one might rationalize it. For the male singers, though, it is heard as a woman's voice, that of the Virgin Mary. At the other extreme lie those musicians who cultivate eccentric and solitary musical fantasies. These are, in effect, fantasies of the musical commodity fetish, of styles of music, of kinds of musical technology, of styles of expertise valued as objects of desire in themselves, the pursuit of which separates these hapless eccentrics from the rich texture of exchange that structures Sardinian village life. Somewhere in between the two extremes, in the middle of this middle position, lie the quasi-professional musicians who supply accordion (*organettu*) music for provincial town dances. A certain amount of tension surfaces over the presence of outside musicians, but this has yet to result in a clear split between professional outsiders and communities. Organettu players clearly relish their fame beyond the immediate locality, but not all deal with this fame equally well. One incident is described at length in Lortat-Jacob's fragmentary *Sardinian Chronicles* (1995).

One organettu player, Salvatore Dillu, has, eccentrically, interpreted Lortat-Jacob's visit as an opportunity to sell his repertory for two million lire. The locals express their outrage and incomprehension. What on earth was he planning to sell, exactly? What gave him the right to dispose of communal property in this manner?

> Salvatore assumed an attitude of detachment that seemed natural to him; he let the others speak while appearing to be holding some logic in reserve. He replied, "when he passes on his practice, doesn't a doctor ask for money from his successor?" At least, that is what he had been led to believe. . . . And didn't he, Salvatore, possess a knowledge equivalent to that of a doctor? Wasn't he passing on to whoever wanted to pay the price for his music the squares and the fêtes to which he had been invited, just as a doctor passes on his practice? If he hadn't been there after the war, when Sardinian music was in such bad shape, music, like his doctor friend's patients, would be dead in Desulo. It was thanks to him, he said, that dance music and the very soul of Sardinia had not vanished from the country. (1995: 15–16)

Lortat-Jacob is at pains to stress that the engagement of Sardinian musicians with commodity logic does not lead inexorably to a situation in which the latter prevails. Indeed, the reverse seems usually to be the case. Efforts such as those of Dillu to treat Sardinian music in commoditized terms invariably run aground. As if to emphasize the point, Lortat-Jacob suggests that Dillu's quest for payment is primarily animated by a personal psychological struggle rather than an engagement with wider historical and economic processes.

The neglect, the decline, and ultimately the entire biography of Salvatore Dillu were all linked by the violence of that death. In fact, it was after the death of his wife that he had stopped playing, in every sense of the word. He had not withdrawn from the village square for a conventional reason, for simple mourning, which traditionally required musicians to stop playing for a month; but quite simply because he could no longer play a note. It was later, when forced by necessity, that he had decided to sell his repertoire in order at least "not to lose everything," he said, and to hear no more about it. (1995: 16–17)

And yet history is not entirely absent. Lortat-Jacob documents the movement of musicians in relation to dancers over the course of the twentieth century in a brief passage in *Musiques en Fêtes*. This is, essentially, a movement out of the dance circle—first into the center of the circle, then onto a dais inside the circle, and then onto a dais outside the circle—which parallels the growing emergence of a class of semi-professional *organettu* musicians in Sardinia (1994: 64). Secondly, Lortat-Jacob alludes, briefly, and with reference to Weis Bentzon's research, to a parallel process of professionalization amongst *launeddas* (pipe) players in the south of the island (1995: 92–93 and 141 b. 38–39). Agriculture, the presence of a commercial artisanat and proximity to larger towns and local elites made possible the emergence of a class of professional launeddas players who enjoyed substantial cross-class prestige. A precise time line is not given. But it is hard to escape the impression that these are clear examples of "history one," in Chakrabarty's terms. It is almost as though a "history one" plan has been repressed—perhaps because it would lead too simplistically to the conclusion that the Morocco-Sardinia-Romania sequence is to be understood as a sequence of historical stages—but only surfaces, expressed all the more forcefully, in odd corners of Lortat-Jacob's work.

Lortat-Jacob's method, then, involves making distinctions between material that might properly be regarded as "historical" and that which cannot. *Sardinian Chronicles* and *Musiques en Fêtes* often seem to conclude that capital's history is resisted by something that admits of no historical explanation itself. The spheres of exchange in which music is embedded in Sardinia, and which imbue it with such tremendous moral force are, as it were, sufficiently strong to withstand capital's historical incursions. It is, indeed, hard to think about what kind of histories might be involved in the forms of musical affect, sentiment, and intimacy he so compellingly portrays, but this, in a sense, is precisely the challenge. Once seen in historical terms, connections, rather than oppositions between localized sentiment and modern disenchantment, might be teased out. In the first instance, and with reference to the Salvatore Dillu story itself, one might note that Lortat-Jacob presents Dillu's efforts to sell his repertory as psychological dysfunction. One could indeed read the episode, following Lortat-Jacob's hints, as a classic Freudian psychodrama, as Dillu attempts to turn his melancholy into a more focused form of mourning. The issue of payment for his repertory somehow, and rather ineptly (on Dillu's part), gets swept into the general process of objectification and psychic separation.

There are, however, senses in which the family sentiments that mobilize his efforts to sell his repertory form a very recognizable history one; indeed, it is a history that has been elaborated endlessly in the sociology of development in the Mediterranean and Middle East. This is the familiar story of the emergence of the nuclear family. Not only is Dillu wrestling with the demands of the performance of a peculiarly "modern" form of intimacy: public grief over the death of his wife. He is also animated by notions of generational progress, and particularly by the possibilities that selling his repertory might present for his sons. In the (somewhat disguised) discussion of this episode in *Musiques en Fêtes*, Lortat-Jacob mentions that Dillu wants his sons to attend music conservatory in Italy. The commodification of his repertory involves not only an attempt to derive cash revenue for his musical labor and expertise but to connect with a world of musical objects and technologies that circulate in an abstracted economy of commodity exchange—a world for which he is trying to prepare his sons. The sentiments and public forms of intimacy involved in Dillu's story, then, have a recognizable history one component. This point is not, of course, incompatible with Lortat-Jacob's analysis.

Lortat-Jacob's writing provides rich material for thinking about dynamics that might be considered under Chakrabarty's rubric of history two as well, though here his inclination to dehistoricize raises precisely the kinds of questions with which I am concerned. One might consider the final chapter of *Musiques en Fêtes* concerning the Romanian *lautari*, and a number of other recent ethnographies of Rom music in Eastern music, in this light (see in particular Rice 1996; Buchanan 1996). Seen in the context of the wider transformations of central and eastern Europe, Rom (gypsy) music might be used to instantiate a history two whose entanglement with, and analytical complication of, a rather more conventional history one type is striking. Lortat-Jacob cites Brailloui's comment that villagers and gypsies constituted a secular priesthood in socialist Romania. This may have been the official view, but the sense of moral antagonism that separates villagers and Rom musicians in the villages is clear in the rest of his analysis. Elsewhere in central and eastern Europe, villager and gypsy are sharply opposed in official discourse, too. Bartok's identification of the "true" Hungarian musical values to be found among the peasantry was made in rhetorical contradistinction to the "false" Hungarian music peddled by urbanized gypsy musicians. Official condemnations of Rom culture throughout the postwar process of central and eastern European state formation resonate with musicological formulations of this kind.

Despite—and ultimately because of—this condemnation, Rom music came to constitute a crucial intimate other in the public space of the central and eastern European states. Through this intimate other, a sense of self *not* articulated by the state, but an emotionally dense complex of biography, kinship, locality, and cosmopolitan fantasy could be performed into existence. Official condemnation, coupled with the marginal moral and geographic spaces that Rom musicians occupied, made for crucial entrepreneurial advantages in access to the vibrant market places of capitalist Europe and the Middle East (notably Istanbul) as the mismanaged and bankrupt Eastern European states collapsed in the late 1980s. During this process, Rom music took on an oppositional cast, accompanied by renewed and increasingly ethnicized persecution, for example in Bulgaria. It assumed a widening transnational prominence in the World Music industry, and finally a role, during the period of "transition," as state-sanctioned symbols of the new and cosmopolitan face of capitalist eastern Europe. What is important to grasp here is the mutual constitution and entanglement of a type one history (the common story of the transition from state-run industrial capitalism to neo-liberal global economy) and a type two history (localized histories of affect as constituted by Rom music).

It is also important to grasp the ways in which this music—breathlessly fast, visceral, and erotic, particularly when seen in contrast to the drab "village" music promoted by the state—not only connected with, but also *constituted* historical process. That is to say, in seeking to understand the historical nature of Rom music, we can do more than simply track its progress over time, measured in the abstract. We can consider the ways in which music *makes* history, in the rather direct sense of modeling—for particular people at particular moments—the way things happen in time. A nuanced account of eastern European history, one sensitive to the ways in which many eastern Europeans continue to experience the uncertainties, but also the visceral excitements of transition might then be one that sought to engage with the turbulent temporarilities of Rom music. One can, I would argue, consider the complexities and subtleties that Lortat-Jacob teases out in more historically mobile terms than he seems prepared to contemplate.

World Music Histories

The problem we face is, then, one of how to consider historical relationships, rather than oppositions, between forms of sentiment and the dynamics of money and the commodity form. The issue has been admirably addressed in Marc Schade-Poulsen's recent study of Algerian Rai (1999), which locates the connections between the two in a detailed analysis of the circulation of money in the world of Rai. A major problem in grasping these relationships is constituted by the enormous surfeit of celebratory language that has accompanied Rai's emergence as World Music par excellence. This is a language that has entrenched oppositions between power and resistance, obscuring Rai as a historical phenomenon. In Algeria, it is commonly argued, Rai resists Islam. It is the voice of young people whose eminently natural desires are denied an outlet by a repressive state and a censorious Islam. Realizing the nature of mounting pressures, which ultimately could not be resisted, the state moved to co-opt Rai in the mid-1980s. Brought into the mainstream, Rai's voice of social and sexual critique might have been substantially dampened, but it was still strident enough to make Rai singers targets for Islamists in the violent and chaotic years that followed. In France and elsewhere in Europe, Rai's reception history has been complex, as Schade-Poulsen notes. On the other hand, its racial connotations have sometimes been downplayed, and transnational stars such as Khaled have been promoted as a Mediterranean Bob Dylan or even a French surrealist poet in the tradition of Apollinaire and Breton. A certain amount of its appeal, however, seems to reside in the notion of Rai as "Islamic," as the resurgence of Europe's repressed other.[5] Those whose only concern is to establish Rai's oppositionality often fail to notice the contradiction between the terms of this oppositionality in Algeria on the one hand and France on the other.

These kinds of discussion make it difficult to grasp what it is that is modern about Rai, in the sense of its connections to the nation-state and the commodity form. They assume "resistance" operating through Rai as a constant and even pressure exerted against state and religion, both in Algeria and France, with no specific historical dynamic of its own. As Schade-Poulsen demonstrates, though, the nature of the nation-state in both Algeria and France has changed substantially over time, and Rai has changed with it. Rai's history is, in other words, entangled with that of the nation and the state, rather than opposed to it. Up to the middle of the twentieth century, Islamic and nationalist institutions in Algeria could, with some difficulty, join in resisting French colonialism. Once the colonial presence was removed, at least in its immediate physical manifestation, their paths parted over their radically opposed views concerning nation-state modernity. Rai could emerge at a time when singers could tap into the radical dichotomies of the anti-colonial struggle, in which Arab and Islamic could be easily conflated, and could be grasped, as Front de la Libération Nationale (FLN) activists were quite quick to do, as opposition. It would, however, become politically construed as a problem (requiring all-too-drastic "solutions") in later years when competing visions of postcolonial modernity took institutional form within the Algerian nation-state. As Rai production moved outside of Algeria, it lost a great deal of its symbolic valence in Algeria (though not France) as a contested sign of modernity.

One must also understand Rai in relation to the emergence of pluralist cultural policies in the social-democratic states of postwar Europe. In the late

1980s and early 1990s, a variety of representatives of France's ascribed pluralism (including Tunisian chanteuse Amina) were selected to sing for France in the Eurovision song contest, in stark contrast to earlier decades. Assimilation in a strongly centralist state thus gave way to ascribed cultural pluralism, carefully monitored and controlled by state institutions. As a consequence, North African popular culture came to attract the attention of French racists in a different and more systematic kind of way, while those involved in resistance to French racism looked to Rai and "beur" culture both for a more globalized and a generationally specific set of strategies. The recording industry was poised to take advantage of the situation. Pluralist political strategies on the part of Europe's social democracies in the 1970s and 1980s coincided with the search for new markets and the cultivation of new tastes by the recording industry. The conditions in which World Music and later "world beat" could flourish were in place, and Rai was an early candidate for global music citizenship. The process culminated in Barclay's signing of Khaled in 1984, and since then the terms Rai and World Music have just about been synonymous. In this sense a historical account of Rai needs to flow into a more general history of modernity, the nation-state and the commodity form, and not be set apart from it. Here we are once again firmly in the domain of Chakrabarty's history one.

But Rai is also full of the kinds of cultural intimacy, affect, and sentiment that we might associate with history twos. The histories that might figure here are varied and complex. Historical preoccupations with the nature of colloquial Arabic are significant. Classical Arabic literature drew on colloquial forms in the Middle Ages (notably in genres such as the *muwashshah* and *zajal*), but in the twentieth century the Maghrebi literati came to consider classical Arabic as cold, objectifying, and distant. Many of the literati, post-independence, even felt that greater literary intimacy could be achieved through the French language, rather than literary Arabic. Darraja, the colloquial language, thus attained a sharpened focus as the language of locality and neighborhood, acquiring positive connotations as the political legacy associated with French and Arabic became ever more problematic. The opportunities Rai offered to cultural legislators in Algeria in the 1980s owed much to the senses of intimacy that Darraja came to shape, and the failure of the Maghrebi literati to develop the North African colloquial language as a literary medium. The politically resonant senses of closeness that Rai musicians were able to shape in the 1970s and 1980s must be grasped in terms of the complex institutional relationship between classical Arabic, colloquial Arabic, and French. This set of relationships is not easy to assimilate with the more conventional narratives of colonization, anti-colonial struggle, and independence.

Significant, too, are the urban intimacies configured by Rai. At a crucial moment in the expansion of commercial recording these brought poor white settler and rural Arab musical cultures into close proximity in specific neighborhoods in Oran. At a crucial moment in the formation of World Music, migration brought Arab and black expressive styles into close and productive proximity in immigrant *banlieus* in Paris. This is a story of music as a means of communication across cultural and racial lines, a story of affective solidarities in European and North African cities. These, again, do not relate in any simple sense to the story of the emergence of the social-democratic state with its traditions of multiculturalism, or narratives of migration and assimilation.

Finally, one also needs to consider the complex histories of gendered expressive culture in North Africa. Rai should be thought of in relation to a number of popular women's genres across North Africa, such as the *ghinnawa* discussed by Lila Abu-Lughod (1986) in western Egypt and, of more direct relevance, the repertoire of the *meddahates* and *cheikhats* in Algeria immediately prior to Rai's emergence (see in particular Virolle 1995). These put the dominant language of patrilinial honor in counterpoint with narratives of vulnerability and weakness, a fact that, as Abu-Lughod and others have repeatedly pointed out, have made them practically invisible to ethnographers and folklorists. Sound recording made women's performance worlds available to a larger, urban, and cross-gendered public, since women could sing in the privacy of the recording studio to relatively little public censure. Worsening economic and political conditions after independence meant lives of increasing marginalization for young men in Algeria, for whom work and marriage were remote prospects at best. The sentiments of pain and loss that had been so central to women's musical repertories in the Middle East began to speak directly to their own situation. As Schade-Poulsen and others have demonstrated, much contemporary productivity in the world of Rai is a matter of "gender-translating" the older women's repertory for a predominantly male audience.

In contexts of cultural intimacy such as these, Rai appears to embody decisively countermodern historical tendencies, at a skew to the modernist historical tendencies embodied and shaped by nation-state, culture industry, and commodity form. How then do we grasp the nature of the relationship between the two tendencies? Schade-Poulsen's explanation focuses on the circulation of money in two different domains. In the first instance, Rai is live music performed in cabarets and at weddings. Events are in the hands of an emcee, the *berrah*, whose job it is to encourage guests to bid against one another, with a great deal of wit and humor, in order to get the singer and the musicians to play a favorite song. The ever-increasing bids are placed in a bowl (the *sni*) on the stage, with much humorous ceremony. When one party wins, the singer sings the song, though usually only the chorus line and a few improvised verses making flattering reference to those present. The process then starts again. The money is usually distributed among the musicians and berrah; occasionally, and often at weddings, the wedding host keeps the money, having sometimes agreed on a fee with the musicians and berrah beforehand. The berrah is the dominant and the musician very much the sub-ordinate party in the transaction, though better musicians may negotiate to get, for example, a fixed fee, or to give the instrumentalists a fixed fee and pick up the sni, depending on which he feels will be most advantageous.

Bids are talked up by the berrah, and repaid with *tabrihas*, words of praise extolling the collective honor of particular groups, whether friends or kin. But this is always balanced, and thrown into question, by juxtaposition with the bid that comes from an opposing faction and the tabriha that returns to it. Schade-Poulsen notes the competitive edge involved in these displays of generosity, locating them firmly in Bourdieu's world of calculated challenge and riposte. But it is also, in Schade-Poulsen's view (1999: 51), a world dom-inated by an aesthetic of "lightness" and good humor. The ideal wedding party or cabaret evening was one in which people became light, *khaffif*, "in such a way that they became a gift to the party, without calculation, strategic purpose, or the negotiation of truth."

This picture predominates in the subsequent discussion of sound record-ing. Rai recording is beset with difficulties as Rai moves from cabaret and wedding party to recording studio. Materials are in short supply, and time is always short. Most Rai is put together in the recording studio, relying on the adaptability of studio musicians, the improvisational skills of the vocalist, and the keen commercial instincts of the *editeur*, the producer. Singers earn little and tend to view the exercise as one of advertising their skills with a view to more lucrative cabaret and wedding party engagements (as in Turkey). One might assume that the fluid and effervescent exchange which predominates in the cabarets and wedding parties, though, would constitute a major problem in the recording studio, increasingly governed by copyright restrictions. In 1973, ONDA (l'Office National des Droits d'Auteurs) took over from the French copyright institution, SACEM (Société des Auteurs, Compositeurs, et Éditeurs de Musique) and attempted, with difficulty and a great deal of resistance from many éditeurs, to construct copyright guidelines for Rai.

Rai's studio form, though, reproduces many if not most of the structur-ing principles of the cabaret. Copyright issues seemed only to strengthen musicians' sense of what could legitimately be considered formulaic, and what needed, in some sense, to be "original" material. It did not, in other words, put much of a brake on the tendency of éditeurs and singers to think of Rai in terms of vocal improvisation, though it certainly changed some of the terms in which they did so. In most other respects it was business as usual. The berrah is absent, but the musician improvises lyrics that refer to the people gathered in the recording studio and friends in the immediate locality. "Thus, in a song, you not only found a voice, a number of formulas, and minor personal statements, but also improvisations emphasizing the direct social and communicative relation embedded in the Rai performance. When recorded, the songs became a continuation on cassette of the live performance" (Schade-Poulsen 1999: 67). These relations continue when the recording leaves the recording studio, as the pursuit of recorded Rai structures patterns of intimacy among the young men who constitute its main audience in urban Algeria.

The world of Rai is a world dominated by the commodity form and by the circulation of money. But the domination of the commodity form and the circulation of money have complex, rather than unitary, effects. Two things happen of significance in the context of this chapter. The circulation of money locates musicians, berrahs, éditeurs, and Algerian consumers in wider systems of exchange, over which they have increasingly less control, and are, ultimately, marginalized. But it also actively generates moral sentiments that both define and constitute local solidarities, rather than dissolving them. These cohere, over time, into patterns that are not always easy to identify historically (given, in Chakrabarty's terms, our inclination towards type one rather than type two histories). It is crucial, however, that we do so, since the interaction between the two does much to shape the complex and plural worlds of North African and French modernity.

Conclusion

With this, we might return to the differences between the Turkish Black Sea singers, Ibrahim and Necmi, with which I began. It is clear now that we have no real grounds in this case for opposing national modernity and the commodity form with a prenational, precapitalist other. This view is entirely partial, coming as it does from the centers of nationalist ideological production in Ankara and Istanbul, with the endorsement of the entrepreneurial inhabitants of lower Agarsar valley. The presence of hazelnuts and a cash economy, and the proximity to the coastal road and to successful, integrating, migrant communities in Istanbul made for a kind of "just-so" tale of Turkish modernity that seemed to explain just how *we* (in the lower valley) ended up modern, and *they* (in the upper valley) failed to do so. The benefits of the critical view we now have are also rather more localized and specific. The assumption that the kemençe will inevitably give way to the saz over time now appears to be rather more loaded than it first appeared. As a consequence of these doubts one can imagine alternative scenarios and understand how, in fact, kemençe and saz come to coexist quite happily in different and non-exchangeable niches, so to speak, in the musical ecology of the upper valley. There is no sense in which the kemençe will inevitably disappear with time.

We might also think about whose history of modernity predominates when we discuss regions on the periphery of Europe, and why. The kind of history one that leads smoothly to national integration was something with eminent and obvious narrative virtues, at least from a lower valley perspective. When somebody like Ibrahim explained the situation to me, he did so along a grain established by the state's educational and statistical apparatus. From this perspective, one might assign Necmi's view of the world to a subordinate status, a "little history," so to speak, whose role is simply to travel on the back of a bigger beast. But there are other ways of looking at this situation. Necmi, as it happens, saw things exactly the other way around. His modernity was one of labor migration to Germany, travel, and cosmopolitanism, in which the Turkish nation-state was something of a parochial irrelevance. Local folklore in the upper valley was an anchor and point of moral reference, but one that was ultimately underwritten by migrant labor remittances (including such things as Necmi's father's German insurance policy). Everybody was well aware of this, not least the musicians. Theirs, then, was a world shaped decisively by commoditized migrant labor in a hostile and exploitative European labor market, in relation to which the musical world of muhabbet, of friendship and love and defiant indifference to the state, had come to attain an enormous resonance. In this context, muhabbet thus emerges as the product of a rather more modern historical sensibility than it might appear (particularly from a lower valley perspective), playing an active role in shaping consciousness of wider processes of historical transformation and mapping responses to it.

Finally it adds weight to the view that Marx's notion of the commodity form's contradictory histories might be more responsive than sometimes assumed to the question of historical difference and the shaping of modern identities in the idiom of closeness and social warmth. The commoditization of music may indeed produce modes of understanding music which increase our fetishization of the musical object or text, and deepen our sense of alienation and moral failing as we struggle to connect ourselves with the otherworldly epiphanies promised (though rarely delivered) by the sublime. But this is only part of the story. Marx provides us with a compelling way of understanding how forms of solidarity and sentiment are fragmented yet also reconfigured by modernity. Grasped in his terms, we might be more alive to the possibilities for radical transformation contained within it.

Notes

1. There are notable exceptions. Qureshi's (1995) account of the circulation in money as a means of mediating between an egalitarian Islam and a hierarchical society in the context of *qawwali* performances in North India and Pakistan is particularly valuable. It directs attention to, among many other things, the complex ways in which the circulation of money shapes the social experience of spiritual intimacy in a firmly and decisively modern and urban world. Waterman's (1990) discussion of the "spraying" of money in the context of Nigerian Juju draws attention to the theatrical, performative aspects of the

payment of musicians, as does Cowan's (1990) account of relations between gypsy performers and Macedonian Greek villagers.

2. Profound thanks are due to Ibrahim and Necmi and their families for boundless hospitality in Istanbul, Trabzon, Beskidüzü, and Salpazari in 1985, 1986, and 1987, and Ibrahim for his hospitality and constant support ever since. Thanks are also due to Tahir Bakal, with whom I conducted a great deal of this research during this period and who provided me not only with companionship in long hikes between villages but put me in touch with hospitable friends and relatives in Akçaabat and elsewhere.

3. The "Kurds" of the provinces immediately to the south, in particular Gümüshane, were for the most part Turks, but they spoke Turkish in a way that is often, in the eastern Black Sea area, assimilated with the ways in which real Kurds speak Turkish. Keen rivalry over highland pastures constitutes one of the reasons the Black Sea Turks use this dismissive blanket term to describe their southern neighbors.

4. Berman (1999: 95) reminds us to put the anti-Semitism of *On the Jewish Question* in the context not only of Marx's later work, but his earlier work, notably his attacks on the anti-Semitism of Bruno Bauer and his circle.

5. One can demonstrate this with reference to the use of Khaled's music in the sound track to Terry Gilliam's science fiction movie *Twelve Monkeys*, which uses Rai to signify the return in the postmodern metropolis of an oriental other repressed and marginalized by modernity. The scene that Khaled's music accompanies in *Twelve Monkeys* is a clear descendant of the famous "bazaar" scene in Ridley Scott's *Blade Runner*, accompanied by Vangelis's orientalist soundtrack.

References

Abu-Lughod, Lila. 1986. *Veiled Sentiments: Honor and Poetry in a Bedouin Society*. Berkeley: University of California Press.

Barth, Frederik. 1967. "Economic Spheres in Darfur." In *Themes in Economic Anthropology*, edited by Raymond Firth, 149–74. London: Tavistock Publications.

Berman, Marshall. 1999. *Adventures in Marxism*. London: Verso.

Bloch, Maurice, and Jonathan Parry. 1989. "Introduction: Money and the Morality of Exchange." In *Money and the Morality of Exchange*, edited by Maurice Bloch and Jonathan Parry, 1–32. Cambridge: Cambridge University Press.

Bohannan, Paul, and Laura Bohannan. 1968. *Tiv Economy*. London: Longmans.

Bourdieu, Pierre. 1966. "The Sentiment of Honour in Kabyle Society." In *Honour and Shame*, edited by John Peristiany, 191–241. Chicago: University of Chicago Press.

Buchanan, Donna. 1996. "Wedding Music and Political Transition and National Consciousness in Bulgaria." In *Retuning Culture: Musical Changes in Central and Eastern Europe*, edited by Mark Slobin, 200–30. Durham, N.C.: Duke University Press.

Chakrabarty, Dipesh. 2000. *Provincializing Europe: Postcolonial Thought and Historical Difference*. Princeton, N.J.: Princeton University Press.

Cowan, Jane. 1990. *Dance and the Body Politic in Northern Greece*. Princeton, N.J.: Princeton University Press.

Erlmann, Veit. 1993. "The Politics and Aesthetics of Transnational Musics." *World of Music* 2: 3–15.

Herzfeld, Michael. 1987. *Anthropology through the Looking Glass: Critical Ethnography on the Margins of Europe*. Cambridge: Cambridge University Press.

Lomax, Alan. 1968. *Folk Song Style and Culture*. New Brunswick, N.J.: Transaction.

Lortat-Jacob, Bernard. 1994. *Musiques en Fête*. Nanterre: Société d'Ethnologie.

———. 1995. *Sardinian Chronicles*. Chicago: University of Chicago Press.

Marx, Karl. 1973. *Grundrisse: Foundations of the Critique of Political Economy*. Translated by Martin Nicolaus. London: Penguin.

———. 1976. *Capital*, Vol. 1. Translated by Ben Fowkes. London: Penguin.

———. 1978. *Marx-Engels Reader*. 2nd ed. Edited by Robert C. Tucker. New York: Norton.

Picken, Laurence. 1975. *Folk Musical Instruments of Turkey*. Oxford: Oxford University Press.

Postone, Moishe. 1996. *Time, Labor, and Social Domination: A Reinterpretation of Marx's Critical Theory*. Cambridge: Cambridge University Press.

Qureshi, Regula Burkhardt. 1995. *Sufi Music of India and Pakistan: Sound, Context and Meaning in Qawwali*. Chicago: University of Chicago Press.

Rice, Timothy. 1996. "The Dialectic of Economics and Aesthetics in Bulgarian Music." In *Retuning Culture: Musical Changes in Central and Eastern Europe*, edited by Mark Slobin, 176–99. Durham, N.C.: Duke University Press.

Schade-Poulsen, Marc. 1999. *Men and Popular Music in Algeria: The Social Significance of Rai*. Austin: University of Texas Press.

Stokes, Martin. 1993. "Hazelnuts and Lutes: Perceptions of Change in a Black Sea Valley." In *Culture and the Economy: Changes in Turkish Villages*, edited by Paul Stirling. London: Eothen.

Virolle, Marie. 1995. *La Chanson Rai*. Paris: Karthala.

Waterman, Christopher. 1990. *Jùjú: A Social History and Ethnography of an African Popular Music*. Chicago: University of Chicago Press.

PART IV

State and Revolutionary Marxism

8
Musicological Memoirs on Marxism

IZALY ZEMTSOVSKY
TRANSLATED BY KATHERINE DURNIN

I must admit that it was difficult for me to agree to the proposal by the editor of this unusual book that I write an article on my "Marxist experience" and my understanding of Marxism in musicology—difficult for many reasons, at once objective, subjective, and a combination of the two. It would take a full-length work in itself to give a full explanation of those reasons.

A discussion of the objective reasons would require not a short article but a solid monograph setting out coherently the history, theory, and practice of so-called Marxist musicology in the former Soviet Union and other countries of the West and East. This would be a worthy and demanding task. The author would have to gather and consider an enormous mass of information. In the years 1917–79 and in the Soviet Union alone, the works of Karl Marx and Friedrich Engels were published in 49 languages of nationalities of the USSR and in 39 foreign languages in publishing runs of some 120 million copies, and the works of Vladimir Ilyich Lenin (including his *Collected Works*) were published in even greater numbers—more than 541 million copies in 66 languages of Soviet nationalities, not to mention the thousands of books and articles in various languages in which these works were endlessly quoted and "discussed." Among these are works by musicologists and "music folklorists," the name by which ethnomusicologists were known for many years in the Soviet Union. The author of such a monograph would also have to understand and distinguish between at least five more or less independent phenomena, namely: (1) the rich intellectual legacy of Karl Marx himself and his collaborator Friedrich Engels; (2) the achievements and mistakes of Western Marxism; (3) the system and practice of Soviet Marxism-Leninism; (4) the politics of the "Marxist-Leninist-Stalinist-and-so-on" structure of the USSR and other countries of what was called the "socialist brotherhood," a politics carried out under the banner of a consciously misinterpreted Marxism; and (5) the most variegated types of camouflage Marxism (if I may so express myself) that were used, for one reason or another, to disguise many philosophical works and even various humanitarian and literary works by Soviet authors. To distinguish between these five very diverse phenomena is not merely important: without doing so, it is impossible to separate objectively the endless streams of empty phrases and the abhorrent demagoguery and ignorant arrogance of pseudo-Marxist criticism from the pertinent and truly serious, rather than oversimplified, research that attempted to delve into questions of musicology and musical aesthetics from a position of "materialist dialectics" or "dialectical materialism," one of the principal Marxist approaches to the analysis of artworks and artistic processes. For example, dialectics, which had virtually disappeared from official Soviet Marxism out of a fear of its merciless logic, continued to be heard from time to time in isolated works of our leading specialists, works that were subject to censorship. The reader of these musicological memoirs of Soviet Marxism should not expect me to carry out an analysis of these five phenomena.

Speaking subjectively and personally, the theme of Marxism cannot be an academic matter in the usual sense of the word, since I spent the greater part of my life and did most of my work in Communist Russia. When I think of Marxism, I cannot help but think of my own fate and the fate of many of my fellow researchers in music and the notorious Soviet cliché for "building the music culture." Our entire lives could be written in terms of the calendar of events that took place under Communism. I was born, for example, in the year of "Stalin's constitution" (1936); I entered university in the year of Stalin's death (1953); I did my first fieldwork in northern Russia in the year of the Twentieth Congress of the CPSU (1956), at which the historical revelation was made of Stalin's cult of personality; and in the year in which the ill-omened 1948 resolution on formalism in music was reviewed (1958), I graduated from the faculty of philology at Leningrad University and began publishing in the national and specialized press. In the year in which Nikita Khrushchev was overthrown (1964), I defended my Ph.D. dissertation, and on the day when some regular Party congress or another (I do not recall which one) opened to the sounds of an incomprehensible speech by Leonid Brezhnev, I defended my thesis for the Russian doctorate[1] (1981). As a matter of fact, it was thanks to that "fortunate" coincidence that the defense took place: the members of the Academic Council in Kiev did not dare miss the meeting on such an important day, and thus the quorum necessary for the procedure, a risky one for me at that time for many reasons, was present in full.

Although I was never a Communist, I was certainly raised in the *spirit* of Marxist—or, as we almost always preferred to say it, Marxist-Leninist—ideology and in the *letter* of Marxist phraseology. The ideology that reigned in the country was considered the sole infallibly correct ideology. Everything was as clear-cut as on the model of imaginary military maneuvers that were played out every week in our courses on military preparation at St. Petersburg University (called Leningrad University when I was a student in the mid–1950s), where there were only two colors, only "us" and "them." Much later I realized that as a result of that "clarity" the Soviet powers-that-be had learned how to deal with only two groups of people: slaves and enemies. The rest, of course, they either physically destroyed or, during rare periods of "diplomatic humanitarianism," exiled from the country.

The combined objective and subjective reasons constitute linguistic difficulties that sometimes seem to me impossible to overcome. It is not just that I personally do not express myself as well in English as I do in Russian. The thing is that it is objectively difficult, if not impossible, to find in any of the Western languages meanings that are equivalent to official Soviet "jargon" and that can adequately convey social and psychological connotations understandable to the Western reader in the same way that they are to former Soviet citizens, so that they would evoke in him or her the same sort of associations, emotions, and feelings that they do in us. Language is not only a way of thought, it is also a way of life. This is all the more true of language in an era of "linguistic oppression," as the philosopher Merab Mamardashvili (1992: 72) once aptly termed Soviet totalitarianism,[2] when life itself becomes an endless process of naming and renaming, and when not just ideological but linguistic insubordination is punished. Hence the heightened attention to language and, consequently, the extreme complexity of translating not only specialized musicological terms but the entire system adopted in modern Russian and set in the clichés of Marxist phraseology. Indeed, it may not be a matter of Marxist phraseology alone but of the entire structure of the language, which was radically transformed during the Soviet era with all of its idiocy and cruelty, all the tragedy and tragicomedy of its everyday life, tragedy and tragicomedy for the victors and the vanquished alike—a language nevertheless printed on the pages of the unique prose of several outstanding Russian writers of prewar times (those, for example, of Mikhail Zoshchenko, Andrei Platonov, Mikhail Bulgakov, Ilya Ilf, and Evgenii Petrov). One must know this literature to understand properly the political context of Soviet life as well as its psychological and stylistic contexts, and that includes its scholarly life, which, we can only hope, has been relegated forever to the past.

As we know, every discipline is made up of four components: an object, a subject, material, and a methodology. In the conditions of total censorship of state Marxism-Leninism we were not ideologically free in any of these four components. We could not freely write about anything, could not freely ask any question we wished, could not freely use any type of material or freely adopt any given methodology or method. It was not just texts that were censored, but the very context of scientific investigation. I will take the liberty in this connection of raising what seems to me a fundamental notion, and will begin by asking a question that may seem quite bizarre at first: Was there any Marxism at all in Soviet Russia?

Russia has always been a country of extremes, and that certainly held true during Soviet times. We inherited Romanticism from the nineteenth century and it continued to exist in various forms of idealization (be it the idealization of certain pages from the "murky past" or the idealization of the "bright future" as a whole). In the arts, even Romantic notions survived according to which the people (envisioned as a "simple people" endowed with a "patriarchal purity") were the keepers of wisdom and of ancient national traditions and ideals. We interpreted Marxism (also inherited from the nineteenth century) in our own way, and as a rule we made it our own by simplifying it, with its proposition that the people are the decisive force in history, the creators of all material values and the founders and bearers of spiritual values. This ideological vulgarization became compulsory in the manner we are now familiar with—both Romanticism and Marxism turned out to be equally unsuitable when put into practice in twentieth-century Russia. Nevertheless society continued to mesmerize itself with their slogans while in fact it turned to an entirely different idea—one that it completely rejected ideologically, at least in words: the ancient idea of shamanism. The idea of shamanism, I will now attempt to demonstrate quickly, was actually realized in Soviet life, actually operated at the most diverse levels from the philosophical right down to the level of everyday life. Here I will call on the phenomenon of Siberian shamanism, well known to modern ethnographers, with its traditional division of the universe into three levels—the lower (underground, dark); the middle (earthly, human); and the upper (celestial, the abode of pagan gods and protectors).

At the level of philosophy, relatively speaking, Romanticism acted as the upper world, with its idealized spirituality, the notorious theory of "socialist realism," which posited the representation not so much of what was really there but of what was considered ideologically desirable. The lower world was the heuristically salvational economic basis of Marx's argument.[3] The middle world—the world of reality, the world of ordinary people—had to be created anew and artificially. It had to be virtually invented. That probably explains why, for a long time, real sociology was dangerous to Soviet power. I remember well how it gradually began to emerge from obscurity late in the life of Leningrad musicologist Arnold Sokhor as he worked to revive it.[4] The middle world was in fact a fiction of real life—partly what American ethnographer Richard Dorson wittily calls "fakelore." The problems of that world were "solved" either from above or from below precisely as in the practice of shamanism, in which the shaman must call on the powers of the lower or the upper of the three existing worlds in order to aid people.

When religion was pronounced the opium of the people in Soviet Russia and was removed from everyday life as well as from ideology, a vacuum was left in its place. As we all know, however, nature abhors a vacuum. A queer mixture began to form of these repudiated religious practices—Christianity,[5] supposedly separated from the state, and shamanism, the most ancient religion, which was viciously persecuted in the USSR. Neither was borrowed from openly, of course, but through a sort of skimming that allowed the most effective of their hidden mechanisms to be used. One unforeseen outcome of that borrowing was that it emphasized the genealogical link between Christianity and shamanism as a pre-monotheistic belief. It may be that any monotheism—that is, any totalitarian ideology—cannot exist without traces and elements of shamanism (see, e.g., Benovska-Subkova 1993). Soviet Marxism armed itself with the ideology and practice of shamanism, which is why it began to persecute shamans as its most malevolent and most obvious—dare I say—competitors! Besides, shamans, with their "pre-Christian cast of mind," unwittingly compromised the avant-garde theories and practices of Soviet communists, by reminding them of their barbaric, savage origins. Soviet rhetoric contained such popular phrases, for example, as this one: "Thanks to the enormous success of socialism, shamanism has now completely lost its significance." At the same time, Soviet rhetoric was an odd mixture of incantations that were shamanistic in style and masks that were carnivalesque in form. The formulae of the totalitarian lexicon, grammar, and syntax seemed to hypnotize people, and were believed to help make predictions, even to "heal"—much as in former shamanistic practice.[6] The cliché-ridden nature of "official language" led to the breakdown of the living language. In this historical context, to remain an academic scholar writing intelligently was something of an exploit.

There was yet another triad in the USSR, not in the sphere of philosophy, but in daily life. This too had three levels: that is, it was grounded in shamanism. The underground world (known as "hell" in Christianity) was formed by the Gulag, in which millions of unlawfully arrested people performed slave labor and perished. People suspected that this world existed—almost as in shamanistic society—but were afraid to speak of it. The middle world was made up of ordinary Soviet workers marching in celebratory parades or in their work brigades, happily (often truly feeling happy for a while in their self-delusion) building Communism, the people whom "songs helped live and build," in the words of the most popular Soviet march.[7] The upper world, as in shamanism, was occupied by celestial inhabitants—the "gods" of the Politburo of the VKP(B), later the CPSU—with the supreme god-thunderer Joseph Stalin at their head. These worlds were of course closely tied to one another, but each of them nonetheless lived as though it were independent, and as if unaware of the others—or of the others as special worlds. And each of these worlds sang (and/or listened to) different songs.

One might well ask, was my generation Marxist? What specifically did we have from Karl Marx himself? Were there really "gentlemen's sets" of quotes from the classic Marxist-Leninist texts, carefully selected and brought together in special "quotation anthologies"? Yes, and among these fragments were some "favorites," the ones quoted most often, a number of which still seem to me quite effective. One of these, for example, is Marx's methodologically important proposition on human anatomy as a distinctive key to the anatomy of the ape. One of my best university professors, Viktor Maximovich Zhirmunsky, liked to refer to this proposition. He developed "linguistic modernism," which was then successfully applied to ethnomusicology. According to this method, the linguistic relations of modern times and of the recent past (for the direct observation of linguistic processes) can serve to help interpret more distant historical phenomena.

One might take from the works of the founders of Marxism the system they proposed which, like any closed system, had the appearance of a dying and internally inconsistent dogma, and from this extract only the method, the merciless dialectic that itself rejects all systems. All Marxists, except the dogmatists, were thus divided into two categories: those who fit into the dead framework of the system that would end in Communism, and those who paid no attention to the system and instead based their work on the dialectic of negation of the negation, and on their enthusiasm for a historical reevaluation of all natural and social processes in their systematic interconnectedness ("The world does not consist of ready-made, finished objects, but is a conjunction of processes"), the fundamental recognition of the irreducibility of complex forms of movement to simpler forms, and above all their call to the "genetic clarification of different forms" and the understanding of "the real process in its different phases."

Behind these last propositions stood what is known as the stage-based approach—the examination of all processes of social development, including art and music, according to the epoch (or stage) of human development to which they correspond. According to Marxist theory, human development followed a strict order. Each stage of historical development, schematically speaking, corresponded to one type of cultural development or another, and in particular, to certain types of musical forms and genres. We felt it essential to speak in terms of types, rather than of specific individual forms. To types of societies corresponded, above all, types of culture with their typical behaviors and modes of expression, and to the latter corresponded given types of artistic forms. In this way a picture was drawn of the development of art at the typological level that seemed perfectly accurate from the point of view of the Soviet humanities. Typology helped illuminate some of the laws that had governed art throughout its historical existence.

In and of itself, typology is related to the most common scientific approach. It is none other than comparison for the purpose of establishing types. One of the fundamental characteristics of our minds is to create types, and this is reflected above all in language. There is no science, therefore, without typology. The characteristic trait of the Marxist interpretation of the typological approach was the attempt to discover the basis of typology not in art itself (in this case, not in music itself or folklore itself), but outside it, in socioeconomic spheres. Typological similarities revealed the system of orderly correspondences conditioned by the unity of the historical process in folklore. The essence of historical-typological similarity in the folklore and music of the oral tradition was explained by the fact that they arose not through direct contact between peoples, but through unity and conformity to the laws of sociohistorical processes, and the repetitious nature of social development. According to this approach, the field of historical-typological analogy encompasses all aspects of ideology, imagery, generic composition, and artistic style of literary works and folklore. Historical-typological links and relationships operate throughout the course of the historical process of folklore and encompass all of its aspects. They are universal, constant, and continuous. Thus V. M. Zhirmunsky, the author of this argumentation, repeatedly used Marx's thoughts on the unity and order of the process of social development throughout history to justify the historical-typological method. It is the orderly nature of historical processes (in the transition, for example, from feudal to capitalist relations) that explains, as Zhirmunsky contends, the possibility of a resemblance among historical phenomena without any direct contact between them. Zhirmunsky bolstered his argument with a reference to Lenin, who spoke in this sense of the possibility of applying to social phenomena the general scientific criterion of repetition in the social phenomena of different countries. That very possibility, according to Lenin, was first scientifically proven in Marx's well-known study of socioeconomic formations.

If one were to ask me today to name the most valuable contribution of the Marxist approach to folklore studies and ethnomusicology—despite the well-known vulnerability of the concept of socioeconomic formation—my reply would still be: the historical-typological approach. Naturally, I am well aware of all the oversimplification and vulgarization of this approach as well, beginning with the works of the linguist Nikolai Yakovlevich Marr and his school of "Japhetic linguistics." But I am also familiar with the excellent works of such Soviet typologists as the philologist and folklorist Ivan Ivanovich Tolstoi, Viktor Maximovich Zhirmunsky, Vladimir Yakovlevich Propp, Eliazar Moiseevich Meletinsky, and Boris Nikolaevich Putilov. The latter (in the post-Soviet era, in the late 1990s) is responsible for the most interesting attempt to break out of the framework of Marxism and, without jettisoning Marx's material, social, and class categories, to focus on the search for factors and characteristics internal to folklore itself. Putilov extended the historical-typological approach and developed it into a historical-typological theory. It was he who stressed the rereading of literary texts, the establishment of the "typological succession" that he himself elaborated, and so on, as the ultimate goal of historical-typological analysis. The main thing is that this theory allows us to understand a great deal that is hidden in literary texts—hidden from other scholarly approaches, including the well-known theories of the anthropological and psychological schools.

I am unable here to develop this important line of thought in sufficient depth. I will simply note that even within the framework of state Marxism, Soviet ethnographers attempted within the bounds of the law to struggle against the artificial political boundaries that had been imposed on ethnic groups "from above," that is, by the Communist government, boundaries that more often than not cut across their true genetic, cultural, and linguistic contacts. In practice, this was the aim advanced and developed by studies of "economic-cultural types" (see Levin and Cheboksarov 1955).

Nor will I discuss here the policy of the Soviet state in the area of concern to us, since I have already had occasion to express my thoughts on that subject (Zemtsovsky and Kunanbaeva 1997). I am more interested in the situation in scholarship, a subject with which I am familiar thanks to my own (considerable) experience.

People of my generation, especially non-Party people, preferred to take from Marxism whatever best allowed them to remain themselves. In my case this was the "Marxist dialectic," which I took the liberty of interpreting more in the Hegelian sense, although I was not remiss in "taking cover" behind well-placed quotations gleaned from the classics of Marxism-Leninism. I will never forget how several specialists from the Faculty of Marxism-Leninism (at L. University) attended one of my methodological papers on the use of dialectics in the study of art (using the example of music folklore as the ideal material, in the terms of the paper). The audience responded so enthusiastically that these specialists did not dare voice their criticism publicly, but during the first intermission they approached me and asked straight out: "Where did you find that, in Marx or Lenin? There is nothing like that in their published work!" These dogmatists knew by heart the entire stock of authorized quotations and were simply at a loss. Without batting an eyelid, I cheerfully replied that I was correct in my reference to Marx, and I named something from his collected works that was rarely referred to.

I must admit that I could never forgo the opportunity for that kind of innovative self-expression under the banner of "dyed-in-the-wool" Marxism-Leninism and, knowing that I was playing with fire, I always acquiesced to a "social order" to write something theoretico-methodological for the regular anniversaries of the "Great Leader and Teacher." Even today I am not ashamed of publications of mine that are openly Marxist by title, including publications such as "Lenin's Theory of Reflection and Problems of Ethnomusicology" (Zemtsovsky 1987) or "On the Systematic Study of Genre in Folklore in the Light of Marxist-Leninist Methodology" (Zemtsovsky 1972). In practice, it was precisely in texts like these, safely girded in the armor of Marxist phraseology, that I found the legal means to promulgate concepts and ideas that, at the time, seemed to me more promising. I will name just a few of these by way of example. My article on the systematic approach to genre in folklore was essentially devoted to the as yet unstudied problem of the relationship between genre and musical "formulae" in the oral tradition. The problem of genre had traditionally stood at the center of Soviet folklore studies and could not be ousted. I took as my point of departure the fact that the system of genres in each local tradition—what Marx called its "rich totality"—is a genetically interrelated complex. While underlining the fruitfulness of the historical approach, I focused on the phenomenon of the "melody-formula"—that is, on that small number of melodies that in a given local tradition are used for many different poetic texts (the texts may vary, but the function is always the same). "Formula" does not imply a literal musical repetition. Often these formulae were not so much melodic in nature (in the contemporary meaning of the word) as they were rhythmic-structural and thus recitational in nature. The period of time over which art took on various social functions was extremely lengthy. Historically, formula and genre are linked. In the phenomenon of the formulaic nature of musical language in music of the oral tradition, I examined the indicator of systematicity in folklore as a whole. I determined that the system of genres is a legacy of the historical development of an increasingly differentiated system of (social) functions. That being the case, a "social function" and its corresponding genre in folklore last for different lengths of time in their history. For example, as a function dies out, the genre continues to exist, or an "old" function gives birth to a new genre. According to my observations, this phenomenon of the musical formula was widespread in the world, particularly in very early traditions. I hypothesized that the formulaic construction of music was established prior to the formation of the system of genres familiar to us through contemporary material. Musical formulaism arose in the pre-genre period. The better a popular-song tradition was preserved (for a given ethnic group), the fewer musical formulae it had and the more genres remained enveloped in formulaism. It was the "Marxist approach" that allowed me at that time to express hypotheses that Soviet folklorists considered highly seditious—hypotheses about the pre-genre period of the oral tradition; about the period of the "common cauldron," in discussions of which it was useful to refrain from using the term "genre" altogether; about the law of inequality in the composition and evolution of poetic and musical elements of songs as special (poetic and musical) genres, according to which there are always fewer musical than poetic genres; and so on. I developed these hypotheses fifteen years later in another "Marxist-Leninist" article. There I interpreted a tune formula of the early folklore tradition as an "anticipatory reflection" of its genre function and ritual meaning. Fundamentally, I still hold the same opinion today. But I no longer have to "swear by" Lenin's theory of reflection: that is, begin each time from the beginning in the light of the Leninist theory of knowledge as a doctrine about art truthfully reproducing reality.

It is no doubt difficult for anyone today, and especially for the foreign reader who has never had to deal with a pathologically vigilant Soviet censor, to understand what exactly was seditious in such speculations, and, it would seem in such ideologically innocent hypotheses, why a "Marxist cover-up"— in fact, often simply Marxist titles on articles—was so necessary just to be able to state them. Often we were aided by the sheer inertia and magic of the classic title used to provide the protective cover, or the appropriate quote from Marx's works used as an epigraph: luckily, the censor did not always check the source. But the truth remains that for several years I could not publish my ideas on the relationship between formulae and genres until I came up with some terminologically safe "Marxist defense" for them.

It is even more difficult to understand properly how such publications could appear as the collection of songs and articles on the folklore of Lenin that I edited thirty years ago. The American scholar Margarita Mazo, who specializes in Russia studies, referred to these publications recently in an article (1996: 379). This reference is so characteristic in its inadequacy in grasping Soviet reality that I will repeat it here in full:

> During the repressive Brezhnev years, when historical, political, and cultural revelations could no longer be made openly, the gap between two simultaneous cultures, the official and the unofficial, was growing. The official one produced plenty of patriotic and "ideologically correct" music in all genres and traditions, including village "folk" songs about Karl Marx, Lenin, and Stalin. (Zemtsovsky 1970, 1971)[8]

This reference misinforms the reader and drastically simplifies a serious problem. My short commentary may help bring the English-language reader a bit closer to the historical reality of those years.

I will first take up the matter of misinformation. The anthologies in question (Zemtsovsky 1970, 1971) contained no *special* songs about Karl Marx and Stalin—they were dedicated only to the figure of Lenin in the folklore of various peoples of the USSR. The editor and authors of the pieces published there avoided repeating previous falsifications that had indeed been perpetrated, and gave preference to songs that were *in essence* popular, both in their lyrical and in their musical language. The quotation marks around the word "folk" are therefore not warranted here. These artworks did not cease to be folk songs in style simply because the name "Lenin" was present. (Indeed, a serious analysis of those publications might have much to offer to ethnomusicology even today. It is a shame that Mazo did not take advantage of that interesting opportunity in her article.) One must also bear in mind that Lenin's name was still sacred to most people in the country, and if not sacred then nearly so. At the very least, it had not been besmirched as Stalin's name was after his cult of personality was denounced. Patriotism was not at that time merely "ideologically correct," it was real patriotism felt by the majority of Soviet citizens, including the authors of the books under discussion. Admittedly, Soviet propaganda at the time exploited the patriotic feelings of Soviet people, needlessly appealing to them too often and thus unwittingly sapping their force. Still, patriotism among the people was never *just* "for show" but was without a doubt genuine. In any event, our patriotism sometimes clashed with the cynicism of the Party *nomenklatura*. I remember well going to Moscow to select the illustrations for that book. There I visited the State Lenin Museum and made a list of the unconventional photographs that interested me, but was filled with amazement and indignation when my request to copy and publish them was flatly refused because they did not fit with the canonical figure of the great leader current in the Soviet press at that time.

It is unproductive to simplify the situation. We were convinced that our anthology would stand up against the total censorship wielded by bureaucrats who feared everyone and everything. We knew that all official attempts to position folklore ideologically "on the right" and to contrast it with left-wing modernism, with its stylistic protest, described in the same article by Mazo, were unjust. Folklore escapes censorship by virtue of its orality. Folklore has always given its own view of history, and this often differs from the politics of the state. A public library once refused my request, for example, to borrow a periodical containing a lament for Lenin by Komsomol members from Siberia. I refused to give up and, armed with a special application from my institute for admission to the closed "special collection," managed to have a look at the item. Only then did I understand why the periodical had been banned: the young people from Siberia had expressed in that heartfelt lament the hope that no one but "Lev Davidovich" would replace Lenin. They were referring to Trotsky, which was enough for that kind of folklore to be banned. (Incidentally, I was later able to refer to the banned publication in my analysis of the music of Russian dirges. The censor missed it, and the reference to a banned book quietly went into print.)

Nor should we forget the circumstances of the historical moment in history when these Lenin collections were being prepared for publication. In those years I was literally fighting for the right to establish two new series: collections of folk songs "From the Collections of Folklorists" (at the "Sovietskii Kompozitor" publishing house) and a series of anthologies of analytical essays on "folklore and folklore studies" (at the "Muzika" publishing house). In order to clear a path for these projects, the publishers insisted that I edit the books dedicated to the hundredth anniversary of Lenin's birth. This was a game of chance, and my participation in it helped: both series were successfully launched. It is true that the first one was immediately removed from my editorship, but the second one continues to exist today as an occasional series by the Russian Institute for the History of the Arts in St. Petersburg. And the long-awaited volume "Slavyanskii Muzikal'ny Fol'klor" ("Slavic Musical Folklore"), the only one of its kind, which I had already prepared in the mid-1960s and which I had long dreamed would launch a new series, was finally brought to fruition in 1972 as the second volume of a series—thanks precisely to that collection of essays and materials on the folklore around Lenin. *The game was worth the candle*, as they say: rare samples of music folklore from different ethnic groups were published in those Lenin collections, including unique songs and melodies of minorities from Siberia and the Far East,[9] and two excellent book series managed, as the expression goes, to get a start in life. "Thank Lenin for that," as one of the clichés had it in those mindlessly celebratory anniversary years.

The situation with folklore and folklorists was much more complex owing to the circumstances that Margarita Mazo describes with such unexpected clarity. Folklore always occupied a large place in Russia, (1) from below, as an unofficial and "left-wing" art, as an uncensored protest against the regime in the form of political songs, *chastushki*,[10] jokes, rumors, legends, and so on; (2) from above, as a demagogic medium for official ideological propaganda; and (3) on the right, as evidence of the popular nature of the regime and the State, and of how folklore connects the people to the principles of education and the educational system. One type of folklore or another existed at every level of Soviet society, without exception, from kindergarten and elementary school right through to universities and the regular national arts and culture festivals held in Moscow, not to mention a whole network of clubs and houses of culture that used folklore and whose purpose essentially was to substitute uncensored, uncontrollable folklore with artistic activities that were subject to censorship and were totally controllable from above. In other words, folklore was at once ideologically necessary as a demagogically reliable justification for the sort of democracy that was imposed from above and at the same time a genuine folklore and a genuine oral tradition in music that were extremely dangerous ideologically by virtue of their unpredictability and the fact that they were not subject to control.

Almost everything in the history of Soviet folklore studies can be explained by this double relationship between the Soviet system and folklore, expressed in the pathological coupling of demagoguery and repression. The struggle against folklore was three-pronged: against the texts, against folklore experts, and with the entire traditional medium as a necessary context for folklore. There were some basic legal means of struggling against folklore, which were employed within written culture. I would use the following terms to describe these approaches: filtration, falsification, substitution, transformation, and banning—either in the form of open repression or simply as an ignoring—that is, acting as if one does not see, notice, or recognize something as a real fact or phenomenon of modern life. The struggle against folklore also took place through a struggle against the bearers of folklore, as well as against scholars of folklore. The ideological criteria and censorship that were applied in the world of literature were transferred to the area of folklore as well. The spoken word as something that is anthropologically and intimately linked to man was stricken at the roots. It became just as dangerous to sing about what one wanted to sing as it was to publish. Repression of the spoken word also began. In these conditions, which made expression very difficult, folklore both consciously and unconsciously adapted itself to Communism. Who knows, it may be thanks to this subtle mimicry that folklore actually safeguarded within the Soviet structure things that might otherwise have been lost. Indeed, it is much more important to maintain creative strength than individual works, and if that creative strength was inscribed in the form of those songs about Lenin, then recording them was ultimately a very significant historical fact. Those songs are a unique document of the era both in the history of folklore studies and in the history of folklore itself. It would be shortsighted to categorize them as "official Soviet art" on a par with third-rate, hackneyed works stamped with the clichés of "socialist realism."

In order to give the reader some notion of the true ideological atmosphere that reigned in the 1960s and '70s and of the daily conditions in which we had to live and publish, I will cite one line from a document that was widely known at the time. It was titled "On the Preparations for the Hundredth Anniversary of the Birth of Vladimir Ilyich Lenin. Resolution of the Central Committee of the CPSU"—that is the full title—and was published in *Communist* (1968, N° 12), the most official magazine of the Soviet era. I quote:

> History has proven that any retreat whatsoever from the principles of Marxist-Leninist teaching and from its international nature, any attempts to substitute a scientific theory with a bourgeois-liberal or pseudo-revolutionary phrase, will entail an irreconcilable conflict with the historical aims of the international working class and the fundamental interests of socialism. (12 (1968): 4)

That is the long and the short of it. It is not difficult to imagine the sort of free hand this document gave to all manner of yes-men and to time-servers[11] with no shame or conscience, and of course to those who completely submitted to Communist censorship. Nor is it difficult to imagine the danger that sort of statement contained at the time. But what is difficult to imagine is what it cost each of us to remain the slightest bit objective as scholars and humanitarians in such an ideologically fraught atmosphere. We continued our academic studies, however, and continued to publish, often using a sort of Aesopian language, and at the same time were filled with pleasure at each secret signal that was missed by the censor, each allusion, each ambiguity, and so on. The philosopher Merab Mamardashvili (1992: 314) to whom I have already referred, once called Soviet culture, in his witty phrase, a culture replete with winks and nods. We lived in that culture, reading with delight every possible sign of "left-leaning" ideas, any suggestion of protest. I think that my musicological memoirs, connected with this art of "double reading," a reading of underlying meanings, will be quite pertinent. I will give just one example.

In the early 1970s I completed my article "On the Problem of Determining Folklore," in which I proposed and argued for a new hypothesis on the *essence* of folklore, a hypothesis that to the Soviet way of thinking was uncanonical. I proposed a determination of folklore not through the standard series of signs in Soviet scholarship (orality, collectivity, anonymity, the existence of different versions, etc.) but through a system of correlative pairs of signs which I schematically outlined in the form of a solar system of interrelated planets with their satellites. I was not allowed to publish the article right then. In the winter of 1973 I had to revise it, adding appropriate quotations from the Marxist-Leninist classics and giving it a new "sellable" title ("Folk Music and Contemporary Times") to make it suitable for inclusion in a book being prepared for press, so that it finally saw the light of day (with myself as one of the editors) in late 1977. Naturally, I had to express my opinion on contemporary folk art, the sacred subject of the era, and of course without confining myself to the application of my gnosiological principle of "multiple correlation." To that end I formulated (at the outset) three paradoxes of the essence of "contemporaneity" as a phenomenon in art as a whole and in folklore in particular, and at the end I added a fourth paradox. My recollection is related to that fourth paradox.

There I announced the dawning of an epoch of primarily non-folkloric forms of popular art. Let me quote twice from my own work:

> The development of contemporary creative artistic activity of the working masses in the areas of literature, music, drama and choreography is moving towards a unique "rectification" of past traditions in folklore, towards the achievement of a greater synonymity in the relationship between innovation and reality. This synonymity, this mono-dimensional quality, is being reached thanks to the particular (monofunctional) concentration of the means of expression, without the complex system of coordinates seen in traditional folklore. (74)

And I went on to ask my "seditious" question:

> But might not this "rectification" of tradition—this development not towards complexity but towards simplification, even the reduction to a common denominator, a kind of levelling universalism in the genres and artistic means used—contain a fourth paradoxical law of contemporary art . . . ?

I will never forget the reaction of my friend, the musicologist Vladimir Frumkin (who now works for "Voice of America"), whom I trusted and who, as my first reader capable of reading "between the lines," exuberantly declaimed these lines about "levelling." He immediately understood the entire subtext of my text, even though I had masked the seditious word "levelling" with the neutral word "universalism," and with a rapture that it is difficult to communicate to today's reader, exclaimed: "You really gave it to them!—You've pulled the rug out from under them, even in this holiest of holies, their ideological speculations about folklore!" (All this, of course, was said in a private and strictly confidential conversation.)

To our great joy, the censors missed (that is, approved for publication) this passage, clearly lulled by the camouflage ending that I had prepared in advance (as though especially for them):

> The more confidently popular art strides into the future, the grander appears its centuries-old history. And the continual creative meetings ["creative meetings" was a common cliché at the time within Composers' Unions, Writers' Unions, etc.] between folklore traditions that are waning and those that are coming into being make the present uniquely beautiful.

The mention of the "beautiful present" was as mandatory in a conclusion as the obligatory optimistic coda in a Soviet symphony or opera. The curtain falls to prolonged, enthusiastic applause. . . .

The thing I feared most in the world during those Soviet years were vulgar economic explanations in musicology. I must admit that I was appalled by the very memory of Roman Gruber's long article "On the Possibility and Limits of the Application of Economic Categories to Musicology" (1928b) with its definition of the work of art as a commodity (see also Gruber 1925). Given the interest in the application of Marxism to musicology, I will take the time to summarize just some of the author's basic theses. Assuming the application of the economic categories of use and exchange value in the analysis of the "artistic product," the author also believes that he himself, in his construction of the science of "music economics," is avoiding the usual errors of oversimplified Marxism. According to Gruber, music—despite of what he calls its "incorporeality," its "non-material nature," its "distance from life," its essentially manufactured aspect, and so on—is nevertheless the key to any social orderliness (to be more precise, says the author, any *capacity for orderliness*), and consequently, is also a powerful factor in the social process as a whole. Music "demonstrates persuasively *what* is being paid for in an artistic commodity: not the raw material (the physical object), but a particular—artistic—fashioning of that material not directly dependent on the use or exchange value of its physical-acoustical components." "An immaterial use value becomes an exchange value . . ." (1928b: 62). It is music, asserts

Gruber, whose materials more than those of any other art make evident the basic laws of dialectics, sometimes in a manner that is impossible for any other material (for example, the *simultaneous existence* of thesis, antithesis, and synthesis).

Basing himself on Marx's dialectical definition of the double nature of the commodity, Gruber translates the relationship between use and exchange value into the language of art and reads them (1) as the relationship between the artistically expressible and the perceptible; (2) as the relationship between artistic creativity and average perception; or (3) as the relationship between the expended high-quality labor of the artist or composer and the average estimation of that labor by society in a given era. Gruber reveals the antithesis: on one hand, the composer disdains real demand, and on the other, he still creates *exchange* value, that is, value whose very essence assumes interest and demand on the part of society. As a result, it appears that the composer creates not with a view to demand, but nevertheless with a view to sales. A resolution of this antithesis is possible, following Marx's thinking, by introducing the category of "imagined" prices. Gruber proposes, however, what to him seems a more convincing resolution. A great artist (composer) creates not with a view to *existing* demand but in an attempt, usually, to *create* demand. For that to happen, the ideology of the creator must coincide with the ideology of a particular group of consumers. By way of "evidence" Gruber cites here Arnold Schoenberg's statement that "the laws of creation of a genius are in essence the laws of future mankind" (58). The most particular quality integral to any "artistic production," according to Gruber, explains the basic antinomy of creation in the area of economics. I will quote his conclusion in full:

> The process of artistic labour (creation), which gives its author a certain sense of self-satisfaction (and consequently is a subjective type of value), also produces an objective, social value. In other words, by satisfying a personal, individual need of the author-creator, artistic labour leads to the satisfaction of an extra-personal, collective need of society, that is, it dialectically elevates itself into its own negation. (59)

I should repeat that I was not attracted by the *economic* analysis of the nature of music as an art:[12] the *sociological* approach seemed to me much more suitable and promising. Naturally, Soviet musicology also went through periods of oversimplification in this area. In the 1930s a bitter struggle took place with "vulgar sociologism" and with bourgeois "false science," and as a result both theoretical and empirical scholarship were banned by the Party. In the obligatory camouflage expression of the mid-1970s, the sociology of music "fell out of use" (Sokhor 1975: 68).[13] The ideologically ominous image of "bourgeois scholarship" entered our anti-scientific lexicon and languished there for a long time.

It is understandable why I was all the more attracted to the sociological approach in the 1960s and '70s. In 1969 I read in Bulgaria a long paper on two aspects of the sociological study of folk music, and it was later published there (Zemtsovsky 1974). The ideas of that paper—on the unity of studying music "from outside" and "from within"—became programmatic for all of my scholarly work. I proposed distinguishing between "external" and "internal" sociology, that is, the study of *the life of music* and, so to speak, of *life **in** music*. For those who are familiar with the *theory of intonation (intonatsiya)*,[14] which I developed for many years, following in the footsteps of Boris Vladimirovich Asafev (pronounced Asáfiev), this should be more or less clear (Zemtsovsky 1997). Later I adopted the experience of basing ethnomusicological study on the "sociology of rhythm" in those same two aspects (Zemtsovsky 1988). There I tried to show how the sociology of rhythm acts through the dialectical unity (*sic!*) of the *external* (the social as, generally speaking, the "class," the "ethnic," etc., determined by history, by the era, by daily life, by the type of music-making, and a whole variety of extramusical factors) and of the *internal* (the social as the genre-style dominant of music articulation and *intonation*, as that which is in some way revealed in the structure itself of the language and speech of music). This latter aspect aims at the study of the social, and its constant transformations can be revealed by "purely" musical means. It was the *intonational approach* that allowed me to do this without resorting to the vulgarizations I found so horrifying.

I am of course aware of the numerous—and, it must be said, clumsy—attempts to vulgarize the intonational approach, and outright attempts to tie Boris Asafev's "theory of intonation" directly to the Marxist phase of Soviet musicology, although Asafev made his discovery before he got to know the ABCs of Marxism. It was not difficult to do that, because in the field of Soviet musicology there really was a great deal of vulgarization and pseudo-Marxist debasement of the intonational approach, which essentially had nothing to do with Marxism as such. The many Soviet (and closely related East European) interpreters of Asafev tried to "translate" him into the language of Marxist teaching, thereby doing him an unintended disservice. The saddest part was—and still is—that the theoretical and analytical works of Asafev are surprisingly unknown to foreign readers, and especially to English-language readers, who must take at face value every ideological and factual accusation brought against the great Russian thinker.

"Asafev and Marxism" is a special subject, and an in-depth, objective study of that subject would be very timely and useful, particularly for the foreign reader. (In Russia few people are fooled by the supposedly Marxist basis of Asafev's work.) Such a study would have to clearly trace what exactly makes up the Marxist method in the study of art and what specific elements of this method are found in Asafev's legacy. Unfortunately, I cannot give these questions sufficiently serious consideration here. I will simply touch on them briefly.

Marx was attempting to create a theory based on the observation of the natural technology of production and reproduction in human life—a social theory that would be grounded in the idea of the existence of objective laws, that is, laws that are independent of consciousness. Consciousness, in Marx's view, is nothing other than the "realisation of a mode of life" (Marx and Engels 1956). Asafev understood intonation as a function of social consciousness, which always comes into existence in a tripartite act of creation, execution (i.e., reproduction), and perception. Does this statement make Asafev's hypothesis synonymous with a Marxist musicology? That is open to question. (See Iranek 1965.)

The accusations against "Asafev-as-Marxist" often target the emphasis he placed on the social basis of musical activity, but they never explain what precisely he understood by "social." For Asafev the social was above all the phenomenon of music-making itself, as well as the nature of music as *a form of address*, of the way in which musical form is directed toward perception and its ability to communicate to people its own purely musical meaning, that is, to "speak" without words. Certainly, Asafev searched diligently to find ways and terms capable of expressing this intuitive *musical* "semantics." His favorite neologism became the two-part word "sound-meaning" (*zvukos-mysl*). He maintained that music is "a thoroughly intonational art, and is neither the mechanical transfer of acoustical phenomena into artistic expression, nor the naturalistic revelation of the sphere of emotion" (Asafev 1963).

Asafev was a realist in his theories, in that he always took into account the *living* aural perception of *real* people—what he called "the ear of the social human being." He was preoccupied with the real "musical vocabulary" of whatever epoch he was studying, and with compiling a musical *thesaurus* of humanity. He was concerned with the mystery of the "collective revelation of music," as he called polyphony. He was concerned with the rhythmic-intonational structure of music in the oral tradition, which he defined (and, incidentally, in a period of universal vulgarization in Russia) in these words: "the varied expression and representation of human energy in melodic formulae and forms closely linked to life and experienced by a number of generations" (1965, 110). He possessed a rare gift for *hearing time*—not just abstract "musical time," but historically concrete time—*in* the music of different eras. Asafev never stooped to vulgar sociologism, even less so to vulgar Marxism. (One should remember that Asafev was never a Communist in the sense that he was never formally a member of the Communist Party, and was in a state of constant philosophical searching, having felt the influence of many and diverse thinkers from the early twentieth century, including a writer as distant from Marxism as Henri Bergson.) We should not, therefore, be too hasty in labeling people, and Asafev is too much of a tough cookie to be broken by a single word, even if that word is "Marxism." Marxism is too complex a phenomenon to render primitive—not to mention just plain stupid—in such an unproductive way. I am reminded of Isaiah Berlin's (1963: 234) harsh but just conclusion: "Exaggeration and over-simple application of its main principles have done much to obscure its meaning, and many blunders, both of theory and practice, have been committed in its name. Nevertheless its effect was, and continues to be, revolutionary."[15]

It is quite evident that I have no intention of using these memoirs to evaluate, much less reevaluate, Marxism as a whole or even Marxism in Russian musicology. I have avoided the cheap temptation of mocking people and judging them. I simply wanted to use a few well-chosen examples in some way connected with my own life to show how difficult it was to exist within the framework of "state Marxism-Leninism." That existence was marked by tragic losses and great discoveries alike. Both losses and discoveries have yet to be thoroughly interpreted. I am convinced that there is a great deal of work yet to be done on the theme I have only touched upon here. The heuristic possibilities opened before us by the in-depth and objective analysis of the specific means employed by Marxist musicology and the conclusions it reached seem to me highly productive ones.

In conclusion I would like to share with the reader one more recollection from those far-off years. Today, forty-three years later, what happened then sounds truly symbolic.

This was in the early summer of 1958. On that sunny morning I arrived at the university in Leningrad, where I had spent five highly interesting years, to sit for some routine mandatory "state exam" that was required to obtain a diploma. This was an exam on the fundamentals of Marxism-Leninism. I will never forget the horror I felt when, peeking through the open door, I saw my beloved folklore professor Vladimir Yakovlevich Propp calmly sitting on the stage of the auditorium as a member of the state committee. I had no idea that my professor was part of the examining committee, and I was struck dumb with horror. I simply could not imagine myself trotting out the required platitudes about Marxism—to Propp himself! A line of students stood at the door waiting their turn. I begged them to let me go in at the very moment when Professor Propp left the room for whatever reason, so that I could pass the exam while he was not on the committee. Luckily, the other students were willing to go along with this. Later, when exams were a thing of the past for me and I had my university diploma, I went to see Professor Propp, who was my supervisor, at his home. Only then did I dare tell him the truth: "You know, I was seriously afraid I might fail the exam when I saw you on the committee! I couldn't possibly give answers to *you* about Marxism!" Propp reacted instantly: with his inimitable laugh, he replied, "But of course. Propp and Marxism are two incompatible things." This was a lighthearted paraphrase of a well-known line of poetry from the short play "Mozart and

Salieri" by his beloved A. S. Pushkin ("genius and villainy are two incompatible things"). I took the full measure of the trust that my teacher was showing me by poking fun at himself, something that was not completely safe at that time. Today, mulling over that humorous phrase ("Propp and Marxism are two incompatible things"), I am aware of its double depth. Yes, Propp was one of the most famous Russian folklorists in the world in Soviet times, and he was neither a Marxist nor a Communist. This does not mean, however, that he worked in some hermetically sealed space or that he never felt the official pressure of Soviet ideology and censorship. On the contrary! But this does mean that living, productive thought existed inside the framework of so-called Marxist scholarship. That a dialogue among scientific schools of thought carried on with recognition of the achievements of Soviet times as well is not only promising but also very necessary.

Yes, Propp and Marxism are two incompatible things, but they existed side by side and continue to do so. As did Asafev and Marxism. As do Propp, Zhirmunsky, Asafev (and many others not even named here), and the present times. We have yet to study the lessons of the "experience of survival" in the conditions of the Marxist state. It can be entertaining at times and is without a doubt educational to study experiences that are difficult to imagine in today's world.

Notes

1. An equivalent to the French Doctorat d'Etat and the German Habilitation.
2. The Soviet political system has already been justifiably called a "logocracy" (Heller 1985: 210), and Patrick Seriot (1993: 100), referring in particular to the book by Andrei and Tatiana Fesenko (1955), maintains that a word-for-word translation into English of the heavy and complicated style of the Soviet bureaucracy, for example, would be essentially ungrammatical.
3. I am not an economist, but I venture to note nevertheless that Karl Marx studied the political economy of capitalism in unprecedented depth. Evidently a Japanese millionaire stated in an interview on Soviet television, with no humor intended, that he owed his success in large part to the study of Marx's *Capital*. Moreover, in 1997, the *New Yorker* published an unusual article by mainstream economist John Cassidy arguing that "the Next Big Thinker" to hit the scene would be none other than Karl Marx (see Munck 2000: 141).
4. See his pamphlet *Sotsiologia i muzykal'naya kul'tura* (Sokhor 1975).
5. See Panchenko and Panchenko 1996 on Lenin's mausoleum and Marxism as a false religion.
6. According to an author cited previously (Heller 1985: 283) the words of the leader, in many respects reminiscent of a shaman's incantation, influenced the life of individuals and of the state and determined the outlines of the future. According to Seriot (1986: 195), "There is a 'Soviet language', known as 'officialese' or 'Sovietese'—it exists and it is a language. This language would have several features: magic, mystery, inconcinnity or maximal opac-

ity." Curiously enough, these features might be attributed, to some extent, to shamanism as well. Konstantin Zachesov and Abdulla Magomedov have written in their article "The Magic of Meanings and Social Reality" (1991) about the magic of words that reigned in the USSR instead of a real science of economics. They conclude that we in the USSR "never followed Marxism" and "having completely lost the ability to see the historical reality behind the magic of words, were left on the margins of the civilized world."

7. Later a bitterly ironic joke appeared in the form of a question to the authors of this popular song: "Where can we lay our hands on a song like that?"

8. The witty expression "unpredictable past" used in Mazo's title is not her creation—it is borrowed from the ironic phrase widely known in Soviet times: "Russia is a country with an unpredictable past," a phrase that had long since passed into the body of folklore of the Soviet intelligentsia. For that reason, these two words (unpredictable past) should have been put in quotation marks. The author is referring to two anthologies (Zemtsovsky 1970, 1971).

9. Although we were not allowed at that time to use examples from gypsy or Jewish folklore.

10. Translator's note: two-line or four-line rhymed poems on a topical or humorous theme.

11. I remember, for example, the following cheerful passage by Siberian folklorist Nikolai F. Babushkin from his ambitious book *On the Marxist-Leninist Basis of the Theory of Popular-Poetic Creative Work* (1963: 138): "Honest people the world over [!] in oral and written poetry alike glorify the grandeur of the deeds of the Soviet people and the CPSU [!]. The theme of Socialism and Communism has become the leading [!] theme of modern world [!] folklore, and is on the lips of the workers and peasants of capitalist countries. . . ." As the saying goes: no explanation required.

12. I remembered where this hypertrophy of the economic approach had led R. I. Gruber himself in the early 1930s, when he argued that the principal peculiarities of music are not that music, like language, is a means of communication, but that music is a "figurative form of ideology" and, moreover, is a "tool of class struggle" (1934: 16). In this he contradicted, in particular, the position of B. V. Asafev, who had compared music to speech.

13. Here the author refers to another article by Gruber (1928a)—an article on the sociological approach rather than the economic.

14. J. Martin Daughtry (2001) defines intonation as follows: "Asaf'ev uses the word 'intonation' (intonatsia) to refer to a complex and dynamic phenomenon that comprises a musical gesture or combination of gestures, its performance or 'articulation,' and the semantic charge (i.e., the meaningful content) that the gesture carries. This charge is ascribed to the musical gesture by the historically situated group of performers and listeners that produce and receive it."

15. I do not feel that it is possible to delve into a large number of statements that are not based on deep insight into the essence of Marxism, but I will take the opportunity of citing one observation, which belongs to an English philosopher: "It is a commonplace—we are all Marxists to this extent—that our society places unrecognized constraints upon our imaginations" (Skinner 1969: 53).

References

Asafev, B. 1963. *Muzykal'naya forma kak protsess* (Musical form as process). Leningrad: Muzyka.

———. 1965. *Izbrannye stat'i o muzykal'noi prosveshchenii i obrazovanii* (Selected articles on music education). Moscow and Leningrad: Muzyka.

Babushkin, N. 1963. *O marksistsko-leninskikh osnovakh teorii narodno-poetich-eskogo tvorchestvo* (On the Marxist-Leninist basis of the theory of popular-poetic creative work). Tomsk: Tomsk University Press.

Benovska-Subkova, M. 1993. "Arkhaichni kulturni modeli i totalitarism" (in Bulgarian, with abstract in English). *Bulgarski folklor* 4.

Berlin, I. 1963. *Karl Marx*. London and New York: Oxford University Press.

Daughtry, J. Martin. 2001. "Russia's New Anthem and the Negotiation of National Identity." Unpublished.

Fesenko, A., and T. Fesenko. 1955. *Russkii yazyk pri sovetakh* (The Russian language and the Soviets). New York: n.p.

Gruber, R. I. 1925. "Ustanovka muzykal'no-khudozhestvennykh ponyati v sotsial'no-ekonomicheskoi ploskosti." (Establishing the concepts of music on a socioeconomic plane.) In *De Musica*, Annals of the faculty of music of the State Institute of the History of Art, no. 1. Leningrad.

———. 1928a. "Iz oblasti izuchenia muzykal'noi kul'tury sovremennosti" (From the area of the study of contemporary musical culture). *Muzykoznanie* (Musicology). Annals of the faculty of music of the State Institute for the History of Art, 40–62. Leningrad: Academia.

———. 1928b. "O vozmozhnosti i predelakh ispol'zovania v muzykovedenii eko-nomicheskikh kategori" (On the possibility and limits of the application of economic categories to musicology). *Muzykoznanie*.

———. 1934. "O realizme v muzyke" (On realism in music). *Sovetskaya muzyka* 6.

Heller, M. 1985. *La machine et les rouages: La formation de l'homme soviétique*. Paris: Calmann-Levy.

Iranek, Y. 1965. "Nekotorie osnovnye problemy marksistskogo muzykovedenia v svete teorii intonatsii Asafeva" (Some basic problems of Marxist musicology in the light of Asafev's theory of intonation). In *Intonatsia i muzykal'ny obraz*, 53–94. Moscow: Muzyka.

Levin, M., and Cheboksarov, N. 1955. "Khoziaystvenno-kul'turnye tipy i istoriko-etnograficheskie oblasti" (Economic-cultural types and historico-ethnographical regions). *Sovetskaya etnografia* 1: 3–17.

Mamardashvili, M. K. 1992. "Mysl pod zapretom" (Banned thought). *Voprosi filosofii* 4.

———. 1997. *Lektsii o Pruste* (Readings on Proust). Moscow: Ad Marginem.

Marx, K., and F. Engels. 1956. *Nemetskaya ideologia* (German ideology). Moscow.

Mazo, M. 1996. "The Present and the Unpredictable Past: Music and Musical Life of St. Petersburg and Moscow since the 1960s." *International Journal of Musicology* 5.

Munck, Ronaldo. 2000. *Marx@2000: Late Marxist Perspectives*. New York: St. Martin's Press.

Panchenko, A. M., and A. A. Panchenko. 1996. "Os'moe chudo sveta" (The axial miracle of the world). In *Polyarnost' v kul'ture*. St. Petersburg: Russian Academy of Sciences, Institute of Russian Literature.

Seriot, P. 1993. "O yazyke vlasti: kriticheskii analiz" (On the language of power: Critical analysis). In *Filosofia yazyka: v granitsakh i vne granits*. Kharkov: Oko.

Skinner, Q. 1969. "Meaning and Understanding in the History of Ideas." *History and Theory* 8.

Sokhor, A. N. 1975. *Sotsiologia i muzykal'naya kul'tura* (Sociology and musical culture). Moscow: Sovetskii kompozitor.

Zachesov, K., and A. Magomedov. 1991. "Magia ponyati i sotsial'naya real'nost' " (The magic of meanings and social reality). *Obshchestvennye nauki i sovremennost'* 6.

Zemtsovsky, I. I. 1970. *Narodnye pesni o Lenine* (Folk songs about Lenin). Leningrad-Moscow: Sovietskii Kompozitor.

———. 1971. *V. I. Lenin v pesnyakh narodov SSSR* (V. I. Lenin in the songs of peoples of the USSR). Moscow: Muzika.

———. 1972. "O sistemnom issledovanii fol'klornykh zhanrov v svete marksistko-leninskoi metodologii" (On the systematic study of genre in folklore in the light of Marxist-Leninist methodology). In *Problemy muzykal'noi nauki*, Vol. 1, 169–97. Moscow: Muzika.

———. 1974. "O dvukh aspektakh sotsiologicheskogo izuchenia narodnoi muzyki" (On two aspects of the sociological study of folk music). In *Izvestia Instituta Muzykoznanie na Bulgarskata Akademia na Naukite*, Vol. 17 (in Russian). Sofia.

———. 1977. "Narodnaya muzyka i sovremennost' (K probleme opredelenia fol'klora)" (Folk music and modernity: On the problem of defining folklore). In *Sovremennost' i fol'klor,* edited by V. E. Gusev, 28–75. Moscow: Muzyka.

———. 1987. "Leninskaya teoria otrazhenia i problemy etnomuzykoznania" (Lenin's theory of reflection and problems of ethnomusicology). In *Leninizm i problemy etnografii*, 147–61. Leningrad: Nauka.

———. 1988. "Sotsiologia ritma (Etnomuzykovedcheski aspekt)" (The sociology of rhythm: Ethnomusicological aspect). In *Metodologia i sotsiologia iskusstv*, 138–47. Leningrad: Ministry of Culture of the Russian Federation.

———. 1997. "An Attempt at a Synthetic Paradigm." *Ethnomusicology* 41 (2):185–205.

Zemtsovsky, I. I., and A. Kunanbaeva. 1997. "Communism and Folklore" In *Folklore and Traditional Music in the Former Soviet Union and Eastern Europe: An Assessment*, edited by James Porter, 3–23, 42–44. Los Angeles: UCLA Press.

9

Making Marxist-Leninist Music in Uzbekistan

THEODORE LEVIN

An all but incalculable distance lies between genteel scholarly invocations of Marxism as a critical tool for probing the social foundations of music, and the unbridled fury which Soviet Marxism-Leninism unleashed on the arts beginning in the 1920s. The devastation that the Soviet state wrought on Russia's artistic elite has been copiously documented by a stream of poets, novelists, historians, filmmakers, and theater directors. Yet, for all their importance as cultural icons, the pantheon of celebrities who became literal or figurative martyrs to Marxism-Leninism—Akhmatova, Mandelstam, Meyerhold, Bulgakov, Shostakovich, Pasternak—represents but one element in the artistic life of the former Soviet Union. Soviet policies aimed to recast popular culture and peasant culture no less than the fine arts, and these policies were implemented not only throughout the vast territory of Russia itself, but in every republic and region of the Soviet empire.

In areas of the Soviet Union whose indigenous populations were predominantly non-Russian—colonies, by any other name—culture policies served four principal ideological aims: combating the legacy of feudalism, embodying atheism, reifying officially sanctioned national identities, and nurturing cultural evolution among peoples who, in the Eurocentric Marxist-Leninist view, lagged behind European Russia's high level of cultural development. "Nationalist in form, Socialist in content" was the slogan that set the course for artistic work in the 15 Soviet republics and dozens of subordinate political entities—autonomous republics, autonomous regions, provinces, territories—where Soviet cultural strategists forged distinct ethnolinguistic identities in literature, art, and music.

In music, the expression "Socialist in content" is of course problematic, since music arguably has no content aside from its arrangement of physical sounds (see, e.g., Stravinsky 1947). Cultural strategists, however, following the lead of Lenin and Anatoly Lunacharsky, the first Soviet cultural commisar, understood Socialist content to refer broadly to styles and idioms readily accessible to the working masses, devoid of associations with religious practice or feudal patronage, and founded on a common language of scales, intervals, and rhythms whose very universality could express the fraternal brotherhood of Socialist peoples. Ironically, this musical lingua franca of the Revolution was rooted in the bourgeois, urban popular culture of Russia familiar to the early Bolsheviks: fin-de-siècle "old romances," popular songs, and sanitized versions of folk songs arranged for piano, concert instruments, and cultivated voices.

The symmetrical diatonic melodies, rich chromatic harmonies, and regular, tempered intervals of urban Russian song could scarcely be a less auspicious match for the highly embellished modal scales, sinuous homophonic texture, and flexible microtonal intervals of traditional music among the Central Asian Uzbeks. Yet fusing Uzbek music with the idiom of urban Russian music (as distinct from Russian village music, whose grating dissonances and bawdy texts were themselves considered anathema by Soviet cultural strategists) to create "Socialist content" was the task undertaken by a pleiade of musicologists, folklorists, theorists, and performers who put their erudition and skill at the service of state culture policy, beginning in the 1920s and continuing until the breakup of the Soviet Union in 1991. Indeed, they had no real choice.

Soviet Colonialism and State Culture Policy

The Soviet Central Asian republic of Uzbekistan was formally created in 1924 from the remains of colonial Russian Turkestan and the defunct Bukharan Emirate. Alim Khan, the last of the Bukharan emirs, had fled Bukhara in 1920 to escape a Bolshevik firing squad, and for a time it seemed as if the resulting power vacuum might be filled by the Jadids, a group of cosmopolitan, European-educated Muslim Socialists drawn from the ranks of Bukhara's social and intellectual elite. The Jadids, however, were fatally tainted by their aristocratic backgrounds and their insistence that Islam was compatible with the establishment of a Socialist state. By the end of the 1930s, most of them had been liquidated as "enemies of the people," stripping Uzbekistan of some of its finest intellectual and artistic talent (see Khalid 1998).

The demise of the Jadids allowed Soviet cultural strategists to begin to build a new society in Uzbekistan, and this task was undertaken with great vigor through the 1930s and 1940s. By the advent of the post-Stalin era in the 1950s, the central government could proudly show off Uzbekistan to potential client states in the Third World as a model of how a poor, largely illiterate Islamic people rooted in feudal social relations could be economically and culturally transformed through Marxism-Leninism into a thriving Socialist

state. While music may seem peripheral in such an all-encompassing transformation, the varying fortunes of indigenous music during the six-odd
decades of Soviet rule in Uzbekistan provide telling evidence of the cultural
mechanisms of state Marxism in a colonial context. The experience of
Uzbekistan is of interest not only for historical reasons, but because it still
resonates in many nations that, willingly or under duress, have adopted
Soviet-inspired models for the cultivation of cultural life.

The strategy and tactics of Soviet colonial rule were unique in the history of empires. Other imperial powers have been content to rule, suppress,
exploit, even enslave their colonial subjects while leaving them more or less
free to speak their own language, practice their own religion, and pursue their
own traditions of expressive culture. By contrast, the Soviets were imperial
micromanagers. No aspect of life or art was too trivial to attempt to bring into
conformity with the prescriptions of Marxist-Leninist doctrine.

In Uzbekistan, as throughout the Soviet Union, colonial rule was nomi-
nally indirect, administered by local cadres schooled in Marxism-Leninism
and loyal to Moscow. The advantage of indirect rule was that these cadres,
rooted in local languages and cultures, were ideally situated to translate—literally and figuratively—Marxist-Leninist doctrine into local languages, customs, and traditions. At the same time that such "Party work" was
spearheaded by local cadres, Russians dispatched by Moscow served as gray
eminences, overseeing, exhorting, teaching, and setting an example for their
local Party brethren. In the arts and humanities, some of the Russians who
assisted their comrades in far-flung regions of the Soviet Union were distinguished figures whose scholarly altruism was fueled by a variety of motives:
ethnographic interest in Russia's vast range of "Oriental" cultures, ideological conviction, fear, or a mixture of these.

The Feudal Basis of Neutral Thirds

An example of how musicology became enmeshed in Marxism is the work of
Viktor Mikhailovich Beliayev (1888–1968), a scholar with wide-ranging
interests in both Russian art music and the musics of the Soviet Union's non-
Russian ethnicities, especially those of Central Asia. Beliayev's *Essays on
the History of the Music of the Peoples of the USSR,* published in 1962,
became a prominent textbook for Soviet conservatory students.[1] Much
less known is his 1933 publication, *Musical Instruments of Uzbekistan*
(Muzykal'nye instrumenty uzbekistana). In this 130-page monograph, Beliayev surveyed the various categories of Uzbek instruments—struck, plucked,
bowed, blown, and so on—offering for the instruments of each category
descriptions of physical appearance, interval measurements, and observations about historical evolution and social function. In the final three chap-

ters, titled "The Use of Uzbek Musical Instruments in Ensembles," "The Surviving Functions of Uzbek Musical Instruments," and "Uzbek Musical
Instruments and Their Use in the Building of Socialist Musical Culture in
Uzbekistan," Beliayev reflected more broadly on the past and the future of
Uzbek music. Throughout the work, he developed his fundamental idea
about musical culture: that characteristics of musical instruments may be
objectively related to a particular level of cultural and economic development
in society, and consequently, that the music intended to be played on any
instrument must embody the social values and attitudes implicit in the level
of development to which it is related. His discussion of the *tanbur,* a long-
necked lute that is the quintessential instrument of the Bukharan court music
tradition known as *shash maqâm,* is a case in point.

The fretting of the tanbur includes whole-tone intervals derived from circles of fourths and fifths as well as "neutral" intervals based on an older system of what Beliayev calls "metrical temperament" (i.e., derived from linear
measurement of the distance between adjacent frets).[2] On the neck of the tanbur, neutral scale degrees occur at the third, sixth, and seventh, creating intervals of more than a semitone but less than a whole-tone. On the evidence of
this combination of interval types, Beliayev dated the origins of the tanbur to
the "middle period of barbarianism" (*varvarstvo*), which Beliayev defined
musically as "that stage of humanity's development when the diatonic scale
existed not only in more advanced, settled agricultural cultures, but also in
nomad cultures" (1933: 85). Moreover, Beliayev attributed the survival of the
tanbur's "primitive" scale, in particular, neutral thirds, to the instrument's
role in a performance tradition that "upheld the taste of the ruling upper class
of the largely settled population of what is now Uzbekistan, an upper class
that strove to preserve feudal traditions in economic, political, and cultural
modes of life" (85).

Beliayev saw the rigidity of the tanbur's scale as connected to "the almost
ritual exploitation and at the same time, ossification of the forms of classical
Uzbek music . . ." (85). He viewed the "archaic" diatonic scale of the tanbur
as antipodal to the more progressive chromatic scale: "Inasmuch as the diatonic scale of the *tanbur* is the basis of the classical musical culture of Uzbekistan, serving the conservative tendencies of feudalism and protecting the
latter from 'foreign' influences, so also it is necessary to consider the appearance of the chromatic scale in Uzbekistan . . . as a factor of a progressive
order, exerting its influence . . . on the *tanbur*'s change of scale, and in this
way, beginning the disintegration of the stagnant culture of Uzbek classical
music" (117). Invoking the doctrine of "nationalist in form, Socialist in content," Beliayev advocated "reconstruction of the scales of Uzbek musical
instruments in the interest of the unification of these latter with [equally tem-
pered] European musical instruments, which must appear as a basic condition

for the possibility of a musical rapprochement between the Uzbeks and other nationalities in the work of creating a socialist musical culture" (124). It can be no accident that such a reconstruction began shortly after the publication of Beliayev's influential monograph.

Cultural Evolution: The Folk Orchestra

In 1934, a laboratory under the direction of A. I. Petrosian[3] was opened to design and build instruments for a newly created orchestra of folk instruments. The fundamental aim of the folk orchestras was to make accessible to native musicians both the masterpieces of the European classical tradition and the newly composed "fusion" music of Uzbek and Russian composers. Such aims necessitated several kinds of changes in the orchestra's instruments. First, the range of individual instruments had to be extended, for example, by adding strings or lengthening fingerboards. Second, instrumental consorts were created to extend a single timbral quality over a wide ambitus: the *rebâb*, a long-necked lute, was cloned into a bass rebâb and treble rebâb, and the *ghijak*, a spike fiddle, gave birth to the *katta ghijak* (big ghijak). Third, in order for the traditional unison orchestra to perform complex harmonic music, both equal temperament and total chromaticism were incorporated into the new creations. By the mid-1930s, experimental instruments had proliferated, and one orchestra counted a consort of five ghijaks, ranging from soprano to contrabass. Until the mid-1940s it was common also to include European instruments—especially trumpets, tubas, and trombones—to provide timbral variety and reinforcement of the bass register. Later, however, these were dropped, and by the mid-1950s, the complete forces of the Uzgosfilarmonia (Uzbek State Philharmonic), directed by Petrosian, included:

> *nai* (end-blown flute) I, II, III
> *koshnai* (soft oboe) I, II
> *surnai* (loud oboe)
> *chang* (struck dulcimer) I, II, III
> *tanbur* (long-necked lute)
> Kashgar *rebâb* (long-necked lute) I, II
> Afghan *rebâb* (long-necked lute)
> *dutâr* (long-necked lute) I, II, alto, bass, contrabass
> *dâyra* (frame drum)
> *naqâra* (kettledrums)
> *ghijak* (spike fiddle) I, II, alto, bass, contrabass

A prodigious body of original works for folk orchestra has been produced by Soviet composers, and a typical program will include selections from this repertory as well as arrangements of classical Russian and European masterpieces. A favorite among folk orchestras is *Eine kleine Nacht-musik*. The solo and concerto repertory has also received wide attention, and for individual practice, instrumentalists tackle the standards of this literature as well as new virtuosic creations by Soviet composers; the Mendelssohn violin concerto and Brahms' Hungarian Rhapsodies are among the most frequently heard.

The ideological legerdemain necessary to represent Europe's great composers not as accomplices of aristocratic court culture but as its hapless victims had already been done for the Uzbeks by cultural strategists in Moscow. Mozart, Haydn, Schubert, Beethoven (who in particular was associated with Lenin and his alleged love of classical music; Zhukov's famous portrait of a pensive Lenin listening to the "Appasionata" Sonata hung in almost every Soviet music school and conservatory) had all received the stamp of approval, and their works became ready targets for the folk orchestra industry. Almost seventy years after folk orchestras first appeared in Uzbekistan, they remain fixtures of state culture policy—de rigueur in music education and ubiquitous on the state-owned radio; monuments to an ideological vision that embraced European high culture as an antidote to musical ossification rooted in the social rigidity of feudalism.

Folk orchestras were not the only musical institutions on the front lines of the ideologically ordained "struggle against the old." Song-and-dance ensembles were transformed from what cultural strategists called "unison collectives," which performed Uzbek music in the traditional monophonic style, to "harmonic ensembles" whose arrangements of folk songs featured densely chromatic harmony. The eventual development of monophonic music into harmonic music was viewed as an historical inevitability. Four-part choruses proliferated, and Uzbek composers explored an increasingly wider variety of European forms and genres. In a book published in 1973, Natalia Yanov-Yanovskaya describes the artistic climate of Uzbekistan between the end of the Second World War and the beginning of the Brezhnev "era of stagnation" in the mid-1960s:

> Party and government decrees on questions of literature and art had a large influence on the development of music in Uzbekistan, as on Soviet art as a whole. These documents oriented composers toward the creation of comprehensible and substantial music, strongly connected with national roots, and democratic in its essence. The decrees especially underlined the fruitful role of the tradition of Russian and Western European classics.
>
> This position received its concrete elaboration in the Decree of the Central Committee of the Communist Party of Uzbekistan of April 8, 1951 "Towards the Conditions of Musical Art in the Uzbek SSR and Measures for its Further Development." It defined the task of disseminating harmonic music among the popular masses, propagandizing Russian classical and Soviet music, and creating artistic pieces on contemporary themes. The

decree condemned attempts at the idealization of archaic forms, the canonization of monophony, the predominance of legendary-fantastical thematicism, and instead underlined the social role of music, its indissoluble link with the life of the people. (7)

While the goals of culture policy have radically shifted in post-Soviet Uzbekistan, the notion of shaping culture by decree has remained very much alive. In 1990, as the Soviet Union was coming apart, a report from the Ideological Commission of the Central Committee of the Comunist Party of Uzbekistan titled "About the Programme of Study, Preservation, and Propaganda of Uzbekistan *Mer'âs* [heritage]" proposed an ambitious plan for the restoration of architectural monuments, the development of museums, the publication of forgotten works of literature and translations and facsimiles of scientific treatises, the revival of traditional festivals such as *Nowruz* (New Year's), and the use of a variety of media—print, film, video, music, theater, sculpture, architecture—to "propagandize the history of the peoples of Uzbekistan," as the report put it. *Mer'âs* became a blueprint for the prescriptive culture policy of post-Soviet Uzbekistan, which through a succession of decrees, campaigns, and strategems has steadily tightened its control over the nation's cultural life.

Embodying Atheism

When the Bolsheviks began their cultural transformation of Central Asia in the 1920s, Islam already had a history of more than a millennium in the region. Bukhara, the capital of the Bukharan Emirate, was known as the "dome of Islam," and the Bukharan Emirate was a theocracy whose rulers invoked Islamic law and tradition in all domains of their rule. Transforming devout Muslims into Socialist atheists was a formidable task for cultural strategists in Central Asia, and an enormous campaign was mounted to undermine Islamic practices and beliefs. Mosques were closed, religious schools shut down and books burned, religious teachers persecuted, and the observance of Muslim holidays forbidden. Wandering dervishes (*qalandar*) who proselytized Islamic values through chants and songs, and story tellers (*maddah*) who gathered crowds to recite morality tales disappeared from the streets. The most sustained ideological battle was against Sufism, the mystical branch of Islam which had many adherents in Central Asia and which has traditionally embraced music and dance as legitimate elements of prayer.

The extent to which Sufism was diffused in works of art, music, and literature has been for centuries the subject of speculative as well as hermeneutic consideration. This is largely due to the nature of Sufism itself, which is a gnostic approach to ontological and metaphysical questions—a world image—more than a rigid doctrine. For Soviet cultural strategists, the presence of Sufi ideas in the cultural tableau of an atheist state was anathema. But these strategists had to face the dilemma implicit in forging historical "great traditions" that provided a basis for national cultural identities while acknowledging that many of the figures central to these traditions were linked both to Sufism and feudalism. To escape the dilemma, Soviet researchers argued that Sufism served medieval Islamic artists and intellectuals as a sort of radical chic in the same way, perhaps, that Buddhism has served American artists and intellectuals in our own time.

Musicologists, following the interpretation of Central Asian music history prescribed by the Ministry of Culture and the Ministry of Enlightenment, saw the locus of Sufi influence in the *maqâm,* the large repertory of art songs and instrumental pieces associated with feudal court patronage. Musicologist Tamara Vyzgo sums up the official position in an article published in 1961:

> During the *maqâm*'s existence under feudal court conditions, the texts changed accordingly, adapting to the tastes of the ruling class. The texts accumulated religious context, penetrated by the foggy ideas of sufism. Thus, court singers and feudal nobility strove to transform these folk compositions. But this did not succeed. . . . At their roots, the *maqâm*s strongly preserved their connection with folk creativity. (216)

Anti-Feudalism Redux

The idea that the roots of the "professional" maqâm tradition are in "folk creativity" is one of the most central and enduring ideological derivatives of both Marxist-Leninist aesthetics and Soviet Nationalities Policy. This relationship was stated repeatedly in Soviet scholarship, for example, by Veksler in 1961:

> All the greatest accomplishment of professional music lean on the tradition of folk creativity. *Maqâms* are an indisputably contradictory phenomenon. Despite certain reactionary characteristics connected with the cultivation of *maqâm* at the courts, they objectively reflect the tradition of folk musical creativity, since they arose on the basis of the latter. (97)

The underlying assumption in Veksler's musical ontogenesis is that music tends to evolve from a sort of spontaneous generation in the pristine state of "folk creativity" to the more complex forms that Soviet musicologists called "professional music." According to this logic, it is only natural that the professional maqâm repertory, arising out of rural folk music, should achieve a higher stage of complexity in the sophisticated urban conditions of Bukhara, Samarkand, Khiva, and Kokand, where the musician could achieve a greater degree of artistic specialization and virtuosic development.

The notion of musical evolution is supported by a concept that became a cornerstone of all modern Soviet (and much post-Soviet) research in music history, theory, and aesthetics. Conceived by the doyen of early Soviet musicology, Boris Vladimirovich Asafev (pronounced Asáfiev) (1884–1949), this concept was coined *intonatsiya* and received exhaustive explanation in Asafev's book of the same name, written in 1941–42 and comprising Volume 2 of his major work, *Musical Form as Process* [Muzykal'naia forma kak protsess].[4] To read Asafev himself is to behold crystallized Marxist materialism trained on the realm of aesthetics:

> Music is a wholly intonational art and is neither a mechanical transference of acoustical phenomena to the arena of artistic imagination, nor a naturalistic revelation of the sphere of feeling. Like every activity of man which is cognitive and reconstructs reality, music follows consciousness and represents rational activity. The feeling, e.g., the emotional tone inevitably peculiar to music, is not its cause, because music is *an art of intoned thought.* It is conditioned by the nature and the intonational process of man; in this process, man does not appear beyond relation to reality. (1957: 260; emphasis in original)

Asafev himself does not provide a terse, summary definition of *intonatsiya,* but Russian music scholar Malcolm H. Brown offered a handy working definition in a 1974 article in the *Musical Quarterly*:

> The concept of 'intonazia' is defined in its primal sense as any phonic manifestation of life or reality, perceived and understood (directly or metaphorically) as a carrier of meaning. In other words, an 'intonazia' in its simplest form is a real sound produced by something, be it creature or natural phenomenon . . . with which meaning is associated or to which meaning is ascribed. Thus, a musical 'intonazia' results when some 'intonazia' from life experience is transmuted into a musical phrase. (559)

According to Asafev, the meanings associated with an intonatsiya become increasingly abstract when the intonatsiya reflects reality not directly, but secondarily, through images or symbols contained in language or in other art forms. Nonetheless, a single intonatsiya—a single semantic meaning—can pervade musics of varying levels of complexity if at root these musics contain common underlying melodies, rhythms, or motifs.

Intonatsiya, then, is the mechanism that for Soviet scholars forged the link between folk music and maqâm. Both types of music could be considered to contain the same intonatsiya, that is, the same kernel of meaning, originating in the same deeply rooted spirit of "folk creativity," and apparent distinctions in the class values of the repertories could be set aside. The great sensitivity of the issue of origins and class values is pointed to by passages such as the following, from a collection of articles on Uzbek music published at the beginning of the 1960s:

Is *maqâm* a product of folk creativity, crystallized through the efforts of many generations of musician-professionals, or is it the creation of a feudal-court milieu, foreign to "the people"? This is a question which for many years has agitated composers and musical figures in Uzbekistan. In several studies of Uzbek music produced in the '30s, the completely incorrect assertion was put forth that *maqâm*s were the product not of indigenous national professional music creativity, but merely an echo, a weak imitation of Arabic and Persian models. (Karelova 1961: 72)

Whatever else they include, these unattributed "studies of Uzbek music produced in the '30s" must certainly number among them Beliayev's 1933 monograph. His depiction of the Uzbek maqâm as a frozen musical artifact emerges as clearly deviant when set against the ideological context that emerged in the post-Stalin era of strong national cultural heritages rooted in autochthonous folk musics. However, Beliayev wrote his monograph before the invention of intonatsiya, and before it became acceptable to trace the maqâm's origins to folk music. Given the time at which Beliayev published his monograph, he could hardly have been too cautious in respecting the ideological currents that clearly affected every kind of music and music scholarship in the Soviet Union.

Reifying National Identities

Soviet Nationalities Policy was founded on Lenin's idea of a voluntary union of nations that would cast down colonial ruling forces and, in their place, establish the right of national self-determination by an emancipated proletariat. The assumption was that once emancipated, the proletariat of each nation would freely choose to unite in the struggle against the forces of capitalist exploitation. Thus the original goal of Nationalities Policy was not primarily to establish and nourish a national identity, but to promote class self-determination, and consequently class solidarity. In the words of the Tenth Party Congress of 1921, Nationalities Policy was meant to help non-Russians in the USSR "develop and consolidate the Soviet statehood in a form corresponding to their own national features and conditions of life." At this Congress, "the People's Commissar for Nationality Affairs, Josef Stalin, listed Bukharans and Khivans, along with Kazakhs, Uzbeks, Turkmens, and Tajiks, as Central Asian nationalities deserving help in developing and strengthening their statehood" (Becker 1968: 163). Music, like language, literature, folklore, plastic arts, film, theater, education, and employment practices, became a vessel for realizing the practical goals of Nationalities Policy.

To sum up briefly these goals for Central Asia, the main thrust of Nationalities Policy was to divide the area into a number of distinct nationalities based on an ethnolinguistic consciousness that was fundamentally alien to indigenous concepts of group identity. Stalin (1942: 12) had defined a nation as "a historically evolved, stable community of language, territory, economic life, and psychological make-up (national consciousness) manifested in a community of culture," and it was this definition that the nationalities were meant to satisfy. Stalin's definition had no place for the fluid and imagined boundaries, hybridity and contested identities, deterritorialization and reterritorialization that figure so prominently in the culture theories of postmodern social science.

From the many fragmented strands of group identity that existed among Central Asian peoples, the Soviet government created five distinct nationalities, each with its own ethnic identity, territorial boundaries, language, and cultural history: Uzbek, Tajik, Turkmen, Kazakh, and Kyrgyz. In addition, a few ethnic minorities (Karakalpaks, Uighurs, Dungans, Baluchis) were given various degrees of autonomy ranging from an autonomous territorial area (Karalkapak Autonomous Soviet Socialist Republic, comprising one third of the area of Uzbekistan), to authorization of separate schools and cultural establishments.

Western scholars writing about Central Asia have focused on the sinister political aspects of Nationalities Policy, concluding that its primary intent was to neutralize the threat of a pan-Islamic or pan-Turkic reformist or separatist movement that would have posed a serious challenge to Moscow's control of the region (the seeds of such a movement had actually been sown by the Jadids, the Muslim Socialist reformist group).

The manipulation of distinctions and similarities—between indigenous Central Asians and Russians, as well as among Central Asians themselves—has been central to the various programs initiated under Nationalities Policy. At the same time that the utopian ideal of breaking down distinctions among peoples to create an international Marxist-Leninist culture remained an abiding element in official Soviet doctrine and propaganda (as was apparent from viewing practically any political billboard in the Soviet Union in the 1970s and 1980s), the threat of unwanted coalitions and convergences of potentially hostile groups has necessitated a delicate and sometimes shifting approach to the nationalities question.

In the Soviet Union, the Nationalities program of the 1920s, which countered the threat of pan-Islamism or pan-Turkism with the creation of national republicanism, was known as "divergence" (*otdalenie*), while later programs to assimilate the peoples of the Soviet Union into one Soviet people were guided by the concepts of "drawing together" (*sblizhenie*) and finally "rapprochement" (*sliianie*) (see Bennigsen and Wimbush 1979: 103; Allworth 1973: 9). The various political trends of Nationalities Policy were reified in official attitudes toward musical performance, pedagogy, and scholarship, all of which were viewed as extensions of issues regarding national identity, and resulted in changes in the style and organization of these activities.

Nationalities Policies affected the *Shash maqâm*—the classical court music repertory patronized by the aristocracy of the Bukharan Emirate—in a number of ways. Most obvious was the cloning of the repertory into two variants, one associated with the republic of Uzbekistan, and another with the neighboring republic of Tajikistan. Most vocalists who performed the Shash maqâm were bilingual in Uzbek and Tajik and sang lyrics drawn from both languages. However, the state publishing apparatus of Uzbekistan published a version of the Shash maqâm that contains exclusively Uzbek texts, while the "Tajik" Shash maqâm was published in Tajikistan in a version containing exclusively Tajik texts. The Shash maqâm became a politically protean symbol of national identity, with scholars adjusting their discussion of the repertory as political expediency demanded. For example, in a 1959 edition of the Shash maqâm published in Uzbekistan, musicologists Akbarov and Kon wrote the following:

> We must suppose that the united effort of historians, orientalists, and musicologists will lead in the near future to clarification of the problem of the origin and historical development of the *maqâms,* which are a remarkable monument to the centuries-old history of musical culture of the Uzbek people. (xxx)

By contrast, in Viktor Beliayev's 1950 edition of the *Shash maqâm,* published in cooperation with the republic of Tajikistan, the following note appears in the introduction:

> The classical music of the Tajik people, which is united under the general name *Shash maqâm,* together with other folk melodies and pieces, and with the musical culture of the great Russian people, is one of the fundamental sources of modern Soviet-Tajik musical culture and musical art. (11)[5]

Of course exponents of neither nation's culture are claiming that the Shash maqâm does *not* belong in some measure to the other. In fact, the absurdity of dividing an obviously unified cultural artifact into two distinct national versions has often been noted, off the record, with irony. Some Tajiks, however, hold that the nomadic Uzbeks are *arrivistes* in the matter of courtly culture and in particular, in the courtly traditions of the Shash maqâm. In their view, the synthesis of a "great tradition" of Uzbek national music and literature has been a sham perpetrated by the exigencies of Soviet Nationalities Policy, and in the post-Soviet era, by the nationalistic culture policies of the current regime.

Culture Policy in the "Period of Stagnation"

By the time of the "Period of Stagnation," as Leonid Brezhnev's rule came to be known during the subsequent era of perestroika, the ideological fury of the early Soviet years had fizzled and sputtered, the government's campaign against the vestiges of feudalism spent and irrelevant to a cynical citizenry. In Moscow and Leningrad, artists and writers famously challenged the metanarrative of Socialism through Aesopian literature and film, not to mention open cultural and political dissidence. In Uzbekistan, by contrast, artists largely remained compliant with the norms of Marxist-Leninist culture policy. Even in 1991, when Uzbekistan became independent by default upon the breakup of the Soviet Union, artists did not immediately rush to overturn the stylistic canons of Socialist Realism. What changed was not so much canons of style and taste, as the ideological use to which these canons were put. In post-Soviet Uzbekistan, it was but a small step from Soviet-style "national" musics identified with a Soviet republic to "national" music associated with an independent nation and its national heritage. "Nationalist in form, Socialist in content" became "Nationalist in form, nationalist in content."

In the strong nationalist climate of present-day Uzbekistan, vestiges of Soviet cultural models created in the 1930s still exist, as they do throughout much of the former Soviet Union and in many parts of the world that forged cultural ties with the USSR in the formative years of post–World War II development: China, India, Africa, the Middle East, Cuba, Mongolia. Nationalistic folk heritage festivals, state-sponsored music ensembles lodged in the sinecure of state-sponsored radio stations, and national folk troupes which perform bowdlerized, choreographed versions of traditional dance and music are but a few of the cultural artifacts that constitute the legacy of Marxist-Leninist culture policy. As the millennium turns and the political system inspired by Marxism-Leninism dissolves or drifts away from its erstwhile orthodoxies, the ideologically dominated and overdetermined vision of cultural life nurtured by the world's largest Marxist-Leninist state remains anomalously, and disturbingly, alive.

Notes

1. The portion of this work devoted to Central Asia was translated into English by Mark Slobin and Greta Slobin and published in 1975 as *Central Asian Music*.
2. This procedure accords with thirteenth-century music theorist Safî al-Dîn's description of linear fret placement (d'Erlanger 1938: 114–15) to produce the neutral third (*wustâ zalzal*) of Persian and Arabic music. The frets for the neutral sixth and seventh, according to Beliayev, divided the interval between the perfect fifth and the octave (a fourth) into three equal parts.
3. Also known as Petrosants.
4. For a complete English translation, see James Robert Tull, "B.V. Asaf'ev's Musical Form as Process: Translation and Commentary" (1977). Ph.D. diss., Ohio State University.
5. Beliayev himself may not have written the brief introduction to his edition from which this quote is drawn. It is signed *"Upravlenie po delam iskusstv pri*

sovete ministrov tadjikskoi SSR" [Administration for Artistic Affairs of the Soviet Ministers of the Tajik SSR].

References

Akbarov, I. A., and I. U. Kon. 1959. *Uzbek xalq muzikasi,* Vol. 5. Tashkent: Gosudarstvennoe izdatelstvo xudozhestvennoi literatury Uzbekskoi SSR.

Allworth, Edward, ed. 1973. *The Nationality Question in Soviet Central Asia.* New York: Praeger.

Asafev, Boris V. 1957. *Muzikal'naia forma kak protsess* (Musical form as process), Vol. 5 of *Izbrannyie trudy* (Collected works). Moscow: Izdatel'stvo Akademii Nauk SSSR. Originally published in 1930 (Vol. 1) and 1947 (Vol. 2).

Becker, Seymour. 1968. *Russia's Protectorates in Central Asia: Bukhara and Khiva, 1865–1924.* Cambridge: Harvard University Press.

Beliayev, Viktor M. 1933. *Muzykal'nye instrumenty uzbekistana.* (Musical instruments of Uzbekistan). Moscow: Gosudarstvennoe muzykalnoe izdatelstvo.

———., ed. 1950. *Shashmaqâm.* Moscow: Gosudarstvennoe muzykalnoe izdatelstvo.

Bennigsen, Alexandre A., and S. Enders Wimbush. 1979. *Muslim National Communism in the Soviet Union.* Chicago: University of Chicago Press.

Brown, Malcolm. 1974. "The Soviet Russian Concepts of 'Intonazia' and 'Musical Imagery.' " *Musical Quarterly* 40: 557–67.

d'Erlanger, Rodolphe. 1938. *La Musique Arabe,* Vol. 3. Paris: P. Geuthner.

Karelova, I. N. 1961. *Voprosy muzykal'noi kul'tury uzbekistana.* Tashkent: Gosudarstvennoe izdatelstvo xudozhestvennoi literatury UzSSR.

Khalid, Adeeb. 1998. *The Politics of Muslim Cultural Reform: Jadidism in Central Asia.* Berkeley: University of California Press

Slobin, Mark, and Greta Slobin, trans. 1975. *Central Asian Music* (adapted from Viktor M. Beliaev, *Ocherki po istorii muzyki narodov SSSR,* Vol. 1, Moscow, 1962. Middletown, Conn.: Wesleyan University Press.

Stalin, Josef. 1942 [1913]. *Marxism and the National Question.* Moscow: Foreign Languages Publishing.

Stravinsky, Igor. *The Poetics of Music.* 1947. Cambridge, Mass.: Harvard University Press.

Veksler, S. 1961. "Uzbekskie makomi." In *Voprosy muzykal'noi kul'tury uzbekistana,* edited by I. N. Karelova. Tashkent: Gosudarstvennoe izdatelstvo xudozhestvennoi literatury UzSSR.

Vyzgo, Tamara. 1961. "Tri proizvedeniia." In *Voprosy muzykal'noi kul'tury uzbekistana,* edited by I. N. Karelova. Tashkent: Gosudarstvennoe izdatelstvo xudozhestvennoi literatury UzSSR.

Yanov-Yanovskaya, Natalia S. 1973. "Muzykal'naia zhizn' 1945–1967 godov," *Istoriia uzbekskoi sovetskoi muzyki,* Vol. 2, edited by I. N. Karelova and F. M. Karomatov. Tashkent: Izdatelstvo literatury i iskusstva imeni Gafura Guliama UzSSR.

10

Central American Revolutionary Music

FRED JUDSON

Music as Social Discourse

Latin America's many musical vocabularies are as evident to consumers and aficionados of World Music as they are to musicians and musicologists.[1] Their variety, beauty, and appeal have engaged and influenced popular and classical music cultures and production far beyond their geographical and social contexts, particularly in Europe and North America. And that influence gathered force during the closing decades of the twentieth century; one need only see or hear the terms *samba, forro, tango, ranchera, salsa, merengue, son, corrido, huayna,* or *mariachi*, for example, to acknowledge it. Though perhaps a cliché, each Latin American musical vocabulary is more than an art form or a cultural expression; it is a social discourse. "Music does not create or realize itself, but is always the result of people doing things together in particular places and times. To understand music is to understand the men and women who make it, and vice versa" (Mellers and Martin 1989: x).

To be Marxist in the understanding of specific Central American revolutionary musics is necessarily to be eclectic and conceptually pluralist. Hence, the analytical point of departure regarding the *subjects* or *social actors* of this music is that of "the people" (*el pueblo*) more than it is of its structural *class* definition. Reflective of the respective Central American *pueblos* the music attributes to the social actors a variety of identities, including those of class (peasantry, proletariat, bourgeoisie), ethnicity (indigenous, black, mestizo and mulatto), gender (the female guerrilla combatant, the mother of the martyred hero, the enduring peasant woman), place (rural, urban, forest, mountain, tropics, province, region, certain towns, etc.), and culture (indigenous, ethnic minority, religious, peasantry, artisans, students, intellectuals, educated, illiterate). It expresses and contributes to a larger, more inclusive and more legitimate societal and national identity than that which prevails and is dominated by national oppressor and imperial social actors. As such, the music is considered as a whole people's cultural expression and thus as *popular* (such usage of the term also refers to the music's production within and alongside the many forms of commercially and socially popular music in Central America) while also political in its role as revolutionary social discourse.

What lends the Central American music examined in this chapter its revolutionary profile is not solely its dramatic social content or its conscious effort to articulate revolutionary social energies and objectives. It is that as concrete cultural production it has been human artifact created and performed in lived social contexts. Those contexts are the respective recent national political, economic, and social histories. The music, its thematic tropes and its forms, are embedded in those histories and in the human and social dynamics that make those histories and shape the respective national presents and futures. In this respect, to understand the music is to situate it in both the larger lived social histories of Central America and in the lived experiences of the music's producers and its "consumers." This chapter examines the themes present in the music with continued reference to those social histories and lived experiences. My own encounters with this music and with selected moments of those histories and lived experiences are central to the "socially constructed understanding" presented in the chapter. From the 1970s through the 1990s, I had the opportunity to act as interpreter/MC at numerous concerts, press conferences, and media interviews given in Canada by Central American musical groups whose work is discussed here. Those experiences provided me with invaluable personal contact with the music and its creators/performers. That cultural exposure was lent context and depth when I served as an interpreter at public meetings and media encounters for activists from various Central American countries who represented social movements and revolutionary political organizations. Research and residential sojourns in Managua, Nicaragua, throughout the 1980s and into the early 1990s put me in a variety of situations in which music was a social actor. To be present at political rallies where some of the groups played the music examined here for the people they intended to hear it deeply influenced my thinking about the music as a repertoire of revolutionary social discourse.

Two examples will suffice to convey the importance of such lived experience for the Marxist-inflected examination of Central American revolutionary music. Attending the 19 July 1985 mass rally on the sixth anniversary of the Sandinista revolution, I joined some half a million Nicaraguans and a scattering of internationalist supporters who sang along with such groups and artists as Mancotal, Carlos Enrique Mejía Godoy y los de Palacagüina, Norma Elena Gadea and Pancasán, whose work is examined in this chapter. To see the faces in the crowd, at times streaming with tears, and to hear the voices rise in songs that had been part of their own revolutionary morale, had been broadcast by clandestine rebel radio or played as part of popular mass in Catholic parishes affiliated with liberation theology during the guerrilla struggle and mass insurrection against the Somoza dictatorship, was an indelible experience. When Salvadorean revolutionary music groups living in exile in Managua took the stage that day, the crowd erupted with repeated slogans (*Si Nicaragua venció, El Salvador vencerá*—If Nicaragua won, El Salvador is next!) and sang the refrains to their well-known and militant tunes. The second occasion was in Managua some months after the Sandinistas lost the 1990 election, at a café where many artists associated with the revolution had performed during the Sandinistas' decade in power. Luis Enrique Mejía Godoy and Norma Elena Gadea sang "Nicagaragua, Nicaragüita," an affectionate, tender expression of love for the small country, as though for a beloved child. It had been performed at virtually all political meetings, as almost a second national anthem, during the revolutionary government, and was closely associated with the sense that the revolution had been a popular victory, an achievement of the whole nation. Needless to say, the café that night was in emotional overflow; it was the first time since the electoral defeat that the two artists most associated with the song had performed together.

Latin American musics as social discourses[2] vary widely. There is music expressing identities, such as the Peruvian black experience on the CD "Música Negra del Perú" (Various Authors 1999) or the contemporary Afro-Brazilian religious expression on the Virginia Rodrigues CD "Nós" (2000). The popularity and commercial success of the Cuban artists gathered under the loose rubric of the "Buena Vista Social Club" (1997) exemplifies, as one of the CDs' titles announces, what is "distinct and different" about Cuban music, and by extension, about Cubans' social experience of the twentieth century. The universe of Latin American music as radical social discourse in the twentieth century, represented, for example, in the LP *1er Festival Nuevo Canto Latinoamericano. Versión Urgente para Nicaragua* (Various Groups 1982), draws on roots of critical expression regarding slavery, colonialism, and foreign intervention in prior centuries. But its central discourses target the exploitation, repression, and immiseration of Latin America's experiences of modern capitalist development/underdevelopment. As well, the Cuban Nueva Trova (or New Song Movement) following the Cuban Revolution and the Chilean Nueva Canción irruption of the 1960s and 1970s, like others throughout the region, melded critical social protest, musical innovation, contemporary poetry and musical forms of oppressed and dominated groups (e.g., prostitutes, the rural poor, Andean indigenous peoples, sugar workers). They sought consciously both to recuperate and represent a "people's music," to legitimate it as popular and to wield music as a weapon in what they understood to be political class struggles, echoing Woody Guthrie's 1930s maxim: "This guitar kills fascists."

At the same time, such musical social discourses were reflective of global/international popular music genres, as they were of the social specifics of their respective national locales. As Simon Frith (1989: 2) writes, "no country in the world is unaffected by the way in which the twentieth-century mass media . . . have created a universal pop aesthetic." There are numerous contemporary Latin American musicians whose work is clearly a social discourse addressing local as well as larger Latin American situations and at the same time containing a "universal pop aesthetic," the Panamanian artist Rubén Blades (1999) being but one, albeit well-known, example. Central American revolutionary music of the 1970s and 1980s is also character-ized by a discursive and artistic content that is equally disparate and transcendent. Central American artists spoke to specific social interclass dynamics while recovering and popularizing musical forms of whole peoples and their histories. They adapted and improvised on those forms and drew upon musical and social discourses from elsewhere in Latin America and beyond, and from the universal pop aesthetic, producing distinctive work with appeal beyond their immediate circumstances. As Nicaraguan artist Luis Enrique Mejía Godoy remarked in liner notes for the Salvadorean group Banda Tepehuani, "They broke the barrier between 'serious' and 'popu-lar' . . . undertaking the deepening of the folkloric roots and popular music of their [Salvadorean] people, integrating elements from universal music" (Banda Tepehuani 1982).[3]

The social discourse of particular musical vocabularies can be intrinsi-cally and explicitly revolutionary, as, for example, the music of some Sal-vadorean groups affiliated with the Farabundo Mart' National Liberation Front (FMLN) written for and broadcast to guerrilla combatants from clan-destine and mobile radio stations (Almeida and Urbizagástegui 1999: 20; Shaull 1990). It can also be revolutionary in specific contexts, where a rev-olution is in power (Cuba, Nicaragua 1979–1990), where an armed revolu-tionary movement is contending for state power (El Salvador, Guatemala, Peru, Colombia at various times in the late twentieth century), where artists identify themselves with revolutionary projects (e.g., in Chile, Argentina, Brazil, Uruguay, Bolivia, Venezuela during periods of repres-sion, dictatorship, and resistance), or where certain musical vocabularies are associated with radical social forces and projects, considered subver-sive and repressed by state authorities. There is also revolutionary music as such due to its internationalism and solidarity with struggles elsewhere. Central American revolutionary music (of Nicaragua, El Salvador, and Guatemala) considered in this chapter meets all these criteria. But just as Frith (1989: 3) declares that "popular music study rests on the assumption that there is no such thing as a culturally 'pure' music," the assumption here is that there is no such thing as purely revolutionary music. It follows that artistic and discursive hybridity, flexibility, dynamism, and variety in Central American revolutionary musical expression are among its crucial characteristics.

A Framework of Understanding

The framework of understanding deployed here contains three general dimensions. One derives from the broad literatures that study revolutions as comparative sociopolitical phenomena, and contains two key assumptions. On the one hand, as Vilas (1995: 9) argues about revolutions in general and the Central American experiences specifically, "[They] are not inevitable, although neither are they accidents. The conditions that fuel and finally ignite a revolutionary process are always particular to each situation, but analysis at the proper level of abstraction brings out recurring elements in the specifics of each case." The "proper level of abstraction" is taken here to be the global character and uneven development of capitalism as the central organizing principle of modern human societies and their governance.[4] Hence, this dimension of analysis falls under the social science category of *political economy*. Following the tenets of that general approach to the study of revolution, represented among others by Moore (1966), Bulmer-Thomas (1987) and Dunkerley (1988), means understanding the social transformations and disruptions of macroeconomic changes, in Central America in the thirty years after World War II, as the crucible for revolutionary upsurges.[5] In effect, the wrenching and rapid modernization of Central America's "traditional" agrarian capitalist societies was the genesis of revolutionary situations.

On the other hand, as Marxist political doctrine and common sense would remind us, objective macroconditions are necessary but not sufficient for revolutionary situations, movements and outcomes to occur. The realm of the subjective, of the consciousness of social forces which may become engaged as revolutionary actors, is just as crucial. This second assumption regarding the causal foundation of revolutionary experiences is embedded in the well-known statement of Karl Marx (1972: 437) that "men make their own history, but they do not make it just as they please; they do not make it under circumstances chosen by themselves, but under circumstances directly found, given and transmitted from the past." It is in the *making*—the collective social action that constitutes history from a Marxist perspective—that consciousness and the realms of the subjective are manifested. Generally, Marxists hold that material life, in particular the human social activity that produces the means to life, determines the content and dynamics of consciousness, hence of culture. Consciousness and culture reflect and represent the ideational, discursive, and symbolic dynamics of those "concrete social relations" and their contradictions, according to Marxist cultural studies.[6] Thus, for example, if social relations are hierarchical, authoritarian, and enforced by violence, it is likely that the dominant cultural values and expressions will be so as well. But it is also within consciousness and culture that "spaces" reside in which ideas and values that contradict a given social order may develop. It is in the relationship between the fundamental social relations of a given society and its culture that revolutionary theorists locate the terrain of subjective conditions.

In the social sciences' inquiries pertaining to revolution and social change, this second general dimension of a framework of understanding derives from the intersection of *political culture* (the study of political values and discourses), *political sociology* (the study of social and class structures' significance for politics), and *political psychology* (the study of political behaviors and their underlying psychological bases). Such inquiries focus on the political syntax of the values and symbolic discourses that maintain or challenge a given socioeconomic and political order, and on those societal and individual processes by which those values and discourses are transformed and become forces themselves in the mass, sustained collective action we call revolutions. A diverse array of scholars and political actors have considered this dimension. Lenin (1975), of course, directly assumed and theorized the historical necessity for the vanguard communist party to mobilize revolutionary ideas, analysis and consciousness in the masses of Russian workers and peasants. Georges Sorel (1925), more representative of the anarchist tradition, focused on the nonrational, symbolic, and mythic structures and discourses of meaning as subjective forces in revolutionary situations. Whereas Marx theorized social contradictions and political struggle as deriving from opposed class interests, and "if . . . both Marx and Lenin stressed the importance of ideas in that struggle, Sorel argued that, in addition to interests and ideas, images and visions propelled human struggles" (Judson 1987b: 20).[7]

This dimension of consciousness, subjective forces and symbolic discourses was famously examined by Antonio Gramsci (1973) in the 1930s, principally through the concept of "hegemony." Gramsci sought to understand the ideological, cultural, and discursive fabrics of class domination under modern capitalism and how practices in those realms interacted with the relations of production and property, arenas of more classical Marxist attention. He also sought to empower subaltern classes and intellectuals through enabling "counterhegemonic" cultures and discourses. And both Marxist and non-Marxist scholarship have shown "in recent years . . . a marked shift from structural explanations of revolutionary processes to explanations integrating more cultural concerns" (Almeida and Urbizagástegui 1999: 14). Charles Tilly (1978), Theda Skocpol (1979), Eric Hobsbawm (1986) and Carlos Vilas (1995) are representative of those who seek to incorporate those concerns.

In combining, then, a political economy or structural dimension of understanding with this broadly cultural dimension, a deceptively elegant argument results: Whatever the structural realities of rapid and wrenching socioeconomic changes (in this case Central America's agrarian capitalist modernizations) people's perceptions and symbolic interpretations of those realities go quite some way in determining their responses to those changes. Those perceptions and symbolic discourses are understood by some, particularly in studies of social movements, as *collective action frames* (Snow and Benford 1988: 14): as dispositions to act. As Vilas (1995: 21) explains, the symbolic elements of a particular culture or society undergoing change do not necessarily orient people to collective action as resistance or revolution:

> Symbolic elements have long offered explanation and justification for the existing social order. Whether the order that is retreating under the assault of the market was objectively better or worse than the new one, therefore, is not the issue; people perceive it as better because the symbolic elements they possess enable them to evaluate it in this way, not merely because the old way of life was objectively less unsatisfactory. Under the old regime, people knew what to expect . . . the arguments that legitimize a social order tend to take on a certain autonomy from their substantive foundations. This is true of any social order and helps to explain the apparently inexplicable "tolerance" or adaptation that people can display under an oppressive or evil order.

Just as the political economy or structural dimension in the framework of understanding elides with that of political culture/sociology/psychology, the latter has a segue with the dimension of *cultural studies*. Almeida and Urbizagástegui (1999) explicitly merge them, drawing on Foran's (1997) concept of "political cultures of resistance and opposition" to focus on the role and content of popular protest music in creating and sustaining a revolutionary mobilization in El Salvador. In their view, popular protest music is a mobilizational resource for a revolutionary movement and is at least an important, even a crucial part of what Gramsci would see as a counterhegemonic culture: "revolutionary movements proffer ideas that emphasize shared injustices and underscore experiences of oppression in a fashion consistent with widespread cultural beliefs" (Almeida and Urbizagástegui 1999: 15). Such music and its conscious political deployment, they argue, achieved a "collective action frame of the insurgent movement in El Salvador between 1975 and 1992, in effect contributing to the movement's mobilization potential" (15) and disseminating a "repertoire of contention . . . the inclusion of contentious repertoires in protest music complements the abstract framing process of general problems, solutions and motivational appeals with precise tactical advice when the moment arises for participants and supporters to engage in collective protest and insurgency" (17).

In a similar elision of political culture approaches and cultural studies that treats Latin American protest and revolutionary music, Rodolfo Pino-Robles (1999: 1) remarks that "to speak of music and social change in the same breath is to speak of a commitment of people exercising this form of art to the service of a social cause." His examples, Atahualpa Yupanqui of Argentina and Violeta Parra of Chile, precede the Central American revolutionary musical discourses but share with them crucial aspects. Their music, in its use of popular forms, "becomes a form of popular memory . . . in which a sense of the past is reconstructed in society questioning and calling attention to the misfortune of those at the bottom of the social ladder" (6). Cuban writer Alejandro Carpentier, says Pino-Robles, captures how such music is "not just a testimony of the past, but a living force which informs the present."

> That music, coming sometimes from remote villages and brought into the city, installed in the suburbs, injected into dances, a lively and inventive music, reinvented daily, it was taking shape, integrating and sketching its own profiles. It was ascending, rising, invading, taking the public taste, to the dismay of those who considered themselves above what they saw as trivial and vulgar. (Carpentier 1977: 13)

Violeta Parra, the Chilean singer who preceded such socially and politically committed compatriot artists as Victor Jara and the world-renowned groups Inti-Illimani and Quilapayun, spoke simply of her connection as a people's artist to her performance materials: "I didn't realize, when I set out to acquire my first song . . . [that] I would learn that Chile is the best folklore reference book written" (1985: 10). Without employing the same conceptual vocabulary, Pino-Robles traces the same sequencing of Chilean and Argentine popular protest/revolutionary music's relationship to macrosocial phenomena of movement, mobilization, and revolutionary commitment as Almeida and Urbizagástegui (1999) find in the Central American experiences.

Themes in Central American Revolutionary Music

This discussion of the three elastic dimensions of a framework of understanding suggests an important enjoinder for contemporary social science: multifaceted social phenomena like Central America's revolutionary experiences and the music that accompanied them may best be understood with combined approaches. The particular framework of understanding presented here, in a certain sense a dynamic synthesis, provides a backdrop of interpretation and meaning for the examination of the music itself. Based in the understanding, a simple content analysis of a score of representative Central American revolutionary music products (LPs and cassettes by Nicaraguan, Salvadorean, and Guatemalan musicians) yields a set of themes. As would be the case with Salvadorean and Guatemalan revolutionary ideologies, a study of *Sandinismo* as Nicaragua's revolutionary ideology/morale (Judson 1987b) had identified several core themes one might expect would be present in the associated music: patriotism and national historical experiential continuity, particularly the linkage of epochs of struggle and figures symbolizing those struggles; anti-imperialism, specifically resistance to United States interventions and control of the region; internationalism and solidarity with similar anti-imperialist and revolutionary struggles, especially in Latin America, but also throughout the world; martyrology, that is, a focus on the sacrifices and losses of those fallen in the struggle, an expressed determination to make the works of the revolution their concrete legacy, and a probing consideration of death's presence for those continuing the struggle; the realm of the future, with its visions, dreams and, in Sorel's terms, *mythes* of the revolutionary society to come. These themes appear throughout Central American revolutionary music's social discourses. In addition to those themes, which together comprise what Central American revolutionaries would call *la mística* or *moral revolucionaria*, several others are evident in the music. Together with the ideological themes, they constitute, as it were, the vocabulary of the social discourses of Central American revolutionary music.

In looking at their respective national societies, Central America's revolutionary musical artists assert the identity of a people as *popular,* as the majority. And they turn that popular identity this way and that, considering class structures, ethnicity, customs, and geographic place. As it is fair to presume, given that the music, by and large, is consciously revolutionary, references to class are prevalent in musical social discourses about who constitutes "the people," *el pueblo,* as the collective social actor. Somewhat in tandem with the theme of solidarity appearing in the revolutionary ideologies, the ideal and practice of unity—of the people, of the revolutionary social forces, and of the different revolutionary organizations—appear frequently. This is especially the case with music that has moved from the raising of consciousness through mobilization to sustaining the political and armed struggle.

In giving discursive contours to the people as protagonist, Central American revolutionary artists, muralists, poets, and painters sharpen the definitions of the enemy. Giving the enemy a collective class name, often "the oligarchy," also serves to show the people as the great majority and the enemy as the powerful and undemocratic few. The instruments of oppression and class rule, the military, police, state security and intelligence operatives, also fall under the category of enemies of the people, though often it is made clear that they are tools and could be morally and patriotically redeemed, especially at the levels of conscript and lower rank. That is not the case with the "enemy behind the enemy," imperialism, the United States government. And in some instances, capital or capitalism is the enemy, though usually the people who control it or serve it are the discursive targets.

With the sharper definition of the enemy, the themes of armed struggle, revolutionary violence and combativity also become more pointed. Metaphors from popular language, intended to inspire courage and diminish the enemy, proliferate, while actual battles add triumphant or angry elements to place names which national and popular audiences are likely to know. And as combat to defeat or repel the enemy increases in ferocity and duration, there are more appeals for unity, discipline and trust in the revolutionary vanguard and leadership. There is direct reference to the life, loves, celebrations, privations and even the diet of the guerrilla combatants or the Sandinista soldiers. In the case of Nicaragua, there is a call to defend the social, political, and material achievements of the revolution. There is also an insistent content given to peace. There are certainly musical expressions of longing for peace and what it will afford for social development, for the flourishing of democracy, for rebeautifying devastated land and communities, for individual and family reunions, for love and life. But peace is not seen as arbitrary or given; it is to be won in confronting the enemy, in maintaining principles at the negotiating table and being forever mindful of the sacrifices of fallen comrades, in being vigilant in the defense of perceived social gains of the revolution in power (Nicaragua, but also FMLN "zones of control" during the Salvadorean conflict) or of the revolutionary struggle's organizational and military gains (El Salvador and Guatemala).

A final element in these revolutionary musical and social discourses, though also primary, recalls the third dimension of the framework of understanding, the cultural studies perspective, and that is the centrality of the popular. It is the language of the streets and markets, fields and jails, of those who have limited opportunity for formal education but who are artisans of language and who love its wordplay, its vibrant metaphors and its humor. And it is the rhythms, musical forms and instrumentations, the social juxtapositions of the music with family and fiesta, with dancing and significant life moments, with *campesino*/peasant,[8] worker and market life and with regional and local identity which lends this music perhaps its deepest and most grounded soul. It might be termed "folk popular," to distinguish it from, but also to acknowledge that popular majorities also listen to and like, domestic and international "pop music."

Revolutionary poetry and liberation theology in Central America found eloquence in the popular and vernacular: "Poetry by Rubén Darío,[9] Roque Dalton[10] or Father Ernesto Cardenal[11] frequently proved more inspirational than obscure Marxist tracts that had little to do with local conditions. Sermons by radical priests and homilies by the martyred Archbishop of El Salvador were often much more influential than quotes from Lenin or supposed directives from Moscow" (Vanden 1986: 1). The same was true for revolutionary music and its creators/performers. As Luis Enrique Mejía Godoy declared in liner notes (1992), "Everyday song is not a fad; it is something always living in the soul of the people."

Nationalism and the Historical Continuity of Struggle

Central American revolutionary thought and practice, which has generally but not exclusively been Marxist, has more often than not been strongly nationalist (Castañeda 1993: 267–325; Liss 1991). This is not surprising, given the national histories of resistance and rebellion, both to colonial rule and imperialism. Such a legacy is a rich resource for the construction of revolutionary discourse, and this theme is one of the most commonly found in the music. The very title of the Nicaraguan group Pancasán's (1983) album *Por La Patria* (For the fatherland) is a portent of the patriotic and nationalist flavor of several of its songs. In "¿Quienes Son?" (Who are they?) Pancasán traces oligarchic complicity with external aggressors to the Spanish "robbery of our Indians," their land and labor power. Pancasán, with perhaps the most militant sound of the Nicaraguan groups, attributes the various invasions and occupations by U.S. troops to "those who made a pact with the Yankees to murder Sandino" (Augusto César Sandino, the nationalist figure who waged guerrilla war against the U.S. Marines from 1927 to 34). They link the FSLN (Sandinistas) to Sandino and prior nationalists who confronted the United States. Time is continuous and mobile in this discourse: "Sandino was here among us, and he is always present," they sing in "El Cuje" (a rural locale). It is an appeal to memory as mobilizer and to a patriotic duty to those who struggled in the past, as Mejía Godoy puts it in his album *Yo soy de un pueblo sencillo* (I'm from a simple people) (1982): "to remember . . . you have to wake up . . . our children will sing what our grandfathers couldn't."

The echo of pre-conquest civilization marks a more distant historical continuity, as well as an alternate indigenous national identity, especially for Maya Guatemala. Kin-Lalat, in their album *Florecerás Guatemala* (1983), sing in the title song ("Guatemala, you will flower") that "we have lived a thousand years of death . . . in the country of eternal spring." The Nicaraguan group Mancotal looks to the precolonial roots for moral, practical and agrarian resources for the struggle to resist aggression and consolidate the revolution. In "Somos hijos del maíz" (We are children of corn) on the LP *Un Son para mi pueblo* (A *Son* for my people) (1981) they draw directly on Mesoamerican indigenous cosmologies. "We will survive," sings Mancotal, "as did our grandfathers, with corn fermented in the blood of heroes . . . corn cultivated here before the cross, the sword, the pirates and capital bloodied our land . . . we've done it for over a thousand sowing seasons." The song counsels Nicaraguans to recuperate the corn-based diet of indigenous peoples, the musicians' voices obviously delighting in listing and pronouncing the many dishes and drinks made from corn, "the irreversible nutrition of the people." With corn, "we will be renewed, we will be fresh corn!" Similarly, Carlos Mejía Godoy and the group Los de Palacagüina (1980) refer to the "millennial presence" of the indigenous community of Monimbó, a district of the Nicaraguan city Masaya. The song features the marimba, an indigenous instrument ("the marimba which plays sounds of liberation"), and links indigenous resistance against "the blond conquistadors" to the role of Monimbó in the popular insurrection against Somoza. Monimbó and its indigenous inhabitants are called "the pure soul of the Nicaraguan people."

The Salvadorean group Yolocamba Ita, in the title song for the album *Canto a la Patria Revolucionaria* (Song for the revolutionary homeland) (1981), pointedly links indigenous resistance to colonialism's commercialization of agriculture and control of labor power to the 1932 rebellion of coffee workers and the armed struggle of the FMLN (Farabundo Martí National Liberation Front) in the 1980s. There have been, their lyrics say, "centuries of lost lives, centuries of overdue revenge for our Pipil [an indigenous people whose remnants were massacred in 1932] land . . . the Indian Aquino [leader of an 1832 rebellion] and Farabundo Martí [leader of the 1932 rebellion] showed us the road we will follow." Both groups consciously took indigenous names, as did the Salvadorean groups Cutumay Camones (Almeida and Urbizagástegui 1999: 20) and Tepehuani.[12] Cutumay Camones also linked the FMLN combatants to Aquino, Feliciano Ama (another indigenous rebel leader in the 1932 events) and Martí: "If you'll glance over there at the mountain, you'll see they've been growing Aquinos in the canefields, Amas in the cornfields, Martís in the coffee groves," went the lyrics of their album *Por eso luchamos* (This is why we fight) (Almeida and Urbizagástegui 1999: 23, 26).

The continuity of suffering, injustice, and truncated sovereignty underlined in the music treating nationalist and patriotic themes finds its response in the appeal to contemporary generations to make good the sacrifices of precursors. An appreciation of national history is validated only by making that selfsame history, continuing and completing its national tasks: liberty, development, sovereignty, as Pancasán's song "Se Está forjando la patria nueva" (The new homeland is being forged) (1979) makes clear even before the 19 July 1979 victory over the Somoza dictatorship. Pancasán's LP *Vamos haciendo la historia* (1981) (Here we're making history) states in the title song: "We go making the history of what will come . . . it costs blows and takes the gun . . . to build the future." Nicaraguan history, plagued consistently by U.S. interventions, is recounted with dates, places, and names in their "Apuntes sobre el tío Sam" (Notes on Uncle Sam). Nicaraguans' pride at Augusto Sandino, known all over Latin America for his resistance struggle against the U.S. Marines, comes to full flower in the song "Adelante Nicaragua" only in the context of the popular insurrection that overthrew the Somoza dictatorship in 1979: "All Latin America is exclaiming: the homeland of Augusto Sandino is battling for its liberty!"

Pueblo, Patria, and Place: Popular Identity

There are several aspects of popular identity that Central American revolutionary music addresses. One of those clearly is social class, while another is nationality and citizenship—a patriotic and nationalist identity. What emerges from listening to this music and its combinations of lyrics, popular language, rhythms, instrumentation, and social discourses is the centrality of the *popular*. It is the music's embrace of the popular that gives its efforts to articulate and reinforce an identity among social forces either engaged or potentially engaged in revolutionary collective action its living discursive content. Collective action frames, as considered by Almeida and Urbizagástegui (1999: 15), "reinforce . . . collective identity, and solidarity among already committed movement members, evoke sympathy from potential supporters, and call the attention of a broader population to a situation that is unjust and in need of change." Particularly in those socioeconomic structures that are *not* what classical Marxism supposed were necessary conditions for socialist revolutions (advanced, industrial capitalist societies characterized by the stark class bifurcation of bourgeoisie and proletariat), a collective action frame has to provide a broader collective identity. Central America's revolutionary music often did that more successfully than did the ideologues and leaderships of the various revolutionary organizations, who tended to replicate vanguardist or Leninist orthodoxies of class (proletariat) and class consciousness.

The key term or trope in the identity discourse of Central American revolutionary music is *el pueblo*. Inclusive, positive, respectful, empowering and democratic are all inferential in the music's articulation of "the people." And it takes poets or musicians who are masters of popular idioms, of the colloquial, of regional and local expressions, to give pueblo its discursive content and form, just as it takes a radicalized and politicized consciousness in those poets and musicians to raise the term to its organic role in revolutionary cultural mobilization. Central America has not lacked for poets and musicians with those attributes. Ernesto Cardenal, Gioconda Belli, Claribel Alegría, Leonel Rugama, and Roque Dalton are among the many names that could come to mind.[13] One of the best-known exemplars among musicians is Carlos Mejía Godoy; Nicaraguan poet Julio Valle-Castillo paid tribute to his gifts in liner notes for the album *Monimbó* (Carlos Mejía Godoy 1980):

> Carlos Mejía Godoy doesn't sing to the people. The people sing in him, through him and with him. A popular voice. Voice and song of the people. Carlos is an eroticist of Nicaraguan speech . . . you can hear the delight of his pronunciation. His lyrics are true poems. Magnificent amorous, social, and political poems. His may be the best libertine poetry—creatively orgiastic—written by the younger generation. These lyrics or poems are in minor meter, octosyllabic even, full of bickering, lines, nicknames, proper names and diminutives: they're a real verbal coitus. (translation by author).

Among the strikingly creative, but genuinely rooted and popular works of Carlos Mejía Godoy is the *Misa Campesina Nicaragüense* (Nicaraguan folk mass) (1977). To sounds of marimba, guitar, accordion and drums, the lyrics identify the pueblo through its faith relationship with God and Jesus Christ: "You're the God of the poor, the human and humble God, who sweats in the street, the God of sunburned and leathery face; that's why I speak to You as my people speak, because you're the worker God, the worker Christ" ("Song of entry"). Such a God, such a Christ are the mirror of the pueblo: "You are there in the pay-line at the harvest . . . I've seen you selling lottery tickets . . . checking truck tires at the gas station . . . Christ, identify with us, not with the oppressor class, but with the oppressed, with my pueblo thirsty for peace" ("Entry" and "Kyrie"). From such a perspective on the pueblo and on faith, the religious credo is: "I believe in You, architect, engineer, artisan, carpenter . . . in You, comrade . . . You shall be resurrected in every arm raised to defend the pueblo against the exploiter's dominion, because You live in the rancho, in the factory, in the school" ("Credo"). The pueblo, in this music, is Christ's pueblo, the "popular classes": "the working class, which from before dawn is on its way to work, which sings to You, Lord, from the plow, from every building site, from the tractor seat, construction workers, tailors, day laborers, everybody equal, stevedores and ironwrights, shoeshine boys in the park" ("Ofertorio"). With the unique ecclesiastical and poetic authority he possesses, Father Ernesto Cardenal, later to be Minister of Culture in the Sandinista government of Nicaragua, paid Carlos Mejía Godoy this homage in the liner notes to *Misa*: "With authentic peasant voices and with the speech of the pueblo which he knows like nobody else, Carlos Mejía Godoy and the Workshop of Popular Sound have composed this Nicaraguan Mass."

The discursive construction of the pueblo as a collective identity has pre-existing materials to appropriate, again particularly in societies with defining features many would term "traditional," or even "folk."[14] When rapid change sweeps through such a society, states Carlos Vilas (1995: 21, 23), like many theorists of revolution, popular social movements and change, people are convinced "that their customs, and the normal order of things, are being violated . . . the speed of change makes custom more difficult to reproduce and to update, and intensifies the feeling of rupture and loss. The development of new modalities of production and access to land, the mercantilization of the labor force, the dislocation of the family, all in the space of a couple of decades, creates an intergenerational break and blocks the transmission of values, attitudes and beliefs." What is crucial for the construction of a revolutionary discourse in these circumstances is that the violated customs, identities, and sense of order take on, potentially, a greater symbolic reality and value than in "normal" or "traditional" circumstances. Vilas (1995: 23) writes: "the fact that the erosion of the traditional way of life arises mainly from an invasion of external factors encourages a certain idealization of the former: the symbolic reality of the traditional order is reinforced at the very moment that its objective reality is vanishing." That "symbolic reality of the traditional" becomes both a discursive space and a resource appropriable for revolutionary symbolic reconstruction. The pueblo's existing sense of itself as people and as *a people* is that cultural resource. As Carlos Nuñez, one of the FSLN *comandantes,*[15] stated in liner notes for the album *Grupo Pancasán* (1979):

> Revolutionary song in our *patria* . . . penetrated our *pueblo*, lighting the flame of insurrection . . . awakening revolutionary fervor in all sectors of the population. It arose from popular throats to sustain us in the hour of defeats . . . opened the doors of our history to show the people the content of their own gestures and actions, their role as protagonists of history. . . . Song has been one of the means for our people to speak of their misery and suffering, of the exploitation. In clandestinity, in underground activity, in combat we have heard those voices singing to life and communicating hopes for the future, demanding bread, freedom, a new regime, a more just society.

Ubiquitous on billboards in revolutionary Nicaragua, and still emblazoned on the pedestal of the monument to the worker-combatant near the old cathedral in Managua's earthquake-ruined (1972) city center, Sandino's declaration that "only the workers and peasants will go to the very end" links the pueblo to genuine citizenship. Classical Marxism (Marx, Lenin, Gramsci, Trotsky) argued that bourgeois democracy was a form of class domination and thus incomplete until the proletariat achieved supremacy and completed the respective national historical projects of democracy with socialism transcending class domination. Similarly, Central American revolutionary discourses, in concert with the precepts of Latin American dependency theory, held that "dependent bourgeoisies" and U.S. imperialism were a historical obstacle to national sovereignty, popular democracy, and concomitant development. Thus the historic responsibility of the *pueblo* as conscious "maker of its own history" was to fulfill those national agendas, as Sandino declared. It would take a *revolutionary pueblo*, conscious and organized, but "when the people have the will, there is no tyrant who can resist them," Tepehuani sings in the progressive salsa tune "Organizete" (Organize yourself) (1982).

The full and historically deserved citizenship which would identity the pueblo with the patria was to result, with the pueblo achieving "an eternal joy when worker/peasant power *is* the power" ("Cuando venga la paz" [When peace comes],) (Norma Elena Gadea 1985). And unlike the selfish, self-absorbed, and oppressive oligarchy, which was incapable of achieving or sharing a true patria and an inclusive national citizenship, the pueblo would know how: "It was the pueblo that most hated you [the torturer for the oligarchy's dictatorship] when the song was in the language of violence . . . but it is the pueblo, now, beneath its red-black [Sandinista and universal revolutionary colors] skin, which has a generous heart . . . [capable] of saying hello to you in the streets without beggars, of ensuring your children have schools and flowers" ("Mi venganza personal" [My personal revenge],) (Mejía Godoy 1982).[16]

The identity of the pueblo, then, is ultimately with the patria, when that patria is liberated, when that patria is fully *popular*. Such an identity is pointedly political, in that it is only realized with access to state power, as well as being nationalist and patriotic. It is also a popular identity of *place*, a theme appearing throughout Central American revolutionary music. There is national, and also natural place, in references to Central America as a region of Latin America and of the world's South/Third World, as a "brother of so many peoples" (from the title song on *Yo soy de un pueblo sencillo*, Mejía Godoy 1982) characterized by being an isthmus of volcanoes, lakes, and earthquakes. *Pueblo* becomes "*mi tierra*" (my/our land), as in Tepehuani's songs "Cumbia de mi tierra" and "El volcán" (Tepehuani 1988), where "earth tremors are human tremors . . . ready to explode . . . boiling up with humanity's love . . . blow, volcano! Get angry, blow now! Be that lava of light, stopping the darkness." One of Luis Enrique Mejía Godoy's songs is "Juan Terremoto" (Earthquake Juan), who has to live in ruins after the 1972 Managua earthquake, when the dictator Somoza appropriated the reconstruction materials arriving from other nations for his own construction companies and the "new mansions were for the rich man" (*Del 70 al 80; Diez Años*). Yolocamba Ita also sings of volcanoes and the combative *pueblo*, literally in the same breath, naming the San Vicente/Chinchontepec volcano where the FMLN maintained control for years: "Above the ravine of Cayetana village, where the male volcano flirts with the female, when the sun has just risen, early in the morning you can see the fighters of the popular movement" ("Canción al FMLN," Yolocamba Ita 1981). The whole country of El Salvador becomes a place defined by its anti-imperialism: "If the Yankees intervene here like they did in Vietnam, if the Marines invade, here they'll find their graves, like Cayetano [FMLN commander Salvador Cayetano Carpio] said."[17]

Place is addressed in two more ways in Central American musical discourses about the pueblo. In the popularization and celebration of the local, this music makes people's, especially rural people's, attachment to place a central feature. It is replete with place names, both in song titles and in lyrics. It tells people that where they are from, and hence they themselves, are important, that the music belongs to them. And place names situate the heroic actions and martyrs of past and contemporary popular struggles in the symbolic firmament of the pueblo. The album *Marimba Revolucionaria* (Hermanos Palazio 1980), for example, has instrumentals with place-name titles of revolutionary significance to Nicaraguans: "Vivirás Monimbó," for the combative indigenous neighborhood of the city of Masaya; "Pancasán," for the site of a failed 1967 FSLN rural guerrilla front in the north-central mountains (the group Pancasán, of course, took its name from that front); "El Niquinomeño," for the "man from Niquinohomo," Augusto César Sandino. Tepehuani (1982) dedicates a song to the Morazán region of El Salvador, where the FMLN established a liberated zone during the war and enjoyed almost complete popular support, effectively establishing governance. The all-peasant Salvadorean group Los Torogaces de Morazán and many of the fifty or more protest/revolutionary musical groups aligned with the revolutionary organizations from 1975 to 1992 all made locales an integral part of their lyrics, in celebrating popular identity and events of the armed struggle (Almeida and Urbizagástegui 1999). And Carlos Mejía Godoy, master of Nicaraguan vernacular and folklore, could have specific locations be nationally known with songs like "Terencio Acahualinca" and "Ticuantepe sin vós" (1980).

Place in Central American folk culture, in tradition and in modernity, is physical and emotional. It is filial and familial, associated closely with life, death and agricultural cycles, and with national, local and personal history. Its very physicality comes from the exuberance and drama of nature and Central American revolutionary music emphasizes the natural aspects of place. Tepehuani's near-avante-garde composition "Madre Tierra" (1982), for example, combines the patriotic and popular sentiment for mi tierra with an ecological sensibility ("Mother Earth") and echoes of indigenous cosmology. Tepehuani uses plants and animals, both to highlight nature in the pueblo's social and symbolic world and as metaphor: "Butterfly, your flight is our flight . . . dreaming of the spring of equality . . . [and] its multiple colors on the horizon" ("Mariposa"); in "Pájaro Guazapa" (Bird of the Guazapa volcano), a song that opens with helicopter gunship sounds, presumably over the slopes of Guazapa, an almost continuous combat zone just outside San Salvador during the 1980s, they sing of "the green bird of my hope . . . the bird of the poor . . . the guerrilla bird" (*El Zamaquión* 1988).

In a somewhat different idiom, Norma Elena Gadea (1985) uses the images and metaphors of birds, trees, and flowers both for highlighting popular identity ("El almendro" [The Almond Tree], in which she sketches the peasant, rural setting of a young girl's life) and to pay homage to the fallen and martyred combatants ("El zenzontle pregunta por Arlen Siu" [The *Zenzontle* bird asks for Arlen Siu]). Nature becomes the *patria* and the very earth, its creatures and its foliage, embrace the pueblo's heroes and martyrs. And nature will celebrate the people's triumph, "when peace comes" (the album title): "the necessary bird, the revolutionary bird, freed from its cage, flies to the future . . . with the Guatemalan bird, the Salvadorean bird"; in that future "the fiesta will be of children and birds."

The Class Identity of *El Pueblo*

In the social discourse of Central American revolutionary music, it has been argued, the *popular* elements of the pueblo's identity are central, and those popular elements can be understood as transcending stricter class characterizations. They can be considered as cultural, as "placed," and as reflections of nationality. Nonetheless, as seen in the references to the Campesino Mass and the discussion of respective national societies' capacities to achieve the historical goals of a nationalist agenda, class is durably embedded in the discourses. Using class categories when singing of the pueblo sharpens the understanding and consciousness of those social forces held responsible for making the revolution and undertaking the nationalist agenda: "Rise up, working class, the time has come to take this thing seriously and liberate El Salvador. The *patria* needs you, with your fist and your voice. Let's fire our guns and shout revolution" (Cutumay Camones, cited in Almeida and Urbizagástegui 1999: 30).

And it is a classically Marxist delineation of social contradictions as outlined, for example, in "The German Ideology" (Marx 1972b), which is articulated in this music, speaking to relations of production and property, to exploitation and the class character of the state responsible for maintaining those relations and suppressing resistance or challenge. It is also classically Marxist in identifying the desired outcome of popular revolution as socialist, even when the music is not so explicit. This is not surprising, as a social discourse which gives a class name to domestic and international enemies, which attributes underdevelopment, dictatorship, and state terror to capitalism, and which assigns to "the popular classes" national historic agendas that the national bourgeoisie is deemed incapable of carrying out, is likely to identify the overarching goal of those popular classes as socialism.

The music locates suffering in the popular classes and connects that suffering to class domination, that is to the unequal structure of property ownership and access to means of production; to the lack of worker's rights and protections; repression of labor organization; to outright forceful appropriation of peasant property for large capitalist farming, and so on. To be "poor and humble" is to be "exploited, peasant, worker" ("Pajarito de la paz" [The little bird of peace], Norma Elena Gadea 1985). It is the Guatemalan highlands Maya peoples "in [peasant] rubber boots," who are the pueblo and the guerrilla fighters in Kin-Lalat's song "Amante Alzado" (My insurgent lover) (*Florecerás Guatemala*). Luis Enrique Mejía Godoy, in "Venancia," recounts how the campesina woman Venancia became a guerrilla fighter after the Nicaraguan National Guard killed her companion "because he was in the union." In "Jacinto," he sings of "María, who shapes tortillas of hope . . . her hands protested the misery of the *rancho* [working for a cruel landlord]," and in "Abajo," returns to the nineteenth century and sings of "the suffering Indian . . . mistreated by the landlord . . . without letters and speech, barefoot and hungry for liberty"(*Del 70 al* 80). For Banda Tepehuani, two main classes, equally exploited by capital and repressed by the oligarchy's state (and by imperialism, by extension) are the protagonists of revolutionary struggle: the peasantry and the workers. Tepehuani points to land reform and worker control of enterprises as their goals in "Llegaremos" (We will get there) (*El Zamaquión* 1988).[18] And when government conscript soldiers become aware of their class identity and allegiance, it shall be "soldiers on our side, with workers, peasants and students," musically and politically aligned with the revolutionary *cumbia* music of "El Zamaquión" (*El Zamaquión*).

Most Central American revolutionary music groups, of course, went beyond class characterizations of the suffering pueblo to laud the worker and peasant origins of specific guerrilla fighters and give a class character to the goals of the struggle, that is a revolutionary socialist society controlled by workers and peasants. In the FMLN's zones of control, such as Morazán or Chalatenango, revolutionary production not only to support the fighters, but also to manifest a revolutionary culture of work, was an objective of the musicians, their concerts in those zones and the clandestine radio broadcasts of their music. In "Producción de Guerra" (War production), Yolocamba Ita plays in a *típica* musical idiom, like a campesino musical group, about producing food for the popular revolutionary army: "Let's ready the plows and machetes, let's prepare the ground for planting, for our liberation . . . here everybody is learning to be organized . . . isn't it great to feel this and be able to work [army sweeps and bombing disrupted much of Salvador's agriculture during the war] . . . we're sowing a delicious revolution" (*Canto a la patria revolucionaria*).

And there was high praise for those who aligned themselves with the two main protagonist classes. The young Nicaraguan student and guerrilla fighter Luisa Amanda Espinoza, killed by government troops early in the 1970s and for whom the Sandinista women's organization was named, had "your girl's heart made grand by the patria . . . the hope of campesinos in your hands" (Norma Elena Gadea, 1985). In the lush, slow tune "Despertar" (Awakening), Banda Tepehuani pays tribute to a guerrilla fighter who "saw injustices before my very eyes . . . strikes and curfews . . . I felt one with my brothers" (*El Zamaquión*). Yolocamba Ita sings of Sister Silvia, a nun who worked as a nurse with wounded FMLN fighters, eventually taking up arms and dying in combat: "You gave your fresh and vigorous blood to your beaten and hungry people . . . your soft nurse's hands grew with the Gospel and you grasped the liberating arms in this holy war of the poor" (*Canto a la patria revolucionaria*). Taking listeners to the loneliness and terror of a political prisoner in the Somoza dictatorship's filthy cells, Pancasán's "Canción para un reo politico" (Song for a political prisoner) reassures: "in the small hours of your moaning, torture embracing you, workers and peasants sustain you" (*Haciendo la historia*).

Unity of the Pueblo, Support for the Vanguard

While the main class protagonists of the pueblo, in virtually all of Central American revolutionary music, are the workers and peasants, the category of pueblo is inclusive. The urban poor, those employed in petty commerce and

services, the small rural producer, and the rural landless who are not techni-
cally proletarian clearly belong to the pueblo. The Sandinista government
spoke of a proportion of the larger capitalist farmers and industrialists as
"patriotic producers."[19] The crucial role of faith communities, especially the
liberation theology current within the Catholic Church, helped make the mul-
ticlass and multi-identity coalitions that gave Central American revolutionary
movements and organizations some unique characteristics. Yolocamba Ita's
"Homenaje a Monsignor [Oscar] Romero" (*Canto a la patria revolucionaria*) is but one recognition of that role, which helped bring literally millions of Central Americans to radical social consciousness. Guatemala's
ethnocultural and linguistic realities[20] made Maya identity a problem for
stricter Marxist doctrines of class issues above all others, but increasingly
focused the attention of revolutionary organizations under the umbrella of
the URNG (Guatemalan National Revolutionary Union) in the 1980s.

Revolutionary music spoke to the reality of disparate social and organizational forces in promoting unity and support of the vanguard, in both a
sociocultural and an ideological sense. In other words, commitment to and
consciousness of the pueblo, including the idea that campesinos and workers
were the two central classes, would qualify anyone for inclusion, no matter
what their class background or position. Students, professionals, clergy,
intellectuals, artists, artisans, small merchants, the "middle class," and here
and there genuinely bourgeois individuals were all present in the popular
mass organizations, in revolutionary organizations and in guerrilla forces.
Rarely, revolutionary music's social discourses articulated a specifically fem-
inist inclusion of women in the pueblo, though individual women martyred in
the struggle received considerable attention.

Musical groups affiliated with specific organizations, and many of the
best-known groups were so affiliated, certainly conveyed symbolic messages
to militants and factions on the need for unity. But they also produced messages cast more broadly to the pueblo on the generic necessity for unity
among revolutionary organizations and for popular unity against the enemy:
"town and country, *barrio* and factory . . . everybody get ready to fight"
(Pancasán 1981); "this thing has gotten really serious . . . enough already,
let's put an end to this shit . . . it's insurrection time" (Tepehuani 1988). Yolocamba Ita, in "El Casor'o de los Compas" ("The multiple wedding of the
Compañeros"), conveys the image of campesinos from different organizations coming together in marriage and in revolutionary unity. And in its fable
"El Baile de los animales" (The animals' ball), the animals, representing different organizations, get together to rid themselves of the oppressor gorillas
(the military), the mean pigs (the oligarchy) and the brutal donkey (U.S.
imperialism): "and so ends this song, which has taught us quite a lesson: if
the animal kingdom can organize, why can't we do the same?"(*Canto a la
patria revolucionaria*). Banda Tepehuani's very album title, *Por la paz, El*

Salvador vencerá (With peace, El Salvador will win) captures the same spirit: it is the pueblo and the patria for whom the struggle is waged.

Spirit is not sufficient; organization, unity, and discipline are required. That is the social discourse of revolutionary music at critical points in the struggle.[21] Kin Lalat's "Canción de la unidad" equates pueblo, organization, and unity, and their hymn to fallen 1960s guerrilla commander and ex-military officer Turcios Lima pointedly notes that he "carried the unitary and liberatory flag" (*Florecerás Guatemala*). Deep into the war against the U.S.-backed Contras, Nicaraguan musicians at the seventh anniversary of the 1979 Sandinista triumph sang "Seguimos de frente con el Frente," a wordplay in Spanish: "We keep up front with the [FSLN] Front." And in "Vamos a la plaza" (Let's all go to the plaza), they urge the pueblo to "celebrate the victory's anniversary; it's a fiesta *and* a responsibility . . . if you're with Sandino, yesterday, tomorrow and forever, you're with the Frente." Responsibility means defense of the revolution: "all arms to the people!" (Various Nicaraguan Groups 1986). In the same vein, Pancasán (1983) links the broad anti-Somoza coalition of the pueblo to the patria and both to the vanguard party, the FSLN: "For the *Patria*, it is our victory, our hope, our dawn. In order to fight, to win, to build, to live . . . to the battle . . . we are millions with the vanguard . . . we demand it for the *patria*." Pancasán's song "Pueblo, ejército, unidad: garantia de la Victoria" (Pueblo, army, unity: The guarantee of the victory) (1981), which spoke to the immediate period after the 1979 victory, was echoed in the FSLN poster slogan of the mid-1980s "One single army in defense and production."

Morale, Mística, and Martyrology

This music's homage to those fallen in the struggle, particularly to the martyrs of the contemporary revolutionary generation, is a natural lament and mourning for the dead which any people, family, or individual would feel and express. As a social discourse, the remembrance, naming, and exaltation of those whose died in the struggle moves into the realm of sacrifice and martyrdom. The music seeks to honor and socialize those sacrifices, to make those martyred a crucial part of the mística and revolutionary morale of both vanguard and pueblo. It links their actions and sacrifices to the goals of the struggle, not just in terms of military victory over the oppressor or the aggressor, but to the expected works and achievements of the revolution in power: democracy, freedom, justice, equality, development, education, health, housing, employment, culture, social services. The mística of those who continue the struggle and the achievements of the struggle are considered the legacy of the fallen heroes and martyrs. At the deepest levels of symbolic discourse, the deaths of martyrs are transcended. They live in the morale and works of the revolution and the revolutionaries. They incarnate *pueblo* and *patria*, symbolically endowing them with popular identity.

It could be argued, and certainly can be the impression for a visitor to Central America, that death is culturally more present than in some of the world's wealthier societies. A socioeconomic and cultural environment that social science quite recently would have termed "underdeveloped" objectively experiences more deaths per population, at earlier ages, as a result of poverty, disease, and marginalization. There is, then, likely to be a popular death trope, as it were, a certain familiarity and informality with death in cultural expression: language, music, literature, art, religion. That trope is imported easily into the social discourses of revolutionary music and gives some surrounding cultural shape and substance to the music's treatment of fallen heroes and martyrs. The music validates and enhances the meaning and symbolic significance of their deaths and of death itself.

Historical continuity and temporal cyclicity are evident in Central American revolutionary music's treatment of martyrdom. The sacrifices of the contemporary revolutionary generation of militants and combatants are linked to those of previous generations and of outstanding national heroic figures, just as they are held up as examples for their surviving comrades and those generations to come. Sandino is told, in Pancasán's "Requiem a la muerte" (Requiem for death) that he lives "forever in your awakened people and the revolution" (*Vamos haciendo la historia*). Carlos Fonseca, martyred leader of the FSLN during the hard years of guerrilla struggle, is exalted in the anthem by Carlos Mejía Godoy and Tomás Borge "Comandante Carlos Fonseca," which every Sandinista militant and much of the country could sing by heart in the 1980s: "you defeated death . . . a bullet found your stubborn saint's heart and spilled your blood into our lives . . . and when the traitors and cowards are but a footnote of an old history, coming generations of the free and luminous Nicaragua will eternally remember you, firing auroras from your carbine" (Frente Sandinista de Liberación Nacional 1979). The "Hymn of Sandinista Unity," also almost universally known in Nicaragua in the 1980s, declares that "the children of Sandino neither sell out nor surrender . . . a new sun will illuminate the whole land which our martyrs and heroes gave us, a land of strong rivers of milk and honey" (Frente Sandinista de Liberación Nacional).

Fallen comrades in current struggles are equally exalted, whether they are specifically named in the music or not. Kin Lalat sings of Guatemala's flowering from "every drop of blood, every tear shed . . . every piece of torn skin, every bullet . . . it's blood that nourishes the cry of freedom" (*Florecerás Guatemala*). The history of the patria, both before and currently, the Salvadorean group Cutumay Camones sings, "is made with the blood of thousands of massacred brothers and sisters" (cited in Almeida and Urbizagástegui 1999: 22). Scores of songs seal the martyrdom of individuals and of the nameless: "from north to south, from sea to sea . . . they sowed the sun . . . life is the harvest of the revolution" ("Canto Final" [Final Song], Various

Nicaraguan Groups, 1986). Some, like assassinated Salvadorean Archbishop Oscar Romero or the Jesuit priests killed by army troops in their dwellings at the University of Central America campus in San Salvador, are very well-known symbols, people who took the side of the pueblo (Romero said: "I am at the service of the organizations of the people") and were killed for it. Father Gaspar García, a Spanish priest who joined the armed struggle in Nicaragua, is celebrated for his internationalism, solidarity, and commitment to the pueblo: "He changed his parish robes and the confessional for the mountains and the gospel of a revolutionary rifle" (Frente Sandinista de Liberación Nacional). His sacrifice is seen as a victory over death: "He knew that death arrives unannounced, but death is a seed when there is a pueblo behind it."

Others, like the 16-year old Salvadorean fighter María Elena Salinas, a "daughter of the people . . . a responsible proletarian," are made examples and are remembered in songs meant for her combatant comrades. To love and honor her, sings Yolocamba Ita (*Canto a la patria revolucionaria*), is to wage "the prolonged war . . . that red love of autumn, your love, announced the springtime of liberation's hopes." And popular musical idioms symbolically identify the popular origins of such martyrs; típica Nicaraguan country music is the idiom in "María Soledad," a working peasant woman who died fighting the Contras (Luis Enrique Mejía Godoy 1986). The music acknowledges the close humanity of martyred combatants, that they have loved ones and that they are loved. The tender love duet "Si me quitan tu flor" (If they take your flower from me) by Norma Elena Gadea and Luis Enrique Mejía Godoy (Norma Elena Gadea 1985) captures the sacrifice of guerrilla lovers who know the risks combatants take. In Norma Elena Gadea's "Te quiero más" (I love you more), from the same album, the lover says "I know I'm not the only love in your life . . . but in pain, in love . . . I love you/share you with my pueblo."

Musically expressed martyrdom arises as mourning and celebration for the life and significance of the fallen and symbolically embraces the martyred in the bosom of the pueblo. As revolutionary social discourse, such a theme is directed to the reinforcement of morale and mística. It encourages militants, combatants, and the pueblo not to weaken, to be more determined, to be inspired. Guerrilla life and underground struggle are not easy, and developing morale and mística is a crucial element.[22] Just as "Sandino fell . . . in order to grow" ("Cantame Nicaragua" [Sing to me, Nicaragua], Banda Tepehuani 1982), the martyrdom of contemporary heroes, as well at the pueblo's suffering and hopes, should make one "happy to be a *guerrillero*, fighting for the pueblo, running off the tyranny" ("Cumbia de mi tierra" [Cumbia of my land], *El Zamaquión*). The pueblo should honor the martyrs by waging "the people's war" (Kin Lalat), "laying ambushes against the army, explosives for their trucks, taking care of business . . . ," just as musicians should wield their guitars "like a machine gun" and the Maya, the "enslaved Indian, illiterate and screwed over . . . [should] rise up to freedom," while guerrilla fighter-lovers know that "our love will be present in the pueblo; if we die, we shall be together in a thought and a song."

Such morale in music is "food, light and encouragement in the difficult hours, remembering fallen brothers . . . it's a stone to smash the enemy" (FSLN Comandante Carlos Nuñez, liner notes, Pancasán 1981). It prepares people to follow the example of the martyred, like Arlen Siu- *la chinita*[23] fought to the very end" (Norma Elena Gadea, 1985). The pueblo has to emulate their grit: "Like a lioness I will defend this land and my cubs . . . they [the Contra] shall not pass . . . we'll defeat these criminal hordes" ("No pasarán"[24] [They Shall Not Pass], Norma Elena Gadea, 1985). For the fallen comrades, revolutionary musicians deploy "this song as a shot . . . guitar, ready, aim, fire and sing . . . a song of love for my brothers and hatred for the enemy . . . firing at the heart of imperialism."

Such music and its martyrology readies people for revolutionary violence, as Luis Enrique Mejía Godoy tenderly acknowledges in "Para amar en tiempo de Guerra" (To love in wartime): "We'll have to kill, but our motive is love" (Luis Enrique Mejía Godoy 1992). The music of *mística* does not have to be sober or solemn, either, in respecting the example of martyrs and stimulating the morale of the pueblo and combatants. It can be humorous and popular, ironic, sarcastic, and full of slang. It uses dance music and lively campesino rhythms. "This lovely little *chavela* [girl] is four years old," sings Luis Enrique Mejía Godoy in "Todas las armas al pueblo" (All the arms to the people) for the fourth anniversary of the Nicaraguan revolution (Various Nicaraguan Groups, 1986). The Contras "came for salad and we gave them yams [slang for "turds"] . . . come get your song, baby!" And to the strains of jumping Atlantic Coast music we hear that "this pueblo is no idiot . . . you [Contras and imperialists] ain't gettin' your *zumba, macumba*! [won't find your jollies here, dudes!]." Just as much bite is in Banda Tepehuani's "La Pelota" ("The soccer ball," a euphemism for the U.S.-made anti-personnel bombs the Salvadorean military used during the war, and also a slang reference to testicles). To jazzy tempos and a pretty melody, Tepehuani sings that "we *guanacos* [colloquial term for Salvadoreans used all over Central America] don't give up . . . you gringos will never know where our blows are coming from . . . you want to fight on Guazapa [the volcano], we'll make you dance, we'll send you to the cemetery, we'll break your teeth, we'll take your 'pelota' . . . so take off" (*El Zamaquion*).

Myths, Dreams, the Future, and Revolutionary Works

In "Salsa Nicaragüense" (Various Nicaraguan Groups, *Bienvenidos a Nicaragua Libre* 1982) the singer joyfully proclaims it salsa *pinolero* [*pinolero* is a colloquial term for "Nicaraguan" used throughout Central

America, taken from the popular corn-based Nicaraguan drink *pinole*]. In the next song, the musician is "singing to you [Nicaragua] because I love you." This direct and simple sentiment as revolutionary social discourse is one of triumph, of being able to equate pueblo with patria and patriotism with revolution. The album's music has a generally light-hearted pop feeling (its title is "Welcome to free Nicaragua"), inflected with some popular and folkloric motifs, but the titles bear the sentiment of cherishing and protecting the revolutionary people and homeland: "I sing to you because I love you," "This great love," "My pueblo," and "They shall not pass." Though there is Guatemalan and Salvadorean revolutionary music which expresses such deep love for pueblo and patria, it was only in Nicaragua that the fundamental *mythe* (Sorel) and dream of revolution, that is, of taking state power, was realized. Notwithstanding that revolutionary shortfall, themes based in that dream appear in all three Central American revolutionary musics.[25]

During the struggle, the future is musically expressed, as has been seen, in the metaphors of birds and flowers, in the imagery of happy children and reunited lovers. The metaphors of maternity and birthing lend the revolutionary future some of the strongest lyrical imagery. In "Mujer, mujer" (Woman, woman, Pancasán 1983), the band combines the combative, violent present with the portent of the future: "Made of fire and gunpowder, woman of time and history, you gained your place in history, leading in combat . . . the future is in your womb." Armed struggle and revolutionary violence can be a national and popular birthing: El Salvador, "in your armed struggle you advance to the future" ("El Salvador vencerá," Pancasán 1983). To "love in wartime" (Luis Enrique Mejía Godoy, *Del 70 al 80; Diez Años*) is "to allow our cause to grow in the womb of history."

The reality of revolutionary power is that some things desired during the struggle have been achieved, but also that they must be defended. The Cutumay Camones song "Las Milicias Populares" (The popular militias) names the people's gains from the armed struggle of the FMLN in the "zones of control" in the Chalatenango region of El Salvador: they are defended against the attacks of government forces, they can organize and participate in popular production, education, health care, and culture. The popular militias, "that's us, thousands of men and women in the countryside and the city, we've come from every part of the popular masses to defend the victories of the revolution" (Cutumay Camones, *Por eso luchamos*, 1984, cited in Almeida and Urbizagástegui 1999: 27). Peace has to be won, in such circumstances, by force of arms. In El Salvador, the FMLN in effect fought the government forces, and behind them the United States government, to a stalemate. The FMLN controlled significant portions of national territory, established effective "dual power" in several regions and achieved some international diplomatic status, eventually engaging in UN-sponsored peace negotiations with the reluctant government of El Salvador. To get to that

point cost many lives and continuing militancy, as Cutumay Camones highlighted in the "Peace Cumbia" (*Patria Chiquita mía*, "My little homeland,"
1987, cited in Almeida and Urbizagástegui 1999: 28): "Thousands of fists are
raised . . . chants are raised because if the issue is peace, the people become
gigantic . . . what we want is social justice, all the people await peace with
dignity. Dialogue is necessary when there is much to discuss, for we have a
war that we want to end. But, one thing, my brother: don't forget that this war
is the product of social inequality."

In Nicaragua's case, musicians declared in the cassette *Seguimos de
frente en lucha por la paz* (We continue in the struggle for peace, Various
Nicaraguan Groups 1986) that "you see, we've grown somewhat . . . now our
house is open in this liberated Nicaragua"; at the same time, defense of the
state is necessary, but it is a revolutionary and popular defense— "here you
see our youth armed with rifles and smiles, smiles we were able to sow
among the ashes" (Luis Enrique Mejía Godoy, "Canción de aniversario").
The Cuarteto Segoviano, in "Hay que hacerle güevo" (You gotta make an
effort), celebrates the revolution's gains, while reminding listeners that
counter revolutionary and external hostile forces require vigilance. With
típica campesino music from north-central Nicaragua, the area bordering
Honduras and experiencing the bulk of Contra attacks from their bases inside
Honduran territory, the Cuarteto urges campesinos to "raise production . . . while our *cachorros* ["cubs," the affectionate name given young military conscripts defending the country] defend the revolution" and secure
peace.

Some of the most moving expressions of that desired state of affairs are
both personal and social; Norma Elena Gádea's ballad "Cuando venga la
paz" (When peace comes) articulates the deep-felt desire to have the violence
cease, however justified it may be from a revolutionary standpoint. It asks
and answers, "What will it be like? What will *we* be like then?" Separated
lovers will be reunited; revolutionaries and the pueblo "will sing the old revolutionary songs . . . and recall the fallen comrades . . . with the [state] power
of workers and peasants" (Norma Elena Gadea 1985). And lovers will have
what they wanted for the future, for themselves and for the pueblo: "to live
fully . . . in a space of sunlight where death does not fit" ("Para luchar y quer-
erte" [To fight and to love you], Luis Enrique Mejía Godoy, *Del 70 al 80:
Diez Años*).

With peace, those in exile will come home, enforced separations will be
ended in the "dreams of a springtime of equality . . . [and] I will not rest until
I find you, along with those who dream of the return home, feeling the delicious fever-chill of peace" ("Mariposa" [Butterfly] and "No descansaré" [I
won't rest], Banda Tepehuani, *El Zamaquión*). It will be a new society, where
"we have cut the distance between human beings" ("Que no se escucha hoy
la madrugada" [Today we won't hear the early morning], Luis Enrique Mejía

Godoy, *A pesar de Usted* 1986), because though "implacable in combat [this pueblo] is generous in victory" and former enemies will have a place; there can be reconciliation within popular power. The pueblo has the opportunity to realize its historic capacities: "As my grandfathers dreamed, we'll have a proud and free patria" ("La Herencia" [The heritage], Luis Enrique Mejía Godoy, *Del 70 al 80; Diez Años*); "as you and I dreamed . . . we are going to make a country and . . . our bird of peace will fly" ("Vamos hacer un país" [Let's make a country], *A pesar de Usted*).

The first few years of Sandinista revolutionary power showed what positive popular social energies might be released. Notable and rapid improvements in social conditions, in access to popular health, education, production and culture and in spaces for popular organization to flourish characterized the 1979–1983 period. It was a time of "a new day advancing" ("A pesar de Usted," Luis Enrique Mejía Godoy 1986), when families "had a son [or daughter] on the border [in defense] or picking coffee" and a time when hopes for rapid improvements in life for the peasantry and the urban poor were being met. The social works of the revolution were felt in every part of the country, as the song "Pobrecito mi cipote" (My poor little boy) (Luis Enrique Mejía Godoy 1982) reflected. It recounts the poverty, hunger, ill health, and scarcity of paid work for campesinos, but "the *compañero* [local Sandinista organizer] says all that will change; the revolution is bringing health workers, vaccination teams, the literacy campaign and food." In a mass popular literacy campaign surpassed only by Cuba's of the early 1960s, Nicaragua saw one hundred thousand mostly young people fan out across the whole of the national territory and rapidly reduce illiteracy. Very lively music, created especially for and about the National Literacy Crusade, captures the excitement, the challenges, and the achievements of that remarkable year of 1980 (Various Nicaraguan Groups, *Convirtiendo la oscurana en claridad* 1980). The album's title ("Converting the darkness into clarity" and its song titles tell the story: "Hymn to literacy," "The ABCs," "You got to learn to read," "The *son* of ABC," "The *Corrido* of the literacy brigade," "Let's together leave ignorance behind," "It's never too late to learn, *Compañero*" and "Josefana's going (to alphabetize)."

The motives of revolutionaries in Central America, on the reactive existential level, are not difficult to understand: outrage at suffering and injustice, resistance to oppression and brutality. Within the symbolic realms of patria and pueblo, a deeply emotional identification with the people and homeland collides with the structural and political barriers to patria and pueblo realizing their potential for freedom, sovereignty, dignity, development, and citizenship. Those strongly nationalist and popular objectives of revolutionary commitment and activity coexist relatively easily in Central American experience with the classically Marxist goals of socialism and the "new man." Central American revolutionary music brought imagery and language articulating all those discursive and symbolic elements together in its notes on and to the future.

Concluding Remarks

In assuming Central American revolutionary music to be a mobilizing and sustaining set of social discourses articulated in the specific historical circumstances of the 1970s and 1980s, this chapter has sought to address both context and content. The framework of understanding presented was intended to give context some outlines, but without falling into analytical or theoretical rigidities. Its three dimensions—political economy, political culture, and cultural studies—were considered as elastic, incomplete and hence still useful, themselves hybrids that borrow and receive from each other and from elsewhere in the social sciences. If not so specified in much of the chapter devoted to the music's thematic content, they were nonetheless present in delineating the tropes of that content and exploring their meanings. Those meanings suggest that an expanded and undogmatic, culturally infused Marxist worldview is appropriate for appreciating Central American revolutionary music as social discourse.

Such a worldview situates the music in the structural political economies of uneven and dependent capitalist (mal)development, with their attendant social stresses, their undemocratic, authoritarian, and repressive political regimes of accumulation, and with their fragmenting of (however unequal or unjust) cultures of consent, consensus, and legitimation. It is a worldview that emphasizes the realm of the subjective in seeking the roots of consciousness moving individuals, groups, and masses to a disposition for revolutionary thought and action. In the cultural, political, and social contexts of Central American societies, such a worldview perforce includes categories aside from class, relations of production and property, and social contradictions arising from those relations. Hence, it considers the key tropes of pueblo and patria from a broader perspective. It gains from a cultural studies perspective an appreciation of Central American revolutionary music's origins in and command of the *popular*, in its language and musical forms. From the strand of social science that studies nationalist political cultures, such a worldview can perceive the organic link of patriotism to Central America's revolutionary organizations and ideologies. And from an encounter with Sorel it can assume an existential outlook with respect to this music's martyrology, mística and the death trope. Perhaps most of all, such a worldview can hear the myriad of life, which is the music.

Notes

1. Brazilian guitarist Paulo Bellinati remarked at a concert in Chico, California, in February 1997 that he was researching twenty-two regional music traditions in Brazil, only one of which was represented at that particular concert.
2. See Foran 1997 for a theoretical discussion.

3. Author's translation. Unless otherwise indicated, all translations from the Spanish are the author's.

4. For a discussion of the concept of "regime" as "organized governance experience," see Judson 1999.

5. For an illustration of the political economy approach as it pertains to Central America, see Judson 1987a.

6. A prime Nicaraguan example is found in the work of Orlando Nuñez (1988).

7. Judson 1984 applies Sorel's approach to the Cuban revolution.

8. The term *campesino* includes almost all rural dwellers and is thus more expansive a category than the English word "peasant." Generally, it does not mean "capitalist farmer," in the sense that the English term suggests sizable holdings and regular employment of wage labor, though many *campesinos* with land produce commodities for the market. Throughout Latin America, *campesino* includes the rural landless, seasonal workers, and wage employees.

9. Nicaragua's poet laureate of the decades around the turn of the century.

10. Salvadorean poet of the 1960s and 1970s.

11. Minister of Culture in the Sandinista government, 1979–1990, who founded the peasant artists' and contemplative community of Solentiname and developed the "folk mass" in the 1960s and 1970s.

12. Personal communication to author by Eugenio Andrade, Tepehuani arranger/composer/keyboardist, Managua, 1993.

13. See the personal and poetic *testimonio* for Leonel Rugama and Roque Dalton by Canadian poet Jim Smith (1998).

14. See Burns 1991 for an elaboration of the concept of "folk society" as applied to Nicaragua.

15. There were nine, all of whom occupied high government posts in the 1979–1990 period of Sandinista government.

16. The lines are from the poem "My personal vengeance" by Tomás Borge, one of the FSLN *comandantes*, written to and about the man who tortured him in Somoza's dungeons.

17. In responding to a journalist's question about a possible U.S. invasion force, Cayetano is purported to have answered: "Our country would become a 21,000 km^2 tomb for the Marines" (Yolocamba Ita 1981).

18. *El Zamaquión* appears to be a rural locale in El Salvador.

19. See the thorough discussion of the Nicaraguan bourgeoisie and Sandinista policies in Ryan 1995, especially pp. 80–90.

20. For merely four informed sources of the hundreds that exist, see Lovell (1995), Noval (1992), Perera (1993) and Bastos and Camus (1993).

21. There are various mappings of these "critical points." See Almeida and Urbizagástegui 1999 for a formulation.

22. See Shaull 1990 and especially Cabezas 1983 and Payeras 1985 for vivid *testimonios* of guerrilla existence. See Diaz 1992 for a *testimonio* about prison and torture.

23. *La chinita*—"the Chinese girl"—visible minority and physical characteristics appear in popular language with much less stigma or social discomfort attached than in "the North."

24. The cry of the legendary Spanish revolutionary "La Pasionaria" during an onslaught of the fascist forces during the 1936–1939 civil war.
25. Such themes could doubtless be found in revolutionary and protest music in the rest of Central America: Panama, Costa Rica, Honduras, and Belize.

References

Almeida, Paul, and Rubén Urbizagástegui. 1999. "Cutumay Camones. Popular Music in El Salvador's National Liberation Movement." *Latin American Perspectives* 26(2): 13–42.
Banda Tepehuani. 1982. LP *Por la paz. El Salvador vencerá* (For peace. El Salvador will win). Managua: ENIGRAC.
———. 1988. Cassette *El Zamaquion*. Managua: ENIGRAC.
Bastos, Santiago, and Manuela Camus. 1993. *Quebrando el silencio. Organizaciones del Pueblo Maya y sus Demandas*. Guatemala: FLACSO.
Bellinati, Paulo. 1993. CD *Serenata. Choros and Waltzes of Brazil*. San Francisco: GSP Recordings.
Berryman, Phillip. 1984. *The Religious Roots of Rebellion. Christians in Central American Revolutions*. Maryknoll, N.Y.: Orbis Books.
Blades, Rubén. 1999. CD *Tiempos*. New York: Sony Music International.
Buena Vista Social Club. 1997. CD *Buena Vista Social Club*. Red Bank, N.J.: World Circuit.
Bulmer-Thomas, Victor. 1987. *The Political Economy of Central America since 1920*. Cambridge: Cambridge University Press.
Burns, E. Bradford. 1991. *Patriarch and Folk. The Emergence of Nicaragua 1798–1858*. Cambridge: Harvard University Press.
Cabezas, Omar. 1982. *La Montaña es algo más que una inmensa estepa verde*. Managua: Editorial Nueva Nicaragua.
Carpentier, Alejandro. 1977. "América Latina en la confluencia de coordenadas históricas y su Repercusión en la musica." In *América Latina en su Música*, edited by Isabel Arets. Mexico: Siglo XXI/UNESCO.
Castañeda, Jorge. 1993. *Utopia Unarmed. The Latin American Left after the Cold War*. New York: Alfred A. Knopf.
Diaz, Nidia. 1988. *Nunca Estuve Sola*. San Salvador: UCA Editores.
Dunkerley, James. 1988. *Power in the Isthmus. A Contemporary History of Central America*. London: Verso.
Foran, John. 1997. "Discourses and Social Forces: The Role of Culture and Cultural Studies in Understanding Revolutions." In *Theorizing Revolutions*, edited by John Foran, 203–26. London: Routledge.
Frente Sandinista de Liberación Nacional. 1979. LP *Guitarra Armada* (Armed guitar). San José: INDICA.
Frith, Simon, ed. 1989. *World Music, Politics, and Social Change*. Manchester: Manchester University Press.
Gadea, Norma Elena. 1985. Cassette *Cuando venga la paz* (When peace comes). Managua: ENIGRAC.
Gramsci, Antonio. 1973. *Selections from the Prison Notebooks of Antonio Gramsci*.

Edited and translated by Quentin Hoare and Geoffrey Nowell Smith. New York: International Publishers.

Hobsbawm, Eric. 1986. "Revolution." In *Revolution in History*, edited by Roy Porter and M. Teich, 5–46. Cambridge: Cambridge University Press.

Judson, Fred. 1984. *Cuba and the Revolutionary Myth. The Political Education of the Cuban Rebel Army 1953–1963*. Boulder, Colo.: Westview Press.

———. 1987a. "Capitalist Crisis, Imperialist Crisis and the Nicaraguan Revolutionary Response." In *Frontyard/Backyard: The Americas in the Global Crisis*, edited by John Holmes and Colin Leys. Toronto: Between the Lines.

———. 1987b. "Sandinista Revolutionary Morale." *Latin American Perspectives* 14(1): 19–42.

———. 1999. "Political Regimes." In *Critical Concepts: An Introduction to Politics*, edited by Janine Brodie, 57–74. Scarborough, Ontario: Prentice-Hall.

Kin Lalat. 1983. Cassette *Florecerás Guatemala* (You will blossom, Guatemala). Amsterdam: KKLA.

Kirk, John. 1984. "Revolutionary Music Salvadorean Style: Yolocamba Ita." *Literature and Contemporary Revolutionary Culture* 1: 338–52.

Liss, Sheldon. 1991. *Radical Thought in Central America*. Boulder, Colo.: Westview Press.

Lovell, W. George. 1995. *A Beauty that Hurts. Life and Death in Guatemala*. Toronto: Between the Lines.

Mancotal. 1981. LP *Un Son para mi pueblo* (A *Son* for my people) Managua: ENIGRAC.

Marx, Karl. 1972a. "The 18th Brumaire of Louis Napoleon." In *The Marx-Engels Reader*, edited by Robert Tucker. New York: Norton.

———. 1972b. "The German Ideology." In *The Marx-Engels Reader*, edited by Robert Tucker. New York: Norton.

Mejía Godoy, Carlos. 1977. LP *Misa Campesina Nicaragüense* (Nicaraguan peasant mass). San José: INDICA.

Mejía Godoy, Carlos, and Los de Palacagüina. 1980. LP *Monimbó*. San José: INDICA.

Mejía Godoy, Luis Enrique. 1982. Cassette *Yo soy de un pueblo sencillo* (I am from a simple people). Managua: ENIGRAC.

———. 1986. Cassette *A pesar de Usted* (In spite of you). Managua: ENIGRAC.

———. 1992. Cassette *Del 70 al 80; Diez Años*. San José: Sony Music.

Mellers, Wilfrid, and Pete Martin. 1989. Preface. In *World Music, Politics, and Social Change*, edited by Simon Frith, vii–x. Manchester: Manchester University Press.

Moore, Barrington, Jr. 1966. *The Social Origins of Democracy and Dictatorship: Lord and Peasant in the Making of the Modern World*. Boston: Beacon Press.

Noval, Joaquín. 1992. *Resumen Etnográfico de Guatemala*. Guatemala: Editorial Piedra Santa.

Nuñez, Orlando S. 1988. *La Insurrección de la conciencia*. Managua: Editorial de la Escuela de Sociología de la Universidad Centroamericana.

Pancasán. 1979. LP *Grupo Pancasán*. San José: INDICA.

———. 1981. LP *Vamos haciendo la historia* (We are making history). Managua: ENIGRAC.

———. 1983. Cassette *Por la Patria* (For the homeland). Managua: ENIGRAC.

Parra, Isabel. 1985. *El Libro mayor de Violeta Parra*. Madrid: Ediciones Michay.

Payeras, Mario. 1985. *Days of the Jungle*. New York: Monthly Review Press.

Perera, Victor. 1993. *Unfinished Conquest. The Guatemalan Tragedy*. Berkeley: University of California Press.

Pino-Robles, Rodolfo. 1999. "Music and Social Change in Argentina and Chile: 1950–1980 and Beyond." Unpublished conference paper, Canadian Association of Latin American and Caribbean Studies Conference, Ottawa, Canada, October, 15 ms. pp.

Randall, Margaret. 1984. *Christians in the Nicaraguan Revolution*. Translated by Mariana Valverde. Vancouver: New Star Books.

Rodrigues, Virginia. 2000. CD *Nós*. New York: Natasha Records.

Ryan, Phil. 1995. *The Fall and Rise of the Market in Sandinista Nicaragua*. Montreal: McGill-Queen's University Press.

Skocpol, Theda. 1979. *States and Social Revolutions*. Chicago: University of Chicago Press.

Shaull, Wendy. 1990. *Tortillas, Beans, and M-16s. A Year with the Guerrillas in El Salvador*. London: Pluto Press.

Smith, Jim. 1998. *Leonel/Roque*. Toronto: Coteau Books.

Snow, David, and Robert Benford. 1988. "Ideology, frame resonance, and participant Mobilization." *International Social Movement Research* 1: 197–217.

Tilly, Charles. 1978. *From Mobilization to Revolution*. Reading, Mass.: Addison-Wesley.

Vanden, Harry. 1986. *National Marxism in Latin America. José Carlos Mariátegui's Thought and Politics*. Boulder, Colo.: Lynne Rienner.

Various Authors. 1999. CD *Música Negra del Perú*. Lima: Producciones IEMPSA.

Various Groups. 1982. LP *1er Festival Nuevo Canto Latinoamericano. Version Urgente para Nicaragua*. Managua: ENIGRAC.

Various Nicaraguan Groups. 1980. LP *Convirtiendo la oscurana en claridad* (Converting the darkness into clarity) Managua: ENIGRAC.

Various Nicaraguan Groups. 1982. Cassette *Bienvenido a Nicaragua Libre* (Welcome to free Nicaragua). Managua: ENIGRAC.

Various Nicaraguan Groups. 1986. Cassette *Seguimos de frente en lucha por la paz* (Let's continue forward in the struggle for peace). Managua: ENIGRAC.

Vilas, Carlos. 1995. *Between Earthquakes and Volcanoes. Market, State, and Revolutions in Central America*. Translated by Ted Kuster. New York: Monthly Review Press.

Yolocamba Ita. 1981. LP *Canto a la patria revolucionaria* (Song to the revolutionary homeland). Vancouver: Goldrush Studios.

Contributors

David Gramit teaches musicology at the University of Alberta. He has served as editor of the *Journal of Musicological Research* and contributed to periodicals and books on subjects including Schubert studies, the social construction of musical meaning, and German musical culture in the eighteenth and nineteenth centuries. Among his recent publications is *Cultivating Music: The Aspirations, Interests, and Limits of German Musical Culture.*

Fred Judson is Professor of Political Science at the University of Alberta. He teaches in the areas of comparative politics, international relations, and Latin American studies. His published work examines Latin American revolutionary ideologies (Cuban and Nicaraguan), the political economy of structural adjustment in Central America, human rights in Central America, and the politics of transition in South Africa. Recently he has written on Canadian commercial relations with Latin American countries, the South in global perspective, and theorizations of political regimes. Presently he is pursuing themes in critical international political economy and interdisciplinary approaches to Latin American studies.

Henry Klumpenhouwer is Associate Professor of Music at the University of Alberta. He has written on the analysis of twentieth-century music, history of music theory, and Marxist-style critiques of culture.

Adam Krims is Associate Professor at the University of Alberta and Director of its Institute for Popular Music. He is author of *Rap Music and the Poetics of Identity,* editor of *Music/Ideology: Resisting the Aesthetic,* and author of numerous articles and essays on Marxism, music, urban geography, and music theory. His current project is a book on music and urban geography.

Theodore Levin is Associate Professor of Music at Dartmouth College. He began studying Central Asian music in 1977 as a graduate student at Tashkent State Conservatory and has maintained close connections with Central Asian musicians and music scholars.

Peter Manuel teaches ethnomusicology at the CUNY Graduate Center and John Jay College, New York. He has researched and published extensively on popular and traditional musics of India, the Caribbean, and elsewhere. His most recent book is *East Indian Music in the West Indies: Tan-singing, Chutney, and the Making of Indo-Caribbean Culture.*

Anthony A. Olmsted received his Ph.D. in anthropology from the University of Alberta. In addition to examining early English public concerts, his work has included applying Marxian theory to the operation and development of Folkways Records of New York. He is currently preparing for publication a monograph detailing the economic life of Folkways Records.

Regula Burckhardt Qureshi is Professor of Music, Adjunct Professor of Anthropology and Religious Studies, and Director of the Centre for Ethnomusicology at the University of Alberta. She is the author of *Sufi Music of India and Pakistan* and coeditor of *Islam in North America* and *Muslim Families in North America.* She has also published widely on poetics, political economy of music, Indian and Islamic musical practices, and ethnomusicological theory.

Martin Stokes is Associate Professor of Music at the University of Chicago. He is the author of *The Arabesk Debate: Music and Musicians in Modern Turkey* (recently translated into Turkish by Iletisim), editor of *Ethnicity, Identity and Music: The Musical Construction of Place,* and coeditor of *Nationalism, Minorities and Diasporas: Rights and Identities in the Middle East.* He has written numerous articles and chapters on music in the Middle East and ethnomusicological theory for *New Formations, The Journal of the Royal Anthropological Institute, Popular Music, The World of Music, The New Grove Dictionary of Music and Musicians,* and elsewhere.

Izaly Zemtsovsky is former head of the Folklore Department at the Russian Institute for the History of the Arts (St. Petersburg), where he has been working for thirty-five years; he has been a fellow at the Institute for Research in the Humanities at the University of Wisconsin-Madison since 1995, and visiting professor at UCLA (1994), University of California at Berkeley (1997–98) and Stanford University (2000, 2001). From 1989 to 1993 he served as Executive Board Member of the International Council for Traditional Music. He has published fifteen books and more than four hundred articles on Russian and Eurasian folk music including the entries on Russian music in the *New Grove Dictionary,* the *Garland Encyclopedia of World Music,* and *MGG.*

Index